PARENTING YOUR PREMATURE BABY

HENRY HOLT and COMPANY · New York

PARENTING
YOUR
PREMATURE
BABY

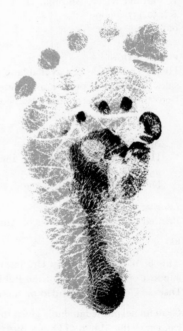

Janine Jason, M.D.

Antonia van der Meer

Published by Henry Holt and Company, Inc.,
115 West 18th Street, New York, New York 10011.
Published in Canada by Fitzhenry & Whiteside Limited,
195 Allstate Parkway, Markham, Ontario L3R 4T8.

Library of Congress Cataloging-in-Publication Data
Jason, Janine.
Parenting your premature baby / by Janine Jason and
Antonia van der Meer.—1st ed.
     p.   cm.
Includes index.
ISBN 0-8050-0880-2
  1. Infants (Premature). 2. Infants (Premature)—Care. 3. Parent and child.
I. Van der Meer, Antonia. II. Title.
RJ250.J37   1989
618.92′011—dc19   618.92011
                                   J 39   88-8367
                                                               CIP

FIRST EDITION
Henry Holt books are available at special discounts for bulk purchases for
sales promotions, premiums, fund-raising, or educational use. Special edi-
tions or book excerpts can also be created to specification.

   For details, contact:

   Special Sales Director
   Henry Holt and Company, Inc.
   115 West 18th Street
   New York, New York 10011

Designed by Claire M. Naylon
Printed in the United States of America

10 9 8 7 6 5 4 3 2 1

This book was written by Dr. Jason in her private capacity. No official
support or endorsement of the Public Health Service or the Centers for
Disease Control is intended or should be inferred.

Grateful acknowledgment is given to Doris Ivey for the photographs on pages
170, 171; to the March of Dimes Birth Defects Foundation for the photos on
pages 29, 46, 52, 60, 63, 94, 113; to Medela, Inc., for the photos on pages 128,
133; to Ruby Ming for the photo on page 91; to Mary Moore for the photos on
pages 114, 115; and to Dr. Susan Reef for the illustration on page 31.

Contents

Introduction

It feels like a long time since I graduated from Harvard Medical School, packed my bags, and drove off to the opposite coast to do my pediatric training at the Children's Hospital in Los Angeles. Since then, I have traveled across two countries in my journey to become the doctor I am today—from the Toronto Hospital for Sick Children, to the Yale University School of Medicine in New Haven, to Atlanta, where I now do research at the Centers for Disease Control.

During all these years, I have seen and cared for many premature babies but never did I think that one of my own children would be born prematurely, that I would become a premie parent. In spite of all my travels, it seems I have never traveled as far as I did in my own personal journey from the premature birth of my second child, Ashley, to the writing of this book. I know that my husband, Bill, also a pediatrician, feels the same way. It was a time during which there was much to experience and endure, and many ways to grow and learn as individuals and as a family. My experiences as the mother of Danielle, my first child, born full-term, and of Ashley, born prematurely two years later, taught me (and are still teaching me) as much as my medical training ever has.

In addition to being a mother, a doctor, and a medical researcher, I am a teacher of pediatrics and immunology at Emory University. In this book I want to reach out to people

who are not doctors and use my teaching skills to share what
I know about prematurity and parenting with you. I hope that
this book's combination of medical information and parenting
experiences will be useful to you.

As parents of premature babies, we face challenges other
parents do not face. And, although each of our situations is
unique, we have all had to deal with the same fears and hopes;
we search for the same reassurances. This book was written to
address those hopes and fears, as well as your need for information. And this book strives to reassure you that in spite of
your fears and insecurities, you have a vital role to play as a
parent of a premature child.

Parenting a premie is very different from parenting a term
infant but can be equally fulfilling and certainly as exciting. I
know the differences firsthand since I experienced both types
of parenting. When my full-term infant, Danielle, was born,
things went perfectly. She was beautiful—she even had a head
of hair. She breastfed voraciously but, of course, like a lady
and we all came home from the hospital in three days. Our
dog, Brandy, would rock the baby's cradle with her nose. Certainly just what a nice couple like Bill and me deserved.

The picture was entirely different when our second child,
Ashley, was born seven weeks early, weighing four pounds five
ounces. I knew that this was a good size for a premie but I
also knew that size wasn't everything. The fact remained that
she was born too soon and I knew her immature system could
cause her any number of problems. My husband and I both
knew all too well about the medical problems Ashley might
have to face. (I had cared for many sick premies as a pediatrician and was often called in specifically to see and help care
for the very sickest.) These years of medical experience taught
me that being born prematurely is a high-risk situation; all bets
are off as to which child will thrive and which will not. I feared
that my daughter would encounter any or all of the problems
I had seen as a doctor.

And yet the essence of Ashley showed through from the
very beginning; she would lie among her tubes and equipment

and smile—as if she had anything to smile about! It broke my heart to think I might have done this to her; I was determined not to fail her any further. It was at this point that my life as a premie parent began.

Before I personally experienced having a premature infant, I saw prematurity from the outside, as a pediatrician involved in the care of very sick infants. Empathetic though I was, I was always awed by the intense, isolating grief of premie parents; these were the parents whom I had the most difficulty comforting. I now know that prematurity is not an experience that can be understood by those who have not endured it themselves. Having a child born too soon is a unique terror, one part irrational guilt that you have somehow caused this event to happen, two parts uncertainty as to the role you can play in this vulnerable infant's care, and three parts anxiety that you will lose your dream child.

The moment I went into premature labor, my family and I entered a nightmare. We felt very much alone. After Ashley was born, I began to look for published information about the causes of prematurity and a parent's role in caring for a premature child. At first, I found nothing. Later, I found the medical facts but little parental perspective. These books did not provide me with the information, support, and reassurance I needed most.

Like other mothers of premature infants, though, I gradually regained my confidence and resolved my anxieties and irrational guilt, in large part by taking a stronger role in the parenting care of my child. Like all of us, I have looked for some good that could come of this experience, some "reason" for it all. Certainly it has helped strengthen our family's bonds and we have Ashley, which is more than reason enough. But also I have had ample time to think about helping other people through this ordeal. I would like to help you feel less alone as a parent of a premature child, more secure about your role in your baby's life from the very first moments, and to feel absolutely no guilt about an event that you could not have prevented.

I am also attempting in this book to provide a bridge for you between your own experience and the medical realities.

Your and your family's emotions are complex and evolving. You may feel very vulnerable, unsteady in the face of medical technology and the possibility of death that is implied. But in fact premature infants handle this technology amazingly well. You may also feel unsure about your place in the hospital's hierarchy of doctors, nurses, and technicians. Know that *you* are your infant's parent in the delivery room and in the newborn intensive-care unit, as certainly as you are in your own home. Believe in yourself and believe me, as a pediatrician and a parent, when I assure you that you should never doubt the importance of that role. You will be the one providing your baby with care, comfort, and security, even in an intensive-care nursery and even if your baby has long-lasting problems related to prematurity. While you should respect, appreciate, and applaud the role of medical caretakers in your infant's life, do not for one moment sell yourself short. It is you, as a parent, who will determine the quality of your infant's life and future, be that life long or short. It is you who will provide him or her with a parent's love.

You and your family will survive this nightmare and gradually feel life return to normal. Along the way, you will learn new things about yourselves and your relationships with one another. I hope I can help you to deal with the premature birth of your child in an informed and constructive way that will allow you to discover your own and your family's strengths.

Note to the Reader

In referring to a premature infant, I wanted to choose one pronoun to use throughout the book, rather than the confusing "he/she." Because my experience was with a "she"—my premature daughter—I deliberately refer to premies in the book as "he," in an effort to include not just my own story, but *all* children, *all* parents, *all* experiences. Although I know premature birth firsthand, my experience is not the only one that matters. In writing this book I had all families and their premature babies in mind, boys and girls.

1. Why Babies Are Born Prematurely

When childbirth occurs prematurely, it's natural to be overwhelmed by fears, anxieties, and guilt. As a pediatrician, I knew that my prematurely born child, Ashley, could die or develop abnormally; as a parent, I was terrified. The experience of having an infant born prematurely and trying to understand why it happened and what lies ahead can be intimidating, confusing, and frightening to all parents of prematurely born and/or small infants.

During my preterm labor and my daughter's birth, I felt devastated that my normally cooperative body had failed me in its most important role. And because it had failed me, I felt I had failed my baby. Once the birth was over, my goal became my infant's survival—I was not going to fail my baby again. In retrospect, this goal was useful for both of us. It motivated me in my role as a parent, allowing me to help my daughter make it through difficult times. In addition, it has helped me resolve the inevitable guilt felt by parents of prematurely born infants.

Repeatedly in those first few weeks and months I asked myself, as I am sure you are asking yourself now, "Why did this happen to me? What did I do wrong?" Early on, these questions are so compelling that they can get in the way of parenting. So before we get on to the central points of the book, let's discuss this question of "What did I do wrong?" Let me reassure you that, almost certainly, you did nothing wrong. Little is understood about the reasons for premature births. Accepting this fact may help to resolve your feelings of guilt.

Occasionally, the reason for a premature birth is obvious, for instance, when it is due to the mother's being injured in a car accident or when it is due to a previously diagnosed uterine anomaly (abnormal womb). More often, no one knows why a baby is born prematurely. Statistically, about 7 percent of all babies born in the United States are premature. Of these preterm births, 50 to 60 percent have no known cause. Most premie parents I have seen or spoken with say they had no idea that anything would go wrong.

As one mother puts it:

"I had a perfect pregnancy. I looked good, I felt good. I ate well, I was strong. I never had any problems—no nausea, no vomiting, no fatigue. I thought, 'Gee, this is easy.' Then at thirty-five weeks, with no warning, my water broke. I checked into the hospital that night and by the next morning my baby was born and my 'perfect pregnancy' had ended for no reason. My son ended up spending three weeks at the hospital."

One mother who gave birth to a little boy at twenty-eight weeks gestation tells how quick and dramatic the whole labor and delivery were for her:

"It was a shock. There are no premies in our family. I was visiting my mother and had been out in the sun all day. When I came in, I noticed my stomach felt very hard . . . but then I decided I was being a hypochondriac. I went into the bathroom, saw I was bleeding, and panicked. My mom and dad drove me to the emergency room. By then, I was hemorrhaging. The medics were unable to find a heartbeat for the baby and rushed me to a larger hospital an hour and a half away. I was pretty sure my baby was dead. When we arrived at the hospital, someone brought in a fetal monitor to try to get a heartbeat. . . . They immediately found one. I was so happy! Grant was born vaginally about twelve hours later. He was so small; it was a very fast delivery.''

If you are like most parents of a premature baby, the birth occurred in a daze and only now have you had time to wonder why it happened to you. You may search your own memory of the pregnancy as well as various medical books to find a *reason* for your baby's prematurity. You may even listen to well-meaning but uninformed friends and relatives who try to supply the answers in the absence of real facts. Their theories often increase your feelings of guilt, since these usually involve something you must have unintentionally ''done wrong.'' These theories can range from the ridiculous to the temptingly rational, from your having eaten the wrong food, to being too active, to lying in bed the wrong way, to taking too many risks, to letting yourself wear down. Just ignore these old wives' tales! They help no one and can only make you feel needlessly guilty.

In fact, every pregnant woman is at some risk for a premature delivery. A few women, though, are at greater risk than others; this does not necessarily mean you should feel responsible, however. The following checklist shows who is most likely to have a premature labor or delivery. It may help you in planning your next pregnancy (also see Chapter 14), and it should answer some of your questions. Those at greater risk include:

1. Women who have previously delivered a premature baby.

2. Women carrying twins. Twelve percent of premature deliveries are multiple births. After a certain point, multiple-birth infants often do better outside the womb; your body may ''know'' this.

3. Women under seventeen years old or over thirty-five years old. (There is disagreement as to whether healthy ''older'' mothers are really at increased risk.)

4. Women who have diabetes mellitus, or diseases of the heart or kidneys. Women with chronic diseases must be

watched closely during pregnancy, for both their own sakes and their babies'.

5. A woman with an "incompetent" cervix. The cervix, or bottom part of the uterus facing the vagina, is supposed to remain tightly closed throughout the nine months of pregnancy. A cervix is "incompetent" if it passively dilates, or opens, too early, without the woman's going into labor. If a pregnant woman is being watched during her pregnancy, this can often be diagnosed and dealt with in operating-room surgery, by stitching (cerclage). If this has been a problem in one pregnancy, it is likely to recur in the next. If cerclage is needed, the optimal time for placement is before sixteen weeks. It can be done prior to pregnancy and left in place for one or more years.

6. A pregnant patient who has undergone fetoscopy and/ or fetal blood sampling during her pregnancy. These tests, used only in extremely high-risk cases when specific fetal problems are suspected, allow the doctor to look directly into the amniotic sac at the fetus and placenta, using a telescopelike instrument inserted through the mother's abdominal wall and into the amniotic sac. Placental and fetal blood samples can also be taken. This procedure is associated with a preterm delivery only very rarely.

7. Those under *exceptional* physical stress. Physical exertion to which a woman is accustomed should not result in prematurity. (The effect of emotional stress is unclear and seems to involve a particular woman's individual pattern of response to such stress.)

8. Women who experience a medical condition known as "placenta previa." Its main symptom is painless bleeding. A complex placenta previa means that the placenta is lying in the lower part of the uterus, over the cervix. This condition necessitates that the baby be delivered by a cesarean section, or C-section, when the woman goes into labor.

9. A woman with a very low prepregnant weight (defined as less than 100 pounds) or unusually short stature (less than five feet tall). Extremely poor weight gain during preg-

nancy, less than one-half pound per week, on average, is also a risk factor.

10. Someone with problems during the pregnancy, such as excessive vomiting, anemia, fever, and infections.

11. A woman carrying a fetus with a congenital defect of some kind. Why this condition might lead to a premature birth is unknown. In any case, it is unlikely that you will know about a congenital defect in advance of the birth, unless you have had ultrasound and/or amniocentesis and chromosome analysis of the infant's cells. Even chromosome analysis can diagnose only a small number of defects.

12. Someone consuming large amounts of alcohol (defined as two or more drinks a day), smoking, or abusing drugs (especially any form of cocaine). Nicotine, alcohol, and other drugs can also lead to intrauterine growth retardation, which we will discuss later, and sometimes addiction withdrawal in the infant. Growth retardation and drug addiction can be more serious for the baby than prematurity.

13. Women who receive no prenatal care, which might have allowed a doctor or midwife to detect one of the risk factors above. Once a woman's doctor has identified her as "at risk" for premature labor, he/she would be able to take certain steps to try to prevent preterm delivery.

14. Women who get pregnant again too soon after a previous delivery. For maternal and fetal health, one to two years should elapse between the time a mother stops nursing and her next delivery.

As you look back over your pregnancy or even as you read through this list of risk factors you will probably still feel guilty—even though you didn't do anything wrong. You may wonder why you couldn't have foreseen the possibility of a premature birth or why your doctor couldn't have prevented it. You may feel you are the cause of your newborn's suffering or medical problems. You may question why you got pregnant in the first place. These feelings are normal. It is something that all of us who have given birth to premature babies must go through. But as parents we must eventually realize that a preoccupation with the why of a premature birth can sap valuable time and energy better spent on ourselves and our babies. So be fair with yourself when you ask, as most of us do, "Did I put my baby at an unreasonable risk?" Most likely the answer is no. You could not have known that you were going to have a preterm delivery.

You might feel somewhat less isolated in this experience by remembering that what happened to you and to me happens to the parents of over 330,000 babies a year in this country. Many, many people know what it feels like to have the anticipation of a special and thrilling childbirth suddenly turn into the emotional trauma of premature delivery. Let's now go back over the events that might have overwhelmed you at that time.

METHODS OF PREVENTING PREMATURE DELIVERY

If you were able to contact your obstetrician soon enough, he or she may have tried to prevent the premature delivery from happening. It is unclear how often medical care can stop labor and how often birth will happen no matter what you try. One problem is that most women don't realize or refuse to admit that they are in labor. They may not want to "bother" the doctor with a "complaint" or they may think, hope, and convince themselves that what they are feeling isn't really labor. In my case, for example, I went into labor around midnight and went into work the next morning, not admitting to myself that this was really labor. Even with all my medical training and a previous delivery, I was able to deny the severity of my pain—because I could not bear to accept this as happening. I finally telephoned my obstetrician around three that afternoon and she asked me if I thought I could wait to see her. Only when I heard myself say no did I begin to admit what was really happening. When I got to my obstetrician's office, a young nurse asked if I were "the one in labor." Then my defense system finally cracked and I responded, "Yes, I guess that's what I'd call this." And two things happened: I began to cry and the contractions suddenly hurt enormously.

My obstetricians were wonderful. They used bed rest and medications for three days to stop my labor, all the while sensing it was hopeless but recognizing that I just couldn't bear to give up. The contractions never slowed to less than once every ten minutes. Finally, they gave me several doses of steroids, in hopes of helping the baby's lungs mature more rapidly.

You, too, may have been given labor-arresting drugs or placed on bed rest before your baby's birth. Let's now go over the methods that might have been used to prevent your delivery. They range from bed rest to oral or intravenous medications, depending on the urgency of the situation: how far the labor has progressed and how far along the pregnancy is.

If premature labor is diagnosed at a very early stage, it can be controlled in 50 percent of cases by bed rest alone. Some obstetricians feel it is probable that in these cases the labor would have stopped spontaneously anyway, without medical help, but there is no reason to take chances. Lying on your back, with the legs and hips elevated, can relieve any pressure the baby may be exerting on the cervix and stop early contractions. Unfortunately, the mother in this situation often must remain in bed, getting up only to use the toilet, since standing up again can bring back the contractions. This can make just about any normal activity difficult, including eating. However, for the sake of the growing fetus, eating must somehow be managed. (Milk shakes, hamburgers, pizza, and fried chicken may become a steady diet.) Sleeping can also be quite unpleasant. But all of this pales next to the experience of premature delivery and parenting. In less serious situations, a doctor may recommend only partial bed rest, advising that you lie down two to three hours each day.

Walking down the halls of maternity wards, I have seen many women hospitalized for complete bed rest to prevent labor and I can tell you that their stays are not easy. As one premie mom who was in the hospital on complete bed rest describes it:

"It was horrific, lying there, not knowing how many more days before I'd go into labor. I was not allowed up even to go to the bathroom. I was placed on a high-protein diet. But how do you eat when you're flat on your back? When I finished each meal, I looked like a baby, with food all down my nightgown. My mother and my husband had to take care of my two other children at home. Most of the responsibility fell on my mom. My children came to see me every day in my room. They were very frightened at first but coming to the hospital helped them to see for themselves that I wasn't dying. They could see I was okay. I told them that whatever happened, it would be God's will, but then I turned around and said, 'Nothing is going to happen to this baby.' I believed that. I had to, for my own sanity. I believed that the Lord had brought me and the baby this far; He was not going to let anything happen now. But in the back of your mind you always know that God may have other plans for you."

Another mother, who had two prior premature births, explains what kept her going through the ordeal of hospitalized bed rest the third time around:

"I'd get out of my bed, walk over to the NICU and look at the babies, and go straight back to bed. I wasn't going to have another one of those!"

When bed rest is not enough or when the labor is too far along to be controlled by bed rest, medications may be used. Referred to as tocolytic agents, these drugs have been quite effective in the prevention of some preterm deliveries. Tocolytic agents act by relaxing the uterus and stopping contractions. These medicines may be given orally, by injection into a muscle (IM), or intravenously (IV). Once the cervix has opened more than three centimeters (about 1¼ inches), however, these drugs will probably not be effective in stopping delivery.

One family of tocolytic drugs used is the β-agonist agents, one of which is Ritodrine (Yutopar). This drug was approved by the Food and Drug Administration (FDA) in 1980. It relaxes the uterine muscles and can often stop or at least slow contractions. Unfortunately, it works on other parts of the body as well. For example, it also causes maternal and fetal heart rates to increase, a significant side effect. Other maternal side effects include headache, nausea, nasal congestion, tremors, jitteriness, and anxiety (just what you need at a time like this!). Ritodrine will not be used if (1) the fetus is less than twenty weeks gestation, (2) fetal lungs are mature and/or the infant's gestational age is over thirty-six weeks, or (3) a mother has high blood pressure or uncontrolled diabetes mellitus. This medication may cause the mother's blood potassium levels to drop, a condition that can only rarely lead to heart arrhythmias (irregular heartbeats). If irregular heartbeats are occurring, potassium may be given intravenously at the same time as the Ritodrine. If the mother's blood potassium level is declining despite this, the amounts given intravenously may be increased, within limits. In high doses, potassium can sclerose (severely irritate) the vein into which it is infused, causing the mother's arm to be tender for several days or weeks.

Some women respond better to one drug than another. Terbutaline (Brethine), frequently used to treat asthma, often can be effective in the treatment of premature labor. (It has not been approved by the FDA specifically for the prevention of premature delivery, but has been approved for use on pregnant women.) Two other medications that are sometimes used to treat premature labor are magnesium sulfate (which is also used as an antiseizure medicine) and (now rarely given) alcohol. At this point in your pregnancy, alcohol will cause no long-term harm to your infant. However, as you almost certainly know, alcohol can cause headaches, nausea, and vom-

iting. One woman who was given alcohol during a premature
birth eleven years ago experienced these side effects intensely:

"I was given alcohol in the veins on Monday morning. I
fell asleep immediately and didn't wake up until Tuesday afternoon. I was crying, and throwing up. I couldn't lift my
head. I was so depressed."

When labor is advanced and/or contractions are frequent,
it is important to achieve quickly high blood levels of these
tocolytic agents. In this situation, the drugs are given intravenously (directly into the bloodstream), or into a muscle. A
number of laboratory tests will be done during the treatment
to monitor the mother's and fetus's status. If the medications
control the contractions, the mother will be switched to an oral
form of one of these drugs.

Most babies, even those born within twenty-four hours of
receiving these medications, have no serious side effects from
them. In fact, these medications are sometimes given to pro-
long labor even when it is unlikely they will actually prevent
it, as long as the fetus and mother are not in distress and there
is no sign of fetal infection occurring. Extending labor might
be done so there will be time for the physicians to give the
mother steroids, such as betamethasone. A number of research
studies suggest that steroids can speed up the fetus's lung maturation, preventing the baby from having some of the problems he might otherwise face because of his prematurity. The
use of steroids, however, is still somewhat controversial, so not
all doctors will use them. Personally, I feel that the current
literature supports the contention that the respiratory benefits
(preventing hyaline membrane disease) outweigh the potential
immune risks to the baby, assuming there is time to give a full
series of injections prior to the infant's delivery. There is, unfortunately, often not sufficient time for this. To be effective,
steroids must be given at least forty-eight hours before the birth,
but no more than ten days prior to delivery. In one study, of
244 babies whose mothers received steroids, 80 percent survived to go home. Fetal breathing problems were less common

and the babies needed less oxygen therapy than those of comparable gestational age (that is, time spent in the womb) whose mothers were not given steroids. At two months after birth, the babies whose mothers were given steroids were heavier and had larger head circumferences than babies whose mothers were not given steroids.

2. Premature Delivery

The birth of your premie probably seemed like a nightmare to you, especially if it happened quickly and without warning. Now that the labor and delivery are behind you, it may be comforting to look back at what happened during the birth so that you can assure yourself that everything possible was done to deliver the healthiest baby.

Instead of having your delivery be a joyous moment, it was a time of tension and shock. You and your husband probably didn't have time to complete any childbirth-preparation classes, usually beneficial both psychologically and practically. You probably did not have the chance to tour the hospital prior to being admitted for premature labor. And, to make matters worse, upon arrival at your hospital, you may have been transferred to another hospital if yours wasn't equipped to handle your high-risk birth. Your chosen obstetrician may not have had admitting privileges there, which means he or she could not deliver your baby. You might have received a new obstetrician or a perinatologist (an obstetrician with additional specialty training in the care of high-risk pregnancies).

Although it is unsettling to be in an unfamiliar hospital

and to have a stranger as your doctor, there are two very good reasons for this move. First, babies born in hospitals with newborn intensive-care units, known as Level III nurseries, have a significantly better chance of survival. (Level I and II nurseries do not have intensive-care units for babies and may not have a neonatologist in attendance.) Second, the mother's womb is the safest "incubator" in which to transport the baby from one hospital to another. If there wasn't enough time to transport you safely, the nearest hospital with a Level III nursery was probably contacted to let it know that your baby would need to be transported there after delivery. Usually, that hospital sends over a resident pediatrician (physician receiving pediatric training) or neonatology fellow (pediatrician receiving training in the care of sick newborns) to assist in the care of your baby in the delivery room and in the transport ambulance or helicopter. (Back in my days in residency training, I was sometimes sent to assist in the care and transport of premies.) But transporting your premie is really not ideal, since this kind of movement and change is traumatic for a fragile infant. It is always preferable to move the baby inside the mother whenever possible.

Whether you were in your own hospital or a new one, any hopes you might have had of using a birthing room were probably not fulfilled. Premature births are handled in a standard delivery room, with the mother on a delivery table, complete with stirrups for her feet. Most likely, you were surrounded by imposing medical equipment and a no-nonsense staff of worried professionals. The equipment you saw around you was there for both you and your baby. Probably not all of it was used. Items that related to your care included trays with forceps and surgical equipment; a cardiac monitor to check your heart rate; an oxygen tank or oxygen outlet, in case you needed extra oxygen; a fetal monitor, to give information on the fetal heart rate, contraction patterns, and the effects of the contractions on the fetal heart rate; IV lines, solutions, and medications; and sterile towels and clean sheets.

When you were wheeled into the delivery room you also may have seen a number of items that were there to help the doctors care for your baby. These included the following:

- A tray and mattress on which to place the baby right after birth, with hot, bright "warming lights" above.
- Oxygen tanks or an oxygen outlet, tubing, and mask, in case the baby needs additional oxygen to help with breathing.
- Suction bowls and tubes for clearing the newborn's airway.
- Laryngoscopes and laryngoscopy tubes. Premature babies may need to be "intubated" right after birth. Intubation means that a plastic tube, or laryngoscopy tube, is put down the baby's mouth (or nose) and into the windpipe (trachea) to the lungs. This ensures a clear airway and gives the neonatologist a clear path for suctioning or resuscitation. Most important, if the baby needs to be ventilated (put on a respirator), this tube will be connected to the machine.
- A scale for weighing the baby. (Just a few hundred grams either way can often make a critical difference in estimating the outlook for these babies.)

The delivery room may have been crowded with any or all of the following people:

- Your obstetrician.
- A perinatologist.
- One or two obstetrical nurses (plus a "scrub nurse" or operating nurse in the case of a C-section).
- A neonatologist (a pediatrician with one to three extra years of training in the treatment of high-risk newborns).
- A pediatrician, if the hospital has no neonatologist on staff. (A pediatrician has three years of training [internship and residency] in the medical care of children, in addition to four years of medical school.)

- A neonatology or pediatric nurse.
- An anesthesiologist, present to administer general, epidural, or other forms of anesthesia.
- An anesthetist, to assist the anesthesiologist.
- One or more residents (doctors receiving specialty training in pediatrics, obstetrics, or anesthesia).
- A fellow in perinatology or neonatology (a doctor who has completed specialty training in pediatrics or obstetrics and who is now receiving additional "subspecialty" training).
- A medical student, assisting a doctor.
- Technicians in radiology and/or respiratory therapy.

In a small, local hospital fewer people would be in attendance. At teaching hospitals or tertiary facilities (a Level III hospital with the most up-to-date technological care), most of the above people may have been in and out of the room at one time or another.

Once your doctor confirmed that a premature delivery could not be prevented, pain medications, like Demerol and Nisentil, were probably not given to you unless absolutely necessary. Demerol and Nisentil are narcotics that can pass through the mother's body to the fetus and may depress a newborn's respiratory abilities. Although narcotics like these are used in term deliveries, they are not advised for a premature birth because a premature baby is at heightened risk of breathing difficulties as it is. Also, drugs could make the premature baby sluggish at birth, delaying spontaneous breathing and making the initial assessment of the baby by a pediatrician or neonatologist more difficult, since it is hard to tell the difference between the effects of the drug and problems related to prematurity. However, if you happened to have delivered shortly after receiving one of these drugs, the baby's respiration can be maintained, even by a respirator, if necessary.

The use of an epidural anesthesia is often recommended for laboring mothers in a premature delivery because it can protect a tiny baby's soft head from the powerful forces of the mother's pushing. Epidural anesthesia decreases the urge to push felt by most laboring mothers, and little if any of this medication crosses over to the baby. The premature baby is much more fragile than a term baby and his journey through the birth canal must be made as smooth and easy as possible.

If epidural anesthesia was used, it was probably administered when your cervix was dilated five centimeters, because progress from five centimeters to birth (at ten centimeters) can be quite rapid when the baby is small. An epidural is a regional anesthesia; it numbs only the lower half of the body and does not put the mother "to sleep." The injection is given through the mother's back, into a space alongside the spinal cord known as the "epidural space"; it is given while the mother is sitting up or lying on her side curled into fetal position with her back arched like a cat's. Often, a small catheter, a plastic tube similar to an IV tube, is inserted into and left in this space, as a passage to the epidural space through which medication can be easily reinjected during labor or delivery.

When I delivered Ashley I asked for epidural anesthesia, more for psychological than for medical reasons. I had had a somewhat difficult time delivering my first baby, Danielle (everything is relative!), and asked for epidural anesthesia after seventeen hours of labor. I had been pleasantly surprised to discover after receiving it that I had no trouble pushing appropriately by timing my pushes with the monitor and had vowed to have it with my next child.

Whether or not you were given pain medication or anesthesia, you were almost certainly placed on a fetal monitor. A fetal monitor is used routinely throughout the labor and delivery of premature babies because these babies are at risk for "fetal distress," usually diagnosed on the basis of various abnormal patterns of fetal heart tones and/or acidosis (the pH of the fetal blood being below the normal range of about 7.2). Electronic fetal heart-rate monitoring is used to evaluate the baby's response to the stress of labor by recording the baby's heart rate. There are two types of fetal monitors that can be used—external and internal.

External monitoring involves placing two lightweight belts

around the mother's abdomen—one that picks up the baby's heartbeat and one that monitors the mother's contractions. Information from the belts is transmitted to a machine that prints it out in a line graph. An internal fetal monitor is more invasive, in that it is inserted through the vagina into the amniotic sac, but it gives a great deal more information about the well-being of the fetus by continuously monitoring the baby's heartbeat and beat-to-beat heart-rate variability. An internal monitor is used only if the mother's membranes have ruptured (her water has broken) either naturally or artificially. A very tiny electrode wire is painlessly attached to the fetus's scalp and records the infant's heartbeat. A thin, fluid-filled plastic tube may also be inserted through the vagina and up into the uterine cavity until it rests alongside the fetus. The information gathered here is transmitted to a machine that prints out a line graph showing the strength and duration of the contractions. In many hospitals, a fetal blood sample may also be taken during internal monitoring, which can permit the identification of any number of fetal problems by measuring the fetus's blood-oxygen level and pH. Many obstetricians still opt for external monitors, although it is difficult to use them to monitor very premature infants.

After the readout from the external or internal monitors, you may have been asked to change position (lying flat on your back can impair your circulation and reduce the baby's oxygen supply) or you may have been given extra oxygen through a face mask. Information from fetal monitoring is also of help in determining whether or not a C-section is necessary. For example, if the baby is showing some signs of stress and natural delivery is not imminent, C-section is the quickest way to remove the baby from a potentially dangerous situation and prevent death or permanent damage.

In order to protect the premature baby's soft head during a vaginal delivery, your obstetrician may have removed the last obstacle to your baby's arrival by enlarging your vaginal opening with an episiotomy. An episiotomy is an incision made in the muscles and tissue of the perineum, the area between your vagina and rectum. An episiotomy serves to minimize the amount of pressure the baby receives in passing through the relatively tight perineal muscles. The episiotomy may also have been necessary if your obstetrician decided to use forceps to assist the baby in being born as gently as possible. Episiotomies cause no permanent damage and usually heal quickly.

Forceps may also have been used in your premie's delivery. You may think it sounds strange, but putting these hard metal instruments around your baby's head can be more gentle than a natural exit through the birth canal. There are forceps that are specially designed for the premature baby. They resemble spoons and fit snugly around the baby's head to protect it from the mother's bony pelvis. Some obstetricians prefer to use their hands to guide the head out of the vagina.

Usually, a premature baby is delivered vaginally, but sometimes a C-section is performed. The C-section rate for premies is twice that of full-term babies. A C-section may be done because of infection, placenta previa, failure to progress in labor, with signs of fetal distress, or a difficult breech presentation (when the baby is positioned with buttocks or feet down; breech presentations are rare at term but much more common in a premature delivery). A C-section can be performed under general anesthesia, with the mother unconscious at the birth, or under regional (epidural) anesthesia, which blocks sensation and muscle control in the lower portion of the body while the mother remains fully awake. With either anesthesia, the surgery is performed behind a screen set across the woman's midsection.

If you had general anesthesia, your husband may not have been allowed in the delivery room with you. However, if there was any time for discussion with your physicians prior to the cesarean, your husband may well have been allowed in the delivery room, to watch over the care of your infant, even if this might not have been the usual hospital policy. If your husband was in the delivery room, he probably played the role of the baby's advocate and guardian while you were still unconscious. With epidural anesthesia, the mother remains awake for the delivery and the father can usually be at his wife's side. If you had epidural anesthesia, you and your husband could both see your baby, but your husband would have been in the best position (literally) to observe your baby's care closely.

As one mother I know of tells it:

"I fought tooth and nail for a vaginal delivery, but because of a uterine anomaly, my doctors insisted on a C-section. I was given an epidural, rather than general anesthesia, so I could remain awake for it, and my husband was allowed into the operating room as well."

As another mother describes it, the C-section seemed to be over before she even knew what was happening:

"My doctor made plans for an emergency C-section. He made the decision at 6:00 A.M. and Emily was born at 7:11 A.M. I didn't have time to panic. I was under general anesthesia. The next thing I remember is the doctor waking me up to tell me I had had a three-pound ten-ounce girl who was breathing on her own. Then I fell back asleep."

IMMEDIATELY AFTER DELIVERY

The events surrounding a premature delivery certainly help to weaken your confidence as a parent. You likely gave birth with feelings of fear and helplessness. Your baby's medical needs were so acute that they took precedence over your need to be with your child. One mother describes the inevitable and immediate separation this way:

"When my baby was born, I heard him cry. I heard the doctor yelling for a neonatologist. I didn't have my glasses on and I'm very nearsighted so I couldn't see the baby. Then they whisked him away. . . . He was born on a Tuesday and I didn't see him until Friday."

As soon as the obstetrician had your baby in his hands, the neonatologist or pediatrician stepped in and took over your baby's care. Everyone in the delivery room may have looked relieved or even said that "your baby looks great." They were coming from a very different perspective, comparing your baby to other premies, not full-term newborns. Or they may have said nothing, always a worrisome situation. In any case, *you* were almost certainly not reassured by what you saw. A premie usually looks more like a fetus than a baby—because that is just what he is.

However things go for you and your husband after the delivery, it is at this moment that you become functional parents, even if you were soon asleep and your baby was moved to an intensive-care nursery. Always remember: there is no magic time when parenting must begin. You do *not* have to hold your baby immediately after delivery to be a loving parent. You do *not* have to find out all you can immediately about your baby's medical status and chances of survival. You may need to rest after the long ordeal of preterm labor and delivery in preparation for the long, stressful months ahead as a premie's parent. You and your husband may decide that he will be the baby's primary advocate and parent in the first few hours or days. There is no right or wrong to these decisions or events, as long as your decisions are based on what is best for your child and your family. That, after all, is what being a parent is about.

Many women I've spoken with said that their husbands were in the NICU (newborn intensive-care unit) well before they were. This mother is a good example:

"My husband saw Emily before I did. He was in the nursery minutes after she was born. When I came to after the C-section, I had no desire to see her. Every time I woke up, all I wanted to do was lie there and sleep. Then at around 4:00 P.M., I suddenly woke up in a panic—I hadn't seen my daughter yet!"

The neonatology staff was busy with your baby and it may have been difficult to get much more than a peek as they rushed to ensure that he was breathing properly. The staff also weighs and tests the babies. All newborns are rated at birth by the pediatrician on what is called an Apgar scale. Babies receive a score of zero, one, or two for each of five categories: color, heart rate, respiration, muscle tone, and reflex irritability in response to suction. A total score of seven to ten is considered reassuring. Sometimes, though, premies who received high scores at birth will later develop respiratory problems. A low score is a signal to the medical staff that immediate resuscitation efforts are needed. The baby's score will be reevaluated at five and again at twenty minutes after birth. Don't put too much stock in Apgar scores, though. They are simply not that reliable as predictors of outcome. One study of Apgar scores points out that much of what these scores measure is specifically related to maturity; using full-term Apgar scales to assess a premie newborn's status is therefore inappropriate. So when you hear your baby's score, remember that your baby is being compared to a term baby.

No matter how sick your baby was, you probably saw him or touched him, at least for a moment. Sadly, you were probably not able to hold him. This is because your infant's condition was unstable. Just holding him for a few loving minutes could have caused his temperature to drop and increased the risk of medical complications. You may worry that without this initial contact the "bonding" process you have read so much about did not occur. Don't despair. Those first few minutes are not the be-all and end-all of bonding. Attachment between an infant and his parents is a process that takes time, work, and love. And there will certainly be plenty of opportunities for that later.

Assuming you gave birth in a tertiary-care center, a special transport incubator was ready to rush your newborn to the intensive-care unit or intermediate-care nursery for further treatment and care. Otherwise, the baby may have been transported to such a facility at another hospital. Your husband may have gone with the baby, leaving you alone. Ideally, you two had the time to agree on this course of action before the actual delivery. In the rush, though, you may not have had the chance to talk about anything, and your husband probably felt painfully torn between going with the baby and being with you.

Even if his going with the baby was your decision, you may have felt alone, deserted, and even guilty for not being with your child. Be comforted that even though you may have had these feelings, it was best that your husband went with the baby. In the end, you probably rested a little easier, knowing that your baby was in safe hands—if not your own, then the next best. Most important, you and your husband gave an important message to the medical staff by letting them know that you were both prepared for and insistent upon taking an active parenting role. One mother says that she did not feel deserted by her husband, only happy that he at least was able to go with their baby:

"My husband stayed with me while I was being sewn up. After that, he went to check on the baby and I was put in a recovery room. I was so exhausted, I don't remember missing or needing my husband."

Sometimes, after the delivery, the mother is given a sedative or painkiller. Many women, however, prefer to remain alert after the birth so that they can find out as much as possible about their premature baby's well-being during those first few hours. One mother says the nurse was insistent on giving her Demerol after her twins were born by C-section at twenty-seven weeks gestation:

"She said I'd need it but I didn't want it because I was so afraid that if I fell asleep the babies wouldn't make it. Eventually, I took a little Demerol and then went to see the babies twice before they were moved to another hospital four hours later. My husband followed the ambulance over there. My dad, mother, mother-in-law, and best friend stayed with me. I remember being very angry with them because I knew they basically felt that the babies would die and they kept telling me to just get some sleep. But I felt that if I slept, I wouldn't be able to take care of the situation."

3.   The Premature Newborn: How He Differs from a Full-Term Newborn

As mentioned before, a premature baby usually looks like a fetus. Or, as one mother put it, like a "Tinkertoy baby"! Parents may feel guilty if they are initially frightened, or even repulsed, by their baby's appearance. This chapter will help you cope with these feelings but, more important, will let you know what to expect of your premature newborn. A premature baby is in many ways very different from a baby born at term.

A preterm baby is by definition any baby born after less than thirty-seven weeks gestation. A full-term baby is born at thirty-seven to forty-two weeks. Although "premature" has a definitional cutoff, there are no absolutes or sudden cutoffs in real-life prematurity. Growth and development are gradual processes, so the degree of prematurity is much more important than the mere fact that an infant meets the definition for prematurity. Premies vary widely in appearance and abilities. Some of this early variation is related to them as individuals, but much of it is strongly related to how premature they are, why they were born prematurely, and how well they thrived while they were still in the womb. They may weigh two pounds or five pounds; they may experience a number of medical problems or only a few. There are as many different looks and personalities as there are premature babies.

Before we get into medical problems, let's take an important side trip and look at the differences between premature babies and other low-birth-weight babies. Much of the research does not distinguish between your baby, born early, and a small full-term baby. Babies born on time but tiny have intra-uterine growth retardation (IUGR). Although the two groups may look alike, many of the problems that a preterm infant has are different from those facing a baby with IUGR. Premature and low-birth-weight babies appear to differ somewhat in their medical risks and long-term outlook. You might be relieved to know that the outlook for premies tends to be better than the outlook for very small full-term infants.

Low birth weight, like prematurity, has a rigid definition in a fluid world: a baby is by definition "low birth weight" if his weight at birth was less than 2,500 grams (about five pounds eight ounces). A baby's low birth weight might be due to his being premature or to the fact that he did not grow well in the womb (had IUGR), or to a combination of both. It is estimated that about two-thirds of low-birth-weight babies born in the United States are small because of prematurity. The rest are small because of growth problems in the womb, which may be related to any of a number of factors, ranging from infection to poor nutrition to heavy smoking. Unfortunately, it is often difficult to be certain that a mother's "dates" are correct, making it a challenge to determine whether her baby was born early, or full-term and small.

Although recent studies have begun to separate premature infants from those born on time but small, much of the available information on prematurity is based on research that does *not* separate those born early from those born small. Keep this fact in mind as you read about studies, some of which are cited in this book. Because people doing medical research are so recently beginning to distinguish between "premature" and other low-birth-weight infants, even up-to-date medical information may not give you a fully accurate picture of your own situation.

When your baby was born he had a "gestational age" (GA) and was probably also classified as premature, intrauterine growth-retarded, or both. Gestational age simply refers to the amount of time, from conception to birth, that the baby spent in the womb. Gestational age is usually figured by counting the number of weeks from the date of your last menstrual period. At times, though, these dates may be uncertain or inaccurate. For this reason, doctors usually score premature babies on a chart of reflexes, appearance factors, and other items to estimate their maturity and gestational age.

In more general terms, low-birth-weight infants are placed into one of four categories:

1.   Premature and small for gestational age (SGA): This means that your baby not only was born early but also was smaller than expected, given the infant's time in the womb (prematurity and IUGR). Your baby may have had growth difficulties in the womb, which may or may not be related to his being born early. (It is also possible, though, that your due date was not calculated correctly and your baby's gestational age is less than originally thought, in which case he is even more premature than originally thought but does not have IUGR.) Babies who are both premature and small for gestational age may have two reasons to be at risk for medical problems, rather than just one.

2.   Premature and appropriate for gestational age (AGA): This means that your baby is the size he should be, given the amount of time spent in the womb.

3.   Premature and large for gestational age (LGA): Although born too soon, this baby appears to have thrived while inside the womb. (There is also the possibility, however, that an error was made in calculating the due date and your baby wasn't born prematurely at all.)

4.   Full-term but small for gestational age: This baby was

born on time (assuming the due date was correct) but seems to have had some difficulties while growing in the womb (IUGR without prematurity).

A PREMATURE BABY'S APPEARANCE

Parents I have spoken with often say they were shocked by their premie baby's appearance. Premies do not look like the fat, round-cheeked Gerber babies of their parents' dreams. When my husband and I first saw Ashley, for example, her neonatologist and my obstetrician tried to bolster our spirits by emphasizing what a big premie she was, compared to what we had all feared. While I appreciated that fact, I was also painfully aware that she had absolutely no fat stores—long and lean, as my husband would say—and was obviously fetal in appearance. We were better off than we had feared, but things were anything but rosy for our little one. I did not, of course, ask to hold her. After one solid look I was eager for them to get her onto the warming table. (I will remind you again and again about how fragile premies are. At delivery, moments away from that warming table can significantly add to your baby's risks.) I almost hung off the delivery table trying to see how things were going with her there! She had real hair, not premie fuzz. I was inordinately pleased with this and saw it as a good omen. I also was acutely aware, though, that even for a premie she was distinctively unattractive. That didn't bother me so much—if anything it made her seem more vulnerable and increased my devotion. Besides, I knew she'd grow out of it. But I worried about it for a very practical reason. All of us, even health-care providers, are drawn to attractiveness. I knew Ashley would get good medical care, but I feared that she might not get the extra, uncalled-for attention a more attractive baby might receive.

Happily, not all parents react with alarm at the first sight of their premie. One mother describes her basically good first impressions of her baby this way:

"Kirsten was two pounds six ounces when she was born but I didn't think she looked weird; she just looked like my baby. I was, ironically, ecstatic—so happy to see her that I didn't really notice what she looked like until I saw her the next morning in the NICU."

Another mother talks about seeing her daughter for the first time in the NICU, not the delivery room. For this mother, a little girl's true beauty showed through all the tubes:

"She was small but we were still proud of her. She had pretty dark hair and dark eyes. She was cute but she was attached to all these machines—a respirator, a catheter in her navel, temperature sensors—and she was strapped down. We could touch her but couldn't hold her."

Often, a mother's first view of her baby is through the eyes of Dad, who reports back from the NICU before the mother has had a chance to get into the nursery herself:

"I asked my husband, 'How big is she?' He picked up a can of my hairspray and said, 'This big.' She weighed two pounds."

If at first sight you noticed that your baby was less than beautiful, you may have felt guilty—after all, love should be blind. You may have expected that parental love would conquer any negative feelings about your baby's appearance. Don't feel guilty if you found yourself put off by your baby's appearance at first; it doesn't mean that you didn't love him. Premies have been described as looking like monkeys, plucked chickens, mice, birds, and even bugs. Some of these are a bit too imaginative for my blood, but don't chastise yourself for possibly having similar thoughts. Soon your premie will look more pleasing and more like the baby of your dreams. But long before then—from the moment he is born—he needs your love and attention. You will find these easier to give if you don't let guilt get in the way. Your attention, after all, means more to your baby's well-being than anyone else's.

At first, your premie will probably seem shockingly small and fragile to you. Some are from head to bottom no bigger than an adult's hand. They are undeniably tiny. While most term babies weigh seven and a half pounds, the average premie weighs five and a half pounds. Some born as early as twenty-six weeks can weigh less than two pounds. One mother of a little girl born at twenty-seven weeks says that her daughter, now four, loves to look at pictures of herself as a tiny premie. In particular, she enjoys a shot of her little hand in her mother's:

"She always says, 'Mommy, I want to see the hand picture.' It's a special picture for her. She puts her hand in the same spot in mine as it is in the photo and says, 'See how big I am?' "

To give you an idea of the small size of a premature baby's head, for example, see the chart below that shows head circumference for various gestational ages.

HEAD CIRCUMFERENCE OF BABIES
BY GESTATIONAL AGE

28 *weeks gestation*	11 *inches (about the size of a large orange)*
32 *weeks gestation*	11.5 *inches*
36 *weeks gestation*	12.8 *inches*
40 *weeks gestation*	14 *inches*

Although during the early months of your pregnancy the fetus got all the basics completed—fingers, toes, facial features—complete maturation of some of the finer points has been interrupted. This is why, aside from being tiny, your baby may not "look right" to you. The abdomen usually looks quite large, which may be in part due to swelling, and yet the rib cage will almost certainly be visible, making the premature infant look like a victim of starvation. Hands and feet may be swollen as well.

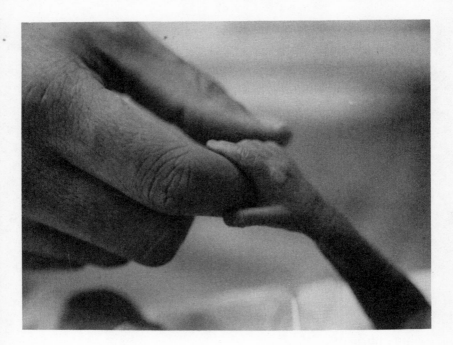

A tiny hand reaches out.

The color and texture of a premature baby's skin are un-
like those of a term infant. The skin is usually quite ruddy and
its texture is generally very thin and almost transparent, with
small drying sections looking thick and parchmentlike. Under
the thin skin, especially on the abdomen and scalp, numerous
veins will be visible. The thicker the skin, the less visible the
vessels. This appearance of the skin is due to the fact that a
premature baby has not yet developed fat deposits underneath
it. It is during the last months in utero that fetuses put on most
of their fat, and your baby missed that stage. There may be a
rash or some cracking and peeling of the skin. If the infant is
anemic for some reason, the skin color may be quite pale rather
than dark red. Black babies born prematurely may look more
white than black at first. Don't worry about this; your baby
will look darker within a week or so. In general, your baby's
skin color may change frequently, depending on his condition
and even on whether or not he has just been moved. Again

remember that these babies are fragile. One of the best signs of their overall status from moment to moment is their coloration. Within minutes it can switch from ghastly gray to a comfortable pink; concern should arise only if poor coloration is prolonged or very frequent.

Your baby may be covered with a thick layer of long, extremely fine hair over his whole body, or at least on the forehead, back, shoulders, and arms. This hair is known as lanugo and is the downy cover on all human fetuses that grows in during the second trimester. Full-term infants lose this downy hair during the last month in utero. The less premature baby may have only a small amount of lanugo at birth, because the lanugo begins to disappear after twenty-seven weeks gestational age; lanugo may be barely noticeable in very fair-skinned and -haired premies. Lanugo will soon disappear by itself and is unrelated to the child's health. It was simply a protective cover for the fetus while in utero and now serves little purpose.

Eyebrows and eyelashes are visible on most premature babies, with the exception of very fair infants or babies born before twenty-eight weeks. Fingernails and toenails are not fully grown out until thirty-five weeks. (For some reason I have found that a number of my patients' mothers are very concerned about this. You really should not worry; the nails will grow in quite normally with time.)

In very premature babies, nipples are barely visible and there is no areola, the dark area around the nipple. Ears may be unformed and shapeless with little or no incurving of the edge. In more mature babies, the ear will be well defined and the cartilage more firm. The bottoms of the feet will not be heavily creased or wrinkled as would a term baby's. By thirty-eight weeks, the creases should cover the sole of the premature baby's foot.

Another noticeable physical difference: the premature baby's genitals will probably not yet be well formed. In boys, the testicles are still high in the scrotum and have not descended. In girls, the labia majora, or outer folds of the vagina, are widely separated and the inner folds, or labia minora, may be protruding. Within the next few weeks, this disconcerting appearance will begin to change and your baby will begin to look more like a "real" boy or girl to you. Again, although the immature genitals may look odd to parents, this will not affect your baby in any long-term way. They will mature quite normally with time.

Until about thirty-eight weeks, the premature baby's skull bones are malleable. Head shape may be affected by the mattresses on which premies lie; some premies temporarily develop an elongated shape to their heads as a result. Some hospitals now have water beds available for use; these may take the pressure

The footprint of a thirty-one-week premature baby weighing 1,270 grams at birth compared with that of a full-term baby weighing 3,600 grams at birth.

off the skull. But either way, this head "molding" should eventually resolve itself.

As time passes and your baby matures, you will become more comfortable with his appearance. Most parents feel better psychologically if they bring in clothes, incidentals, and toys that make their baby more of an individual and that help define him or her sexually. Nurses and doctors may be so busy in the basic medical care of your infant that they are not always sensitive to this parental need. I still remember spending precious time late at night making Ashley bows after I had returned home from the nursery. I would bring them in, tape one on her head, and leave the rest in the drawer below her incubator, only to find them all tossed out the next day. It was equally upsetting to see her with her genitals clearly visible in a urine collection bag, only to have the nurses refer to my "she" as a "he." These situations are not infrequent and you should try to be patient when they occur. But whatever the response, don't stop what you are doing or feel foolish about it! All these small, affectionate actions make your baby more of an individual and are part of the bonding process that you and your premie urgently need, as much as he needs his medical care. Keep them up; they are part of becoming and being a parent. Both you and your baby will develop better because of them.

Obviously, your baby's appearance and sexual identity have a great deal to do with how you come to love that child as a person in his or her own right. Sometimes, when the hospital staff is very busy and stressed, some of them may forget that each baby is an individual and that babies and their parents have nonmedical needs. But the important thing is that you as a parent don't forget your baby's, your family's, and your own needs. If you show strong concern about your baby's needs, this will come across to the medical staff and they will be more aware of those needs, too.

A PREMATURE BABY'S POSTURE AND REFLEXES

The way your baby holds himself may distress you. He may lie limply, with legs extended. The premature baby has minimal muscle tone at birth. For example, at about thirty weeks gestation, a premie will flex his little legs at the thigh; by around thirty-four weeks gestation, the characteristic full-term infant's froglike flexing of the legs will be evident. (Term newborns, as you may know, keep their limbs strongly flexed.) Because he has little muscle tone, the premature baby's heel can be brought all the way up to his ear and his arm can be wrapped around his neck like a scarf. As the baby grows older, his arms and legs become more resistant, and muscle tone improves; it would be impossible to perform either of those moves then. A premature baby also has little or no control over head movement. If you pull a premature baby up from a supine to a sitting position, the head will lag behind with little or no control. A term baby would tend to hold his head forward as you pulled him up. This "righting reflex" is not evident in premies.

The Moro, or startle, reflex is strong in term babies but weak or not evident in premature babies. When a term baby hears a loud noise or loses his balance momentarily, he should react with this startle reflex, tensing and arching his body, thrusting arms and legs out and then quickly inward as if trying to grab on to something. Term babies also have surprisingly strong hand grips. Premies, however, are unable to grasp in this way, so don't be too disappointed if, the first time you offer your finger to your baby, he doesn't give you that reassuring squeeze you crave. This ability will come in time.

Many reflexes that we associate with a baby's survival, such as sucking and swallowing, are just not developed in a premature baby. So not only does your baby not look like the baby of your dreams; it may seem to you that he doesn't act like a real baby either. This is because many reflexes simply are not part of an infant's repertoire until after thirty-four weeks gestation.

Rooting is the name for the reflex that enables babies to turn toward a nipple to eat. In premature babies, this reflex is usually weak and slow. Sucking is also usually weak. Sucking is more complicated than it may seem, since it involves using the lips and gums to form a seal around the mother's areola, then using the tongue to press the nipple against the roof of the mouth, and then moving the tongue backward to express the milk. Babies born after thirty-two weeks gestation, however, will *begin* to have a stronger sucking reflex. Swallowing is the reflex that naturally must occur after rooting and sucking, but in premature babies, swallowing, too, may be a reflex not yet developed. Swallowing can be difficult because the baby must monitor the amount of liquid in the mouth so that he doesn't have more than he can swallow at one time. The baby must also breathe while eating and be able to gag if he happens to swallow too much or chokes. In other words, the simple act of feeding or nursing is not easy at all and involves a number of complicated abilities and reflexes. Weakness of any or all of these reflexes will obviously have a great effect on the method of feeding available to your infant. (For detailed information on nursing, bottle feeding, and tube feeding, see Chapter 7.)

HOW IS A PREMIE DIFFERENT ON THE INSIDE?

Your baby doesn't just look different on the outside; he's different on the inside as well. Your baby's organs are immature. They will continue to grow now that he is outside the womb, of course, but the immaturity of your baby's organs will have a great effect on what he can and can't do right now and on what may or may not happen to him medically. Parents of premature babies find out right away that it's what's *inside* that counts. As one mother of a premie who *looked* better than most tells it:

"Jonathan was born weighing five pounds two ounces. He was eight weeks early, but I have very big babies. The doctors told me if I had carried to term, he would have weighed over ten pounds. But then I found out that birth weight has nothing much to do with a premie's problems. There were babies at the hospital weighing only four pounds who went home sooner than Jonathan did. Jonathan's lungs, liver, and heart were all very immature."

Let's go over some of the ways *your* premie's immaturity may affect his health in the early weeks and months of his life.

As you probably know by now, breathing is one of the most serious sources of difficulty for premature babies. As a fetus, your baby did not have to use his lungs to get oxygen. Oxygen was supplied directly by the mother, through the placenta, and the inactive lungs were filled with fluid. By the end of twenty-four weeks gestation, the fetus's lungs *begin* to manufacture a substance known as surfactant, which becomes very necessary once the baby is born and must breathe on his own. Surfactant is constantly being made by cells lining the insides of the lung's air sacs, or alveoli, and works to prevent these sacs from collapsing completely after exhaling. With surfactant, the lungs can refill easily with the next breath. Without it, the alveoli are like a withered bunch of grapes and cannot accept the new breath of air. Also, the alveolar sacs themselves undergo some development in the last trimester. Many premies who are born before they are able to make enough surfactant and before the alveoli are fully developed will have respiratory-distress syndrome (RDS), also known as hyaline membrane disease (HMD).

A premature baby's cardiovascular system also may not be fully ready to cope with the demands of surviving outside the womb. Remember that in utero the lungs are not being used to oxygenate the fetus's blood (see above). In utero, fetuses have a connection between the blood vessels just outside the heart, known as the ductus arteriosus. This connection permits blood going to the fetus's lungs to mix with blood going to other parts of the body. Once the baby is outside the womb, this opening must close so that the blood going to the lungs to receive oxygen does not mix with blood going to the rest of the body. Following birth, *after* blood goes through the lungs, it goes back to the heart and then passes to the rest of the body. In most term babies, this connection spontaneously closes up within three to seventy-two hours after birth. In a premie, however, the closing of the ductus can take as long as three weeks; sometimes the ductus in premature babies reopens after closing.

The brain and nervous system are in many ways immature even in a full-term newborn, and it is not surprising that they are even less mature in a premature baby. This is probably the single most important thing to remember when getting to know your premie. An immature nervous system affects your interactions with your baby in the first few weeks, months, and even years ahead.

Much brain growth occurs in the last trimester of pregnancy. An immature brain does not in any way mean your baby is or will be retarded. The brain should continue to grow and develop, and there is increasing evidence that the way you interact with your premie can have an effect on that development. There is every reason to assume that intellectually your premature baby will be completely normal.

Head circumference is the best measurement of brain growth and will be followed closely in the first few weeks and months of your premie's life. There are defined patterns of normal growth. Sudden changes can be worrisome. For example, if head size increases too rapidly, this may be a sign of hydrocephalus, a condition in which the fluid around the brain does not circulate normally and instead builds up, applying pressure to the brain tissue. (See the chart on page 28 for the normal head circumferences at various gestational ages.)

A premature baby's liver is often immature as well, leading to an extremely common problem among premies: hyperbilirubinemia, causing jaundice, or a yellow coloration of the skin and the whites of the eyes. Rare is the premie who escapes this problem! Bilirubin is a colored pigment that comes from the normal breakdown of red blood cells. If the levels are too high in the bloodstream, the pigment will get deposited in many places in the body. It does little damage in most places, but if it is deposited in the brain, it can cause permanent brain damage. This is why high levels of bilirubin must be prevented. The most common cause of hyperbilirubinemia in premies is an immature liver. The liver's job is to break down the bilirubin into small pieces, which can then be flushed out of the body in the urine and stool. Immature livers cannot do a good job of breaking down the bilirubin pigment.

Infections are also a very common problem in premies because their immune system, which fights infection, is extremely immature. The majority of premies who are in the hospital more than a week will be treated for one or more serious infections. It is very hard to diagnose infections in premature infants because even serious infections often show as nothing more than general symptoms that can also occur just because of everyday premie fragility: poor color, poor appetite, low body temperature, and the like. Although antibiotics have risks (because of side effects), it is better to prescribe them right away rather than wait for the results of a "culture." Otherwise, there is the risk that a baby could die or be permanently disabled from an untreated infection. When an infection is suspected, blood, intravenous lines, urine, and the like are "cultured" for possible bacteria. The cultures are grown in a laboratory; results take several days. Until results are known, the baby is put on antibiotics. If any culture is positive, the antibiotics will be continued for a period of time; if the cultures have no growth, antibiotics will be stopped.

Kidney function is also immature in a premie. Even term infants do not have fully mature kidney function. Ordinarily, this does not cause any real problems, assuming the baby is doing well. But if problems develop that require certain medications, these medicines can strain the kidneys' function. For example, immature kidneys may have trouble processing the sodium that is in some antibiotics. If a premie has heart problems, he can go into heart failure, just as your grandparents or parents might do. Heart failure can strain the kidneys and cause fluid retention. If your premie is very ill and has short periods of time with very low blood pressure, or even cardiac arrest (heart stopping), the kidneys can be harmed by the decreased blood supply during that time. In other words, some medical problems and some medical treatments can have effects on your premie's immature kidneys. Happily, in the majority of instances these problems resolve themselves within weeks.

SOME OF THE MEDICAL PROBLEMS PREMIES MAY FACE

Now that we have covered many of the ways in which premies are physically immature, this section will cover a number of the early medical problems your premie may face as a result of these immaturities. Before you read it, bear in mind that your baby won't necessarily experience any of these. Still, you may be frightened—just knowing about all the things that *can* go wrong may feel worse than not knowing about the problems at all. If you feel this might be the case for you, you should read about only those issues that apply to your baby's health right now and refer to additional sections if and when you need to.

Apnea, bradycardia, and tachycardia.   Apnea is a problem in breathing regulation. It does not mean that your baby has lung problems. Bradycardia is a problem in heart-rate regulation. It does not mean your baby has heart problems. Both apnea and bradycardia are related to your premie's immature nervous system. Normal breathing at rest is slow and regular. Premies' breathing sometimes slows too much; a premie may go twenty or more seconds without a breath. This is called apnea. Thirty percent of premies born weighing less than 1,750 grams (or three pounds fourteen ounces) suffer from apnea. It is not easy to differentiate between periodic breathing (occasionally going fifteen to thirty seconds between breaths, without discomfort) and apnea (frequently turning pale and clammy while not breathing). Apnea occurs almost routinely after a young premie is fed. When a baby has an "apneic spell," he usually starts breathing again on his own, but sometimes requires gentle stimulation to be "reminded to breathe" (tapping of feet or hands, flexing a leg, rubbing the skin, or tapping on the isolette wall). Apnea is more worrisome if it requires vigorous stimulation, is very frequent and not in association with feeding, is associated with noticeable clinical signs, or occurs in association with bradycardia, a slowing of the heart rate.

Apnea is a less serious sign of nervous system immaturity and is less worrisome than bradycardia. Apnea in and of itself is not a major problem, but if it is severe, it may be a sign that the baby's problem is not just an immature nervous system but rather that some medical problem exists, such as an infection, for example. Premies prone to apnea are placed on a machine called an apnea monitor, which beeps whenever there has been an unacceptably long pause in breathing. The monitor can be set to go off at different breathing levels. An episode of bradycardia or tachycardia (rapid heartbeat) will also set off this alarm; again, the level at which it goes off must be set. Babies with moderate or severe apnea are frequently on stimulant medications, usually theophylline (often used for asthma because of its effects on the lungs) or caffeine. Both stimulate the respiratory center in the brain but may have the side effect of an increased heart rate and stomach irritation.

The stomach irritation is important for you as a parent to know about, since you may well bring your baby home on this medicine. As a doctor, I never thought twice about the logistical problems associated with this side effect; I would just write an order about when to give medicines and when to feed and, with the expertise of the nurses, it was done. But stomach effects became of real concern to me the day I took Ashley home. In the process of getting her discharged and driving her home, we had to let her feeding and medicine schedules go out of

cycle. This certainly added to the stress of her home adjustment. Her theophylline doses were coming very close to her
feedings. If I delayed a dose, her monitor would start beeping,
but if I gave it to her and then fed her, she would vomit up
her breast milk—and her theophylline dose. Since she was fed
every two hours, we had to schedule feedings and medicine
quite tightly. It took days to get her back on schedule!

Jaundice.   As discussed earlier, jaundice is usually a sign of
liver immaturity. Even healthy full-term babies often have
jaundice, but it resolves within the first week or so of life.
Premature babies have a harder time. If your baby shows signs
of jaundice, usually on the fifth or sixth day of life, nurses will
probably take blood samples from the heel every six to twelve
hours to test for the amount of bilirubin in the bloodstream.
The real danger of jaundice is that, left untreated, bilirubin
levels could climb high enough to cause brain damage. Treatment in most cases involves the use of special light bulbs; the
light breaks down the pigment being deposited in the skin and
removes bilirubin from the rest of the body, too. Since the
wavelengths in these bulbs can damage the retina, the eyes
must be patched while the lights are on. In very severe cases,
the bilirubin can be removed directly from the blood by re-
placing the baby's blood in an "exchange transfusion." This
is avoided if possible, since, as we've already discussed, there
are always risks to putting a premie's body out of equilibrium,
in this case by rapidly changing the blood pressure and a number of other things during the exchange. A promising new
medicine may be available in the near future; this drug (Su-
protoporphyrin) lowers bilirubin levels and may help doctors
avoid exchange transfusions in the years to come. (For more
about the treatment of jaundice, see Chapter 5.)

Anemia.   During the last weeks of gestation, red blood cells
are normally produced in great numbers. Because premies are
born too soon, they usually have an insufficient number of
iron-rich red blood cells, leading to anemia. A full-term baby

is born with enough iron to last for six months but a premie may have only enough iron for one month. Often the premie's problem is compounded in two ways. First, your baby's umbilical cord may have been cut immediately after delivery in order to perform life-saving actions. This means that some of the blood that normally flows from the placenta to the baby through the cord did not have a chance to empty into the newborn's bloodstream. Second, because your baby has to be watched closely for signs of all the problems we are discussing, his doctors must order a great many blood samples to be drawn from the baby for a variety of tests. Some tiny premies can become anemic after just 10 cc are drawn from them, so this blood is usually replaced on a routine basis through transfusions. Many parents are unnecessarily concerned that these transfusions might put their baby at risk of AIDS. The risk of contracting AIDS from a blood transfusion is now extremely low, since blood donors are tested for this infection. In fact, the risk of being hit by a car when you cross the street is greater than the risk of acquiring AIDS from a blood transfusion. As an AIDS specialist, I promise you that if one of my girls needed a transfusion, I would not think twice about AIDS.

Infections. As discussed above, premature newborns are at increased risk of infection because of their immature immune system. There are two other reasons that their risk is increased. First, they may have become infected in the womb. This may have been the reason for their being born early or it may have happened during labor, especially if your waters broke many hours prior to delivery. Second, being in the intensive-care unit increases your premie's risk of infections as well as his chances of survival. In particular, the very necessary IVs, shunts, and catheters can provide entry for organisms. The intensive-care units are, of course, kept as clean as possible, but infections cannot always be prevented. As you well know, parents and medical staff must scrub to the elbow for two or three minutes before entering the nursery. I often have the raw skin to prove it! This is to help remove some of the bacteria that are always on the skin and thus lessen the likelihood of your premie's becoming infected. Gowns, by the way, although a tradition in nurseries, have never been clearly shown to affect the rate of infection.

As I mentioned earlier, infections in newborns can be difficult to diagnose, and antibiotics are given if infections are even suspected, at least until samples can be checked for bacteria. New ways to treat and prevent premie infections are being looked at very carefully; this is a very exciting, active area of medicine. Some of these new ways include giving the baby immunoglobulin, which contains antibodies that help fight some infections. It takes infants months to begin making antibodies on their own. A full-term infant receives some of his mother's antibodies through the placenta in the last trimester; a premie has not had time for this. So giving certain premies or infected premies antibodies makes a lot of sense; studies so far suggest that doing so may help prevent or treat infection in some premies and does not have major side effects. Doctors have also given white blood cells (the cells that fight some infections) to premies with very serious infections. But white blood cell transfusions can have serious side effects, and it is not clear if they make a difference in the premie's ability to get rid of infections.

Patent ductus arteriosus (PDA).   As explained earlier, the connection known as the ductus arteriosus, which permits blood going to the lungs to mix with blood going to the rest of the body when the baby is still in utero, must close once the baby is born because blood now is going to the lungs to receive oxygen for the rest of the body. When the ductus arteriosus is open, it is called "patent." About 20 percent of premies will have a PDA. Smaller, more premature babies are at greatest risk. Although PDA sometimes does not cause problems, it occasionally leads to serious difficulties such as congestive heart failure and fluid buildup in the lungs, because extra amounts of blood are being pushed by the heart through the PDA and into the lungs. If a PDA is causing clinical problems, it can be closed with medicine or surgery. Surgical closure was a dangerous procedure as recently as ten years ago, but now is a relatively routine, albeit serious, operating room procedure.

Necrotizing enterocolitis (NEC).   This is an intestinal disorder affecting about 2 to 15 percent of very small premies. Its cause remains one of the great mysteries of neonatal medicine; many researchers, including myself, have tried to solve this puzzle. We do know that the more premature a premie is, the greater his risk of NEC, but large, thriving premies about to go home have also gotten NEC. NEC outbreaks sometimes occur in nurseries: that is, many babies in one nursery develop NEC during a single time period. This suggests that NEC is caused by an infection, but no one has yet found an organism that causes it. NEC is diagnosed when a baby stops absorbing his feedings (in other words, he has milk remaining in his stomach at the next feeding), his abdomen becomes distended, and his stool has small amounts of blood in it. The diagnosis can be confirmed by an X ray, which would show air in the intestinal wall, and a blood test showing a decreased number of platelets (cell parts that help blood clot) in the blood. NEC occurs more often in babies who are fed by mouth or tube, but can occur in babies being fed just by vein. NEC is more common in babies receiving formula rather than breast milk, but can occur in either case. When NEC is diagnosed, oral or tube feedings are stopped and antibiotics are begun because there is a risk of the intestines rupturing, and feeding might increase this risk. We all have bacteria in our intestines—this is normal—but these bacteria must not get into the abdomen, which would happen if the intestines ruptured. In most cases, the premie recovers from NEC with no permanent damage. Occasionally, however, the intestines may rupture or be so damaged that portions need to be removed, and a colostomy tube inserted temporarily. This tube collects fecal material from the intestines and diverts it to a bag attached to the lower abdominal wall. In cases where a great deal of bowel needs to be removed, there may not be enough left to absorb food. In this situation, the baby may need to be fed intravenously or given a special liquid diet for months or even years.

Central nervous system (CNS) bleeding.   Remember that all parts of your baby's body interact. In particular, even subtle changes in lung conditions, heart status, blood pressure, infection, pH (acid) status of the blood and the fluid around the brain, and any number of other factors can cause the fragile blood vessels around the brain to rupture and bleed. This is called "central nervous system bleeding" or "CNS bleeding." Small amounts of bleeding, never noticed clinically, appear to be quite common in very small premies. This does not necessarily cause any long-term problems; the blood just slowly gets reabsorbed into the bloodstream. But severe bleeding can damage brain tissue and can lead to permanent problems such as mental retardation, seizures, or hydrocephalus. The amount and location of CNS bleeding are now commonly assessed using one of two very modern techniques: ultrasound, in which sound waves are painlessly bounced off the baby's brain matter and skull, and computerized axial tomography (CAT scan or CT scan), an X-ray technique that can differentiate blood from brain tissue. Ultrasound is more commonly used because it can be done right in the baby's bed, without subjecting him to the trauma of a trip to, and a wait in, the radiology department. It is also much less expensive and quicker. Of course, your doctor will also monitor your baby's head circumference continuously, on the lookout for any sudden or rapid increases in head size, which may be a telltale sign of CNS bleeding.

CNS bleeding is occasionally caused by the rough trip through the birth canal which, as we explained in Chapter 2, can be damaging to a premature baby's soft head. This is why many premies are delivered with forceps or by C-section. Most CNS bleeding occurs within the first seventy-two hours after birth. Bleeding is more common in premies who had respiratory distress at birth and needed "continuous positive airway pressure" (CPAP), a way of blowing air into the lungs to expand the alveoli, during the first few days of life. This does not mean that RDS or CPAP cause bleeding; they may just be a sign of a premie's fragility and prematurity, both of which increase the risk for CNS bleeding, along with his other problems.

The severity of CNS bleeding is scored on a scale of one to four, as follows:

GRADE 1: The blood remains in a small area in or around the brain.

GRADE 2: The blood has extended into the ventricles, the spaces within and around the brain tissue, normally filled with clear cerebrospinal fluid, or CSF. CSF brings nutrients to brain cells the same way blood brings nutrients to other cells, and fills the ventricles and the spaces around the spinal cord.

GRADE 3: The ventricles have become dilated, or enlarged. A Grade 3 bleed means that either the blood has filled the ventricles or it is interfering with the drainage of the CSF from the brain to the spinal cord.

GRADE 4: The blood has spread into the brain tissue itself. (Blood is extremely irritating to brain cells.)

If your baby's doctor suspects CNS bleeding, he or she may do a spinal tap to see if there is blood in the CSF around the spinal cord. Remember that the brain and spinal cord are all one system, so if there is bleeding into the ventricles, the blood will eventually appear in the CSF around the spinal cord. Grades 2 to 4 CNS bleeding can interfere with this CSF flow between the brain and spinal cord, causing the CSF to be trapped in the brain, creating pressure on the brain cells. This is called hydrocephalus; in our grandparents' day it was also called "water on the brain." Left untreated, hydrocephalus can cause mental retardation, so if your baby was diagnosed as having hydrocephalus, a shunt (a tube to help drain off the CSF fluid trapped in the ventricles) might have been placed surgically. (CSF is constantly being made in the ventricles, so your baby's ventricles will never become dry, even with a shunt.) The tube is surgically inserted into one of the baby's ventricles, runs inside the neck, and empties into the abdominal cavity. The shunt must be surgically replaced with longer tubes as your baby grows, so it will continue to reach the abdominal cavity. Your baby may not need a shunt forever. With time, drainage may begin to occur in the normal fashion and the shunt can be removed. The single biggest risk of a shunt is the danger of its becoming infected and the infection's spreading to the brain. How to watch for this and how it is handled are discussed in Chapter 12.

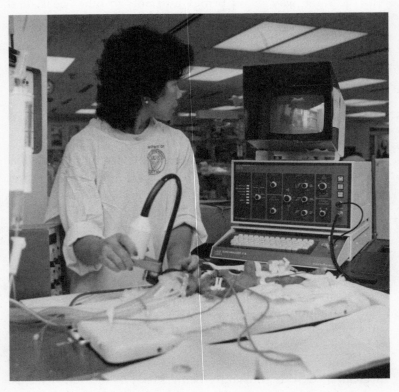

A technician uses ultrasound.

Respiratory-distress syndrome (RDS).   As many as 10 percent of premies suffer from this lung problem. Less than 1 percent of full-term infants will have respiratory-distress syndrome. Premies are at even greater risk for lung problems if they weigh between 1,000 and 1,500 grams (between about two pounds three ounces and three pounds five ounces). Also, the shorter the gestational age, the greater the likelihood of developing lung problems. About two-thirds of premies born at under thirty weeks gestation will develop respiratory-distress syndrome. Although RDS is the most common premie lung problem, it is not the only one. Severe lung problems require supplementary oxygen, which may be given through the use of an oxygen hood, CPAP (continuous positive airway pressure), or possibly respirator therapy (ventilation). A new treatment, involving the use of surfactant, is also available. For more on all these treatments for RDS, see Chapter 5. Lung problems are a primary reason why premies end up in the intensive-care unit. Ventilator, or respirator, therapy takes very intensive monitoring.

This chapter should have given you an overview of prematurity and its related problems. You may wish to come back to it in the future, but more details on some treatments and tests for these problems and others can be found in the following chapters.

4. What a Premature Newborn Can Do

Now that you have a picture of why your baby may have problems with the world outside the womb, let's begin to look at what he *can* do, what you can reasonably expect from him, and what kind of help he can use from you.

At the moment your baby is born, he can:

1. See
2. Hear
3. Sleep (with very different patterns)
4. Cry (theoretically)
5. Taste
6. Smell
7. Respond to touch
8. Feel pain

Let's look more closely at these abilities, and limitations.

Seeing. Although premature babies can see, they do not really focus in on anything until a gestational age of thirty weeks or more. At this age, a premature baby will begin to widen his eyes to look at a particular object, perhaps your face. Like a term baby, he seems to prefer patterns to solid-color objects, and will see most clearly at a distance of about a foot. All babies, premies included, are drawn to the human face. They probably do not recognize color until at least seven weeks of age but eventually like bright objects in primary colors such as red and yellow. Sick babies are likely to be less visually alert. Premies do not like to be stared at. Attempting to maintain prolonged eye contact with your premie will stress him and he may show it in very real ways: his color may turn gray, his breathing may decrease (apnea), and his heart rate may slow down (bradycardia). Remember that your premie's nervous system is not well organized yet; that is what we mean by an immature nervous system. He *does* want to look at you and get to know your face, but it has to be on his terms. Try this: look into his eyes. Remember that if he is very sick, he may not look back at all. Don't panic about this, give him time. When he looks back at you, after just a second, gently move your eyes away from him; focus to the side of his face. This gives him a chance to look at your face without being overwhelmed. After a few seconds, you can glance back into his eyes. This eye contact is amazingly important to both of you and, if done right, will very much help you two become comfortable with each other as parent and child.

It is also a nice idea to leave a small soft toy or patterned picture in the isolette for your baby to look at. This doesn't just help your premie; it also helps you to begin thinking of him as a real baby—your real baby.

Your baby's eyesight will be checked periodically. He will be given eye tests prior to discharge from the hospital.

Hearing. Even very premature babies can hear. If muscle tone allows, a newborn will turn toward a sound at birth. A test called Auditory Brain Stem Evoked Potentials (ABR) can measure the acuteness of the baby's hearing. Babies hear their parents' voices even when still in utero. Outside the womb, they respond to voices and tend to become alert and quiet when they hear a female or high-pitched voice. A newborn learns to recognize Mother's voice very quickly, so be sure to *talk* to your baby as much as possible. You may want to make a tape of your family's voices and have the nurse play it when you are not there. Be sure this is done softly, perhaps with the recorder covered with a sheet or washcloth.

One mother who left tapes for her daughter notes:

"My husband made a tape for Kirsten. He read long stories to her. It seems silly to me now. The nurses would play it for her when we weren't there. I'm not sure I'd recommend this, though, because since then I've heard that sound can really reverberate off the walls of the isolette and may do more harm than good."

The NICU is a very noisy place, and the noises are anything but what a baby normally would hear—various machine hums, clicks, and alarms, and a babble of many different human voices. Your soft voice can help counteract this situation by providing comforting, human sounds that your premie can identify as directed *to* him and not around him.

Your premie's hearing will be checked repeatedly while he is in the hospital and before he is discharged. Even if he is born with perfect hearing, any number of things occurring during his time in the hospital (e.g., jaundice, CNS bleeding, infections, and treatment with antibiotics) can cause hearing loss, although this is uncommon.

Sleeping.   Premature babies sleep almost all the time, as they would if they were still in the womb. But it is an active, not a heavy, sleep; this is why you see them moving frequently, breathing irregularly, and making various facial expressions, including "smiles" and "grimaces." Quiet sleep actually requires a more mature brain function and is not usually achieved until after thirty-two weeks gestation.

Physicians and nurses are becoming more and more aware that the twenty-four-hour routine of an NICU is extremely disruptive to a premie's sleep cycle. Researchers are beginning to think this may have long-term effects on premies' brain and nervous-system development. It certainly is part of the reason premies have more trouble settling into a normal sleep routine at home, once they are discharged from the hospital. In addition, a disrupted pattern of sleep may have a very real impact on your baby's growth and ability to handle medical stresses, such as pulmonary problems and infection. For all these reasons, more and more nurseries are instituting "quiet times," during which lights are dimmed in the intermediate-care nursery and the isolettes of stable babies in the NICU are covered. During these periods, no one is allowed to bother a baby, even a doctor, unless it is medically absolutely essential.

Crying. You may notice that you almost never hear your premie cry. Premies are born with the right equipment for crying but don't use it. It's not clear why. Premies will occasionally cry weak cries, but it will be many months before they cry with the strength and frequency of a full-term baby. I have been surprised at the number of parents who have asked me if that means there is something wrong with their premie. Be assured that there isn't. Interestingly, once a premie does cry out loud, his cry becomes one of the main sources of parental stress. (For more on this, see Chapters 9 and 10.)

Tasting and smelling. Although there are no studies that specifically look at premature babies' senses of smell and taste, full-term newborns have been studied and have been shown to distinguish smells and have preferences for sweet over salty tastes by five days of age. It is likely that a premie's senses of smell and taste are also developed at birth or soon thereafter. Certainly the hospital provides the premie with an assortment of smells. Why not supply one that your premie can associate with you? For example, you may want to use the same perfume, aftershave, or soap each time you see your premie, so that your infant will be able to recognize your smell immediately whenever you visit. It has also been suggested that you leave an object of yours in the isolette with the baby—for example, a hanky or a used but clean breast pad. Smelling "you"

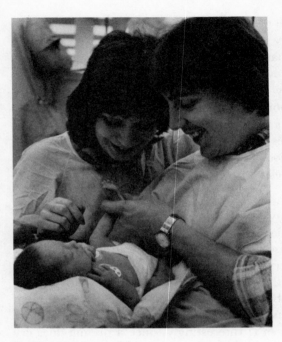

Your loving touch is important.

may be particularly comforting for the baby when he is stressed and you cannot be there.

Responding to touch.   Being touched affectionately is very important to a premie and is perhaps just as important for the parent. Your baby is constantly being touched, but unfortunately often in uncomfortable or painful ways. Recent research is suggesting that comforting touch, by one caretaker and individualized to the baby's personality and responses, can actually enhance a premie's weight gain and development; these effects can last long after the baby is sent home. In one study, premature infants who were massaged for fifteen minutes three times a day gained weight 47 percent faster than those who were not touched. Their nervous systems matured more rapidly as well and they became more responsive to people and toys. The massaged infants left the hospital six days earlier than the other babies. Eight months later, the massaged premies still weighed more and scored higher on tests of mental and motor ability than did the control group. It has been theorized that the babies respond to touch in this way because touch affects nervous system "hormones" whose main role is related to primitive survival instincts. The theory is that babies depend on their mothers for survival; therefore, if the mother's touch is absent, the premie "shuts down," lowering his metabolism and need for nourishment in an attempt to improve chances of survival while awaiting the mother's return. In other studies, babies who were touched more frequently had fewer episodes of apnea (slowed breathing) and also scored higher on tests of mental and motor development in the first year of their lives.

So have no doubt that your touch is important. It is essential! A reassuring hand every day, beyond the amount involved in routine care, certainly provides emotional comfort, and may help your baby to grow stronger—it is developmental gold. Although your premie may be very fragile, talking and touching your baby appropriately will not overstress him. What is appropriate? Well, remember what I've said about your premie's immature nervous system and fragile response to outside stimulation, stresses, and changes. It is very important to stimulate your premie in just one way at a time, so as not to overload him. Do not talk to him, touch him, *and* try to make eye contact all at the same time; that would *not* be pleasant for a premie. Be sensitive to his responses; if he looks uncomfortable, his color worsens, or he has apnea or bradycardia, ease up on the stimulation—just be there, without actually touching, if that is all he can handle. When he is in a more stable state, try lightly massaging your baby's back, legs, and arms. This is also helpful if he seems to be in pain or has an obvious reason to be in pain, for instance during a heel stick to take a blood sample. Remember that a pleasant sensation can distract him from a unpleasant one—you can actually decrease his discomfort!

Being held or having their position changed, however, can be very upsetting to some premies in the early weeks of life. All newborns tend to regurgitate a bit, but for premies this is an even greater problem. The slightest change in their position (and therefore the position of their diaphragm, which divides the lung cavity from the abdomen and is important in breathing) can cause them to regurgitate and to aspirate this fluid into the lungs. The intestinal tract of a premature baby is not mature enough to handle a lot of movement, especially after eating. This is not to say that you should not try to hold your newborn premie; you should. It is a wonderful experience and a good "bonding" interaction. Just do it cautiously, especially after feedings, and get advice and direction from your baby's doctor and the more experienced nurses.

Feeling pain.   Yes, your premie can feel pain. This is something that many parents sense intuitively but which, surprisingly, was until recently a matter of some medical debate. Recent research indicates that parents are correct here and has led doctors to take strong stands on the prevention of unnecessary pain in newborns. In the not-too-distant past, sometimes even major surgery was done without anesthesia, which was deemed dangerous for premies. The art and practice of anesthesia have now progressed to the extent that premies can be given anesthesia quite safely. This advance, coupled with recent information on premies' responses to painful stimulation, has led to very impressive changes in premie operative care. In the last few years, the American Academy of Pediatrics, as well as other organizations and individual physicians, has strongly advised that no surgery be done on a premie without anesthesia.

What about less severe procedures? Well, this is a more difficult area. We doctors cannot quantify your premie's pain and your premie can't tell us when he hurts. Pain medication can depress breathing and affect the heart, so it isn't usually given for minor procedures. I would not be surprised if this changes in the next decade, but for now we must make the best decisions we can, given the current state of knowledge. You as a parent are probably very aware of the painful side of routine care: heel sticks, lung suctioning, and the like. I'm sure it bothers you more than you can say, but we doctors do not have any good answers just yet. Certainly, if you think tests are being taken too often, ask for an explanation. Most important, remember this advice: use your comforting touch as much as possible to distract your baby from his pains.

5.   The Newborn Intensive-Care Unit

You may find it depressing to think of the newborn intensive-care unit (NICU) as your baby's *home,* but nonetheless that is where your baby will live for the first few days, weeks, or months of his life. In a way, the hospital will become your second home as well. This chapter is intended to help you feel more at ease in this clinical environment. Once you know the ins and outs of the NICU, the sounds and the activities, you may feel less intimidated and better able to care for your new baby. I routinely give medical care to infants in NICUs as a doctor, but even now, when I am called in to evaluate a premie in an NICU where I have not lately been, I feel like an outsider. This is not surprising and in a way is a good sign. An NICU is a very isolated, very high-tech environment run by physicians and nurses who know one another very well. Like any tightly knit group, the NICU team will make you feel like an outsider, even though that is not the group's intent.

So here you are, already exhausted, frightened, and feeling like a failure, coming into this very alien world. For someone who is not a medical professional, the high-tech side of this is overwhelming. You will not know what to do, where to go, or who the players are. Your feelings of helplessness, frustration, and guilt will be multiplied by the isolation of being a "visitor," unfamiliar with this very unique hospital environment. But it's important to you and your baby that you feel at home here quickly. No matter what your personality, you must force yourself to be aggressive about this settling-in process. The goal of this chapter is to help you make your baby's little corner of the NICU your own temporary home. Let's set some ground rules first, for the sake of you, your baby, and the medical personnel.

First, you are not a doctor or nurse and shouldn't try to be. You are paying impressive bills to have the real doctors and nurses fill that role; they are trained for it. You should not get in the way of medical care and should not get involved in the care of the other premies.

Second, you have a right to know everything about the care of your premie and to understand what you are told. You do, however, have to make some allowances for other demands on the doctors' and nurses' time. Also, some medical professionals are better than others at explaining procedures and problems. Never doubt your right to know, though.

Third and most important, you are your baby's parent. No one can do this job except you and no amount of money can get someone else to do it. Parenting a premie in an NICU is not fun; it is a big responsibility and heartbreakingly stressful. But it is very important to your and your baby's future. Be polite, but do not let anyone get in your way. Although your baby has medical caretakers right now, you are still the most important person in that baby's life. Doctors and nurses will be making crucial medical decisions for your baby, but you are in charge of your baby's emotional and developmental needs—and future life.

It is not only the NICU's staff and equipment that make you feel alone and out of place. All the preparations you have made for seeing your baby—getting a babysitter for an older sibling, driving to the hospital, getting to the NICU, scrubbing up, donning a gown—can make you feel like a real foreigner, removed from your baby and his care. When you are a "visitor" in your baby's "home," it is sometimes hard not to feel useless and out of place. You need to become familiar with the NICU, the hospital, and their routines. Find out about little things that can make your life easier, which the medical staff may not think to mention, like parking passes, breast pumps, a private spot for breastfeeding, places to rest or change, telephones, microwaves for warming food and drinks, nearby places to eat, possible in-hospital childcare for older siblings, in-hospital educational material for premie parents, hospital chaplains, personnel with whom to talk about expenses and billing, social services personnel and programs, etc. Ask about the layout of the hospital and the nursery, the routine schedules of the doctors, and the nursing shifts. For example, Ashley was in the hospital a week before anyone told me there was a breast pump on the floor (I hand-expressed all that time!) or that parking passes were available; everyone assumed that I just "knew." I had never attended at this particular hospital and simply did not know about all these resources.

The more you know the ins and outs of the place (and the more you use all available facilities), the more comfortable you'll feel there. And "belonging" is a major step toward more effective parenting. You'll be less likely to defer all care and decisions to nurses. The majority of parents I have spoken with found their physician willing to listen to their opinions and to try ideas that sounded reasonable.

One mother tells us that speaking up is not always easy in the beginning. At first she didn't want to question anything the medical staff was doing. Later, as she became more sure of herself, she became more vocal. She describes her growing willingness to be assertive and her doctor's response:

"The first night I was in the NICU with my daughter, she was having a number of episodes of tachycardia [rapid heartbeat]. The monitor kept going off. I felt the nurse wasn't handling it properly. I thought the nurse should have called a doctor, but at that point I didn't speak up. Later on, I wasn't so shy. When my instincts told me something was wrong, I acted on them. For example, Kirsten was taking the drug theophylline and this bothered me. I had read that one of the side effects of the drug was rapid heartbeat, which was already one of Kirsten's problems, so I spoke with the doctor and said, 'This doesn't make sense to me.' He listened, he took her off the medication, and sure enough, the number of her tachycardia episodes declined."

At first, you will probably be bewildered and confused by the NICU and your baby's condition. Your child's life seems to be dependent upon a confusing jumble of wires, machines, and medical therapies over which you have very little control. Part of your difficulty in understanding all that is happening to your child is that the medical personnel do not have all the answers. Diagnosing premies' medical problems can be very hard; each premie's condition can change from hour to hour, and from day to day. Because of this, your doctors may tell you one thing one day and another thing the next. One day, your child may be looking and doing very well and the next day there may be a crisis. This emotional roller coaster is sometimes unbearably hard to ride. Medical care of premies has improved incredibly and I can sincerely advise you to be optimistic, but premie parents must learn never to take anything for granted.

The first time you enter the NICU, the look, sound, smell, and confusion may shock you. It doesn't look like a nursery for a baby. There's nothing "cute" about it at all. The first things you will notice are the bright lights, beeping monitors, busy nurses, tense parents, and babies looking incredibly small compared to everything they are attached to. Next, you will focus in on your own baby. On your first visit to the NICU, your baby may look to you like an experimental animal: naked, lying flat on his back or down on his tummy under bright light on a metal tray, with tubes and wires running every which way on his tiny body. You will probably be struck once again by your newborn's vulnerability and fragility, how much he looks like a fetus and how thin and tiny he is.

As one mother describes her first look at her son:

"I didn't go into the nursery for three days, while I recovered from a C-section. I saw some pictures of Jonathan before I went into the NICU, though. The first time I looked at those Polaroids, I almost died. When I finally did get to see him, the nurses had 'dressed' him for my visit with a hat, little booties, and toys in his incubator. That way, I wasn't totally crazed.''

Your baby is in an intensive-care unit because this is where he can get the best possible care. Observation of your baby is constant, and medical equipment is always in use or at the ready. Premies who are not very sick will not be placed in the NICU. They will go to an intermediate-care nursery instead, assuming your hospital has one. If your infant was placed in an intermediate-care unit, you may want to skip ahead to Chapter 6, but this chapter is still useful for information on specific medical treatments and how a parent can fulfill an important role in a hospital environment. If your infant is in the NICU, read this chapter, but remember that not everything in it will apply to your situation. The medical information here is not intended to frighten you. Not all the medications, pro-

The NICU can be a busy, intimidating place.

cedures, and health problems mentioned here are relevant to your baby's situation.

EQUIPMENT

Most likely, your baby will be on an open, radiant warmer tray. This is a bed with an overhead heating source; premature babies (and other low-birth-weight babies) have little fat tissue, so they lose heat quickly. Premature babies have the added problem of being unable to control body temperature effectively. The radiant warmer tray is open, which allows the medical staff to reach immediately any baby who may need emergency treatment. A temperature probe is taped to the baby's skin so that the amount of heat needed can be regulated. Some babies are placed in isolettes, or incubators, instead. Isolettes have the baby in an enclosed space, so these are not usually used for sick premies who may suddenly need emergency care. Isolettes may look more serious and technical to parents than warming beds, but actually isolettes mean that less intensive care is expected.

There is debate recently as to whether premies in the NICU do better on their backs or on their stomachs; there are pros and cons to both positions. You may see your premie in either position, but the "standard" position is on the back. At some hospitals, babies can also be placed on tiny water beds. Some researchers hypothesize that the gentle movement of these water beds simulates life in the womb and helps to stimulate the infant's breathing and lessen the likelihood of an apneic spell.

You may also notice that your baby is under very bright lights other than the warming lights. These lights are known as bili lights and are used if your baby has hyperbilirubinemia and is jaundiced, as many premies are (see Chapter 3). This treatment is known as phototherapy. The bright lights change the molecular structure of the bilirubin in the bloodstream so that it is more rapidly excreted. One side effect of phototherapy is rapid fluid loss from the heat, so the staff will be especially careful that your baby has enough liquids and is not getting dehydrated. They will also check the baby's temperature often to make sure the baby doesn't get overheated under all the lights. A baby under bili lights will have patches over his eyes to protect them from the lights. This wavelength of light can hurt the baby's retinas, just as a sunlamp can hurt yours. You can ask the nurses to turn off the lights and remove the patches during your visit, so that you and your baby can occasionally make eye contact. Allowing time for eye contact will make both you and your baby feel closer to each other, but don't forget to use the flirtatious sort of approach we discussed in Chapter 4. Occasionally, phototherapy cannot control the jaundice and an exchange transfusion is needed. For an exchange transfusion, an intravenous tube (catheter) is placed in a blood vessel, usually in the baby's navel. Through this tube, or "line," jaundiced blood is withdrawn, discarded, and replaced with fresh, unjaundiced blood from a blood bank.

In addition to warmer trays and bright lights, your baby will have at least several wires and tubes and attachments sticking here and there. Sometimes just knowing what each wire does can make you feel a little bit less anxious about seeing it there. But even if you prepare yourself by reading this book and looking at pictures, the first few times you see *your* baby with those intrusive-looking tubes and lines, it will surely be emotionally painful for you. You may never become 100 percent used to seeing your baby like this, but remember that it will not last forever. To make matters worse, each time you come to the hospital you (and your baby) may have a new and different piece of equipment to get used to. Also do not be surprised if you come in and find your baby moved—and moved more than once. This can happen fairly frequently, sometimes because of changes in the medical care of your baby or other babies and sometimes just because of changing space demands. It can feel very odd to come to your baby's "bed" and find it, and him, gone!

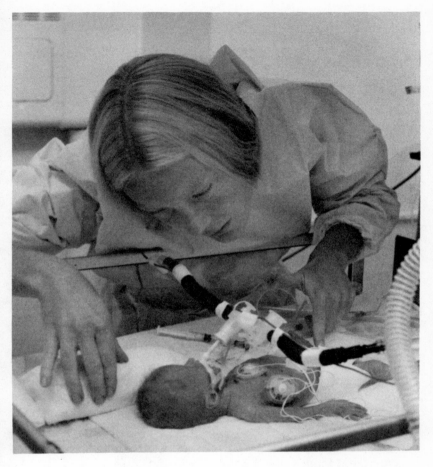

It may seem as though every square inch of your baby's body is covered with tapes, tubes, or wires. Sometimes just knowing what each does can make a difference.

Here is how the mother of a baby girl born at two pounds six ounces describes her introduction to her baby in the NICU:

"The first time I saw my baby there, I was sad . . . but more than that I was angry. Later, I became more accepting of the fact that she had to be hooked up to all those machines."

A baby in the NICU must be monitored continuously

because a premie's condition can change at any moment. Rather than rely on a nurse's vigilant but obviously intermittent observation, a number of electronic monitors will be attached to your baby. The cardiorespiratory monitor keeps tabs on your baby's heart rate and respiratory rate. An alarm sounds if your baby's heart rate or breathing changes beyond the limits set on the monitor by the physician's orders. (The monitor's limits are set individually for each newborn, since normal breathing and heart rates vary from baby to baby.) For babies with apnea, bradycardia, or tachycardia (all discussed in Chapter 3), this monitor is essential. In addition to an alarm, the monitor will show the current heart and breathing rates on a digital readout. The leads from the monitor attach to the baby's body with stick-on disks, which can sometimes irritate a premie's skin. (Although the leads look cumbersome, the stick-on disks don't pinch or hurt the baby; premies move so little that leads don't really get in the baby's way.) Another monitor measures the baby's blood pressure. This monitor is connected to a small plastic cuff around the infant's thigh or upper arm. Another very new device, on your baby's hand, measures the oxygen in your baby's blood by shining a light through his finger, to measure the color of the blood flowing inside. This device is called a pulse oximeter. It has been available only for about a year and has made it possible for doctors to avoid many painful blood tests used to check the level of oxygen in a baby's blood.

Your baby may also have several mini-hoselike plastic attachments, known as catheters, inserted into veins, arteries, or the urethra (going to the bladder to collect urine). When a catheter is in a small artery or vein, the medical staff will refer to it as a (peripheral) "line"; when it is in a large artery or vein, it will be called a "central line"; when it is in the urethra, it will be called a "urinary catheter." Through the lines to arteries or veins, a nurse or doctor can give medication or nutrition to the baby. The more commonly used peripheral lines are inserted into the baby's hands and feet, or the top of his head. A peripheral line is held in place with tape and a makeshift cup surrounding the spot where it enters the skin, to protect it from getting bumped; on the arms or legs, it will also be splinted against movement that might pull it out, usually with a tongue depressor (these babies are *very* little!). These devices may all look a little strange, as though the baby had been in a skiing accident, but are simply precautions taken to prevent the baby or someone else from dislodging the line.

Central lines are used on babies in more critical condition because they can remain in place for a longer time, give the doctors access to less fragile vessels, and often can have blood drawn through them. Almost all babies in the NICU have a central line at one time or another. It is usually inserted through a blood vessel in the umbilical stump, a major vein in the leg, or through the subclavian vein in the arm/shoulder. Its correct placement will then be checked with an X ray. The central line can be used to deliver medication or food. A central line inserted into an artery can be used to check continuously on the levels of oxygen in the bloodstream. Central lines are obviously very good in many ways, but they do have risks. Infection and, on rare occasions, blood clots may develop at the site where the catheter was inserted. Infections from central lines can spread rapidly through the bloodstream. To minimize these risks, central lines are always removed as soon as your baby's condition improves enough for the doctors to be able to use peripheral lines instead.

There may also be a urinary catheter inserted. If your baby is a boy, you will notice a little line inserted into his penis; if a girl, into her urethra. This is used to measure the amount of a baby's urine or to obtain a urine culture. Do not permit your doctor to stitch this line in; this is painful and unnecessary. Urine may need to be measured to make sure that the baby is producing urine at a normal rate; it is often done if the baby has heart problems that put him at risk of fluid retention. Urine cultures are done to check for infection in the kidneys and urinary system, a common source of infection in premies. However, it is not uncommon for a urinary catheter itself to cause a bladder infection, so again, this catheter is not left in if it can be avoided—for instance, if a plastic urine bag can be used to collect the urine instead.

Whether or not your baby is being fed intravenously, he may receive breast milk or formula through an orogastric or nasogastric tube. This tube runs through the mouth or nose directly into the stomach and is used for feeding babies who cannot yet suck and swallow well. Although the tube may be left in place constantly, your baby may not be fed constantly. The tube is often left in to spare your baby the discomfort of repeated removals and insertions. Find out when your baby will be fed. Even with a nasogastric tube inserted, you may be able to hold your baby during a feeding. Also, sucking on a plastic nipple, turned into a pacifier by the nurses, will help his suck become coordinated. Feel comfortable asking the nurses if holding your baby can be arranged; even if one says no, feel free to ask a more senior nurse. She may agree with you. Many parents I have worked with do find holding a premie more frightening than fulfilling at first, but it's a start.

Many of the premies in the NICU have serious respiratory problems, most commonly hyaline membrane disease (HMD, or RDS, as discussed in Chapter 3). As we explained in that chapter, immature lungs make little surfactant and are not supple enough for the demands of breathing. Much NICU care is related to the respiratory problems of very premature infants.

The simplest method of providing air mixed with extra oxygen to your baby is through an oxygen hood. The hood is clear plastic and big enough to cover the baby's head and upper body. A hose from the hood is attached to an oxygen tank or outlet. The oxygen hood may appear foggy, preventing you from seeing your baby's little face. The fogginess is caused by the warming and humidifying of the air. The air that we normally breathe is only about 20 percent oxygen, but inside the oxygen hood the baby is breathing air with an oxygen concentration of about 30 to 40 percent. For many small premies, though, the oxygen hood is not enough. The next level of oxygen supplementing is continuous positive airway pressure, or

CPAP (pronounced *see-pap*), a forced-air system that keeps those sacs in the lungs open so that they cannot collapse between breaths. This is given through plastic "nasal prongs" (small plastic tubes going into each nostril), a mask, or a plastic tube that goes down the baby's throat and into the airway. No matter which of these routes is used, air with extra oxygen is gently pushed into the baby's lungs. This certainly must be uncomfortable and will obscure your baby's face somewhat, but many babies begin to improve after a few days. However, if your baby's blood tests show that even with CPAP he is still not getting enough oxygen into his blood, or, more commonly, if he just does not have the energy to keep trying to breathe on his own, your premie will be placed on a mechanical respirator, also called a ventilator.

It is not uncommon for most of the babies in the NICU to be "attached" to ventilators at some time during their stay. The ventilator breathes for your baby, although the baby may also be taking some breaths on his own. Sometimes babies will be given sedatives or other medications to stop them from breathing on their own, since if they are not breathing in rhythm with the respirator they will tire themselves out and also may damage their lungs. It's important that you be told this has been done, since these medicines will prevent your baby from responding to you in any meaningful way.

Many times, a baby who fights the respirator is showing that he is ready to breathe on his own. One mother says that her baby knocked the ventilator out of her mouth and began to breathe on her own—so well, in fact, that they took her off a little earlier than expected.

To put your baby on a respirator, the doctor will first insert either an endotracheal or a nasotracheal tube. It is through this tube that your baby will receive oxygenated air with pulses of pressure. An endotracheal tube is inserted through the mouth, down the throat, and into the trachea, the tube to the lung commonly known as the windpipe. A nasotracheal tube is inserted through the nose, down the throat, and into the windpipe. When oxygen is given on a ventilator, it is usually "pushed" into the lungs with a little pressure; this helps to expand the alveoli and, in a sense, does the job of the missing surfactant. Unfortunately, like all other treatments, respiratory therapy carries with it some risks. A baby's lungs can get stiff and lose their elasticity from being too long on a ventilator. This is known as bronchopulmonary dysplasia, or BPD, and is an ongoing problem that is discussed in Chapter 12. It is also possible that the pressure from the respirator will cause air to leak out of the lungs and into the chest; this is known as a pneumothorax. A small pneumothorax may cause only some additional difficulty breathing; in healthy premies the air may simply be reabsorbed into the lungs. A more serious pneumothorax may create too much pressure or even cause a lung to collapse. In this case, a chest tube may be inserted between two of the baby's ribs to drain out this air under light suction. The next twenty-four to forty-eight hours may be quite tense, as a baby in this condition often has some continued difficulty breathing and may have other problems as well.

Your baby will be tested regularly while on a ventilator to see how he is faring. Doctors and nurses will check his skin color, heart rate, respiratory rate, and skin temperature. They will also take blood samples to discover the levels of carbon dioxide, oxygen, and acidity in the bloodstream. You may feel awful that your baby is continually being pricked and poked at, not just for essential medical care but for numerous tests. But these tests *are* essential, to make sure that current medical treatments are working and to know how to adjust the ventilator settings. In particular, it is important that blood-oxygen levels are in the correct range, so that enough oxygen gets to all parts of the body without the levels' becoming so high that the risk of retrolental fibroplasia (RLF) is increased. (RLF is a long-term vision problem related to high oxygen levels; it is discussed in Chapter 12.) So the tests are directly related to optimal medical care for your baby. That does not mean that these tests are not painful for your baby; if he is stable enough, a gentle hand of a premie's parent on the back, arm, or anywhere reachable during or after them always helps.

In a very new form of therapy for respiratory-distress syndrome, surfactant can be put into the baby's air sacs to supply what the baby himself cannot make. The method of introducing the surfactant to a premie is simple. A fine mist of surfactant is put into the baby's oxygen mixture by mask or respirator. As the infant breathes, he takes the surfactant down into the lungs and into the alveoli. So far, it seems that surfactant works best if it is first given right after delivery and if "natural" surfactant, obtained from animals' lungs or human amniotic tissue, is used rather than synthetic, manufactured surfactant. Natural surfactant is more difficult to obtain and may not be widely available for a while.

SOME ROUTINE TESTS

As we explained above, tests may be annoying to your baby, but they are important to his care. Babies are always weighed at least once a day, sometimes as many as three times a day. Their weight is recorded in grams instead of pounds. In the first week it is not unusual for newborns to lose weight rather than gain. It often will take more than two or three weeks for a premie to get back to his birth weight. Don't worry about this weight loss or about any temporary setbacks in weight gain. In a few months, you'll be looking at weekly or monthly gains and day-to-day tallies will be just a bad memory. Even the baby's diaper may be weighed, to determine the amount of fluid being passed through as urine. If your baby doesn't wear a diaper, a urinary catheter or bag may be used to collect urine for the same purpose.

Blood may be drawn from a central line, as explained above, or into a syringe from a needle inserted into a small vein in the arm, leg, or even scalp. An easy and commonly used method for drawing blood samples is the "heel stick."

The baby's heel is pricked with a sterile needle or the tip of a very small scalpel blade, usually after the heel is warmed to increase blood flow. The blood that flows out is collected in small, thin tubes. The bleeding usually stops immediately afterward, but it is nice to have a parent wrap or gently hold a cold washcloth on the heel, to minimize bruising. Premies *do* bruise easily and their blood may not always clot quickly. Not all blood tests can be done from blood drawn by a heel stick, so your baby will probably have blood drawn more than one way. If you feel that the number of sticks is excessive, ask why the tests cannot be combined; there may be very good reasons and you may feel better to know this. At times it is just poor planning, and stating your question in a nonconfrontational manner will remind your doctors and nurses to plan ahead a bit better.

Premies in NICUs usually need so many blood tests that they will periodically get small blood transfusions to replace the red blood cells they are losing; these will be given through one of the baby's intravenous lines. Your baby will look and act much better after one of these, since it literally gives him an oxygen boost—but don't think that if a little blood is good, more is better; more would cause problems. Again, as we mentioned in Chapter 3, do not worry about your baby getting AIDS from these transfusions. Since the spring of 1985, blood donors have been screened for antibodies to the virus that causes AIDS.

X rays are commonly taken of the abdominal cavity, chest, or entire body, using a portable X-ray machine, often to make sure all tubes are properly inserted or as an evaluation for possible infection. X rays can show the condition of the lungs, brain, and other organs. A very sick baby in the NICU may be X-rayed as many as ten times a day for short periods of time. You may be worried about the level of radiation your baby is receiving. The amounts of radiation used are extremely small; during their entire hospital stay these babies usually get no more radiation than the average person gets per year living in the outside world. Low doses of radiation do not cause sterility or cancer. If you just cannot sleep for worry about this, however, you can ask for a tiny lead shield to be placed over your baby's reproductive organs during X-raying. Be assured that I was not concerned about this with Ashley; we premie parents have too much to worry about as it is!

Sonograms are very much like X rays in that they literally give a picture of what is going on inside your baby. They are done by special technicians and read by radiologists, physicians with special training in reading X rays, sonograms, and assorted scanning techniques, such as the CT scans mentioned in Chapter 3. As stated in that chapter, sonograms (also called ultrasound) work just like radar, bouncing sound waves off the baby's internal organs.

PERSONNEL

Who are all these people who appear and disappear at your baby's bedside? What role do they have in your child's medical care? Who is really in charge? With whom do you speak about medical problems, procedures, and prognoses? With whom do you talk about how to breastfeed? To whom do you go with your questions and complaints? In the NICU, your child will be cared for by doctors and nurses and will be seen by therapists and technicians. It can be difficult to sort them all out at first.

Physicians. The bewildering array includes neonatologists, the pediatrician you have chosen (see Chapter 9), pediatric residents, consultant pediatric specialists (like me), medical students (who help and learn from the residents and neonatologists), and fellows (licensed pediatricians training in a subspecialty, such as neonatology, infectious diseases, or cardiology). Realize that some of the doctors may well be working up to thirty-six straight hours without a break, so while they may be quite accessible, they also may at times be tired and cranky.

The doctors are the people with whom to speak about your medical issues. You have a good deal of flexibility here. In general, you would deal most with the neonatologist or your pediatrician, but if you feel more comfortable with one of these other individuals or find them more accessible, there is no harm in dealing with them instead or in addition. One word of caution, though: experience *does* count for something here. For example, a medical student may not understand everything going on and may sometimes misinterpret things. Ultimately, your neonatologist and pediatrician will have to agree to all major medical decisions. Ideally, as you take your place as an NICU premie parent major decisions will be made *with* you.

Nurses.   Neonatal nurses are registered nurses with a specialty in newborn care. Your baby's nursery may also have one or more nurse practitioners, who are nurses with additional training; they can perform a number of medical acts on their own but remain under the supervision of the neonatologist. Ideally, your baby will have the same nurses each day, but this may not always be possible. Nurses work eight-hour shifts, although it is not uncommon for a nurse to work two or even three shifts in a row.

Not surprisingly, most nurses prefer to work the daytime shift. What this means is that the nurses with the most experience (i.e., with the most seniority) tend to work in the daytime. Thus, the nursing care may not be quite as good in some of the very hours you cannot be there, although NICU nurses in general are the "cream of the crop." When Ashley was in the hospital, I found that the daytime nurses tended to be quite helpful and understanding but the night nurses were young, overly defensive, and sometimes rigid. Clearly, this may not be the case for you. For example, you may be more comfortable with the younger nurses on the night shift. In any case, it is to your benefit to try to meet them or have some contact with them. One mother who lived thirty miles from the hospital and was unable actually to be there at night says:

"In the middle of the night I would call in and check on the baby. Because you don't get to see the night nurses—at least this way they knew who I was."

Nurses are wonderful sources of advice on how to feed, comfort, hold, and care for your baby. Try to get to know as many of the nurses your baby has as possible. For advice, go to the ones with whom you feel most comfortable, the ones you trust the most. Realize, by the way, that this may not be the person with whom your spouse feels most comfortable. But that's all right; two opinions never hurt, as long as you remember that they are just that, opinions.

Respiratory therapists. These people monitor the machines that help your baby to breathe, and they help keep the tubing—and your baby's airways—as clear as possible.

Technicians. Technicians handle everything from audiometry (hearing tests) to EKGs (electrocardiograms for the heart), EEGs (tests for brain waves), ultrasound studies, and X rays. These technicians do not spend all their time in the NICU; they work all over the hospital. But they do feel quite comfortable about what they do and are used to being in the NICU setting. They may offer their own "readings" of a test they have just done. Although technicians may be quite good at giving the tests, they are not trained to interpret them, so wait for the specialist's reading! Some technicians, on the other hand, have been taught not to discuss the tests with anyone and may refuse to tell you what they are doing or why. If this happens, just quietly go to your baby's nurse or doctor and ask what test is being done and why.

Neonatal social workers. Social workers at the hospital can provide you with needed emotional support, as well as put you on the right track for financial advice; they are not only for people on welfare or in financial difficulty. They may arrange parent support groups and should know about groups in your area. They may have a good deal of experience with the stresses having a premie places on a parent and a family. Even if you are very independent, you and your family may profit from some support and guidance. Parenting a premie is a stressful experience, and the rewards are anything but immediate. Until these rewards begin to come, in the months and years ahead, try to make things easier on yourself and your family in any way you can.

Let's just summarize all this for a minute. Although there are a lot of people working on your baby's case, the doctor in charge is the neonatologist. It is to him or her that questions about your baby's care and prognosis should be directed. The nurses will fill you in on how your baby is doing and what new things might have come up while you were out of the hospital. Technicians and therapists are there to do specific jobs, as ordered by the neonatologist or other specialist. They may be able to answer some of your questions about the procedures themselves, but the results of these tests should be discussed with the neonatologist, not the technician.

Because there are so many different people working together to help your baby grow, everyone but the technicians meets as a team once a day to make rounds and discuss each baby's case. Do not try to speak with the neonatologist during his rounds or none of the babies will get the care they need! Instead, find out when he or she is expected to be in the NICU after rounds and arrange to be there then for a talk. If you always seem to miss the doctor ("always" being more than a day), ask when and where you can set up a meeting to discuss your baby's status, both this time and on a regular basis. The neonatologist may have an office just down the hall from the nursery. If you want to speak with this doctor immediately and are not comfortable talking to one of the other doctors, you can have him or her paged. Things are often so busy in an

NICU that the only time a doctor may make a point of seeking you out will be in an emergency. This is not an ideal doctor/patient relationship, so do not be embarrassed to be politely aggressive. Try to at least touch base with the doctor every day, even if it is just over the telephone, but pattern these meetings to his or her schedule as much as possible. If your neonatologist knows you and understands what your concerns are, he or she will be more likely to tell you in advance about the procedures being planned for your baby, even small ones. The neonatologist may inform you more fully or explain problems in greater detail because you have displayed this interest. You, in turn, will likely have more trust in a neonatologist with whom you speak on a routine basis. One last, probably disappointing note: if you are in a large or teaching hospital and your baby is in the hospital longer than one month, you may have to get to know a new neonatologist, just as you were getting comfortable with the old one. Many major hospitals rotate their attending doctors; for example, I take infectious diseases/immunology consults for one-month periods. This rotation helps to keep doctors fresh. Residents and fellows also change in one-month cycles, but these changes are staggered, so that your baby always has someone there who has known him for some weeks. Nurses and nurse practitioners don't rotate and will be there for you from month to month, although, as mentioned above, the ones caring for your baby may change from day to day.

Not surprisingly, given the intensity of the NICU setting, parents have strong emotions and strong memories of the doctors and nurses who cared for their premies. Interactions with individuals frequently become generalized to "all nurses" and "all doctors."

Some parents I have dealt with have very good memories of the care their premies received. As one mother remembers:

"The nurses ran the NICU. At my hospital, the nurses were great. They loved those babies. I saw them cry. They didn't care who the baby's parent was. That parent could have been the biggest pain in the neck and it didn't matter when it came to looking after the baby. I was allowed to visit morning, noon, and night. Sometimes, the nurses would pick me up and drive me to the hospital. If I had been there all day and was too tired to go back at night, I would call up to see how Jonathan was doing. They'd say, 'Don't worry. We'll feed him, we'll take care of him.' "

Another mother had a very different experience and was not as pleased with the attitude of the nurses and doctors. She remembers somewhat bitterly:

"Since my baby was born, I've learned so much—not from doctors, but from books. I was really annoyed that they didn't keep me more involved. They volunteered *nothing*. My baby had BPD [bronchopulmonary dysplasia], and they didn't even discuss that with me. He was on a respirator for three weeks and I was very worried about RLF [retrolental fibroplasia] but they didn't discuss that with me, either. I think this left us at a real disadvantage. One day, I saw the nurse putting some medication into my son's IV. I asked, 'What's that? Aminophylline?' She was very defensive and wanted to know how I knew that. I would have been lost without my books. My son was always at risk for a lot of things. I guess they felt that if I knew about all those things, I'd be a basket case. But I'm not like that."

You should use this book to try to avoid a similar situation. Not all doctors and nurses are reasonable people; not all *non*medical people are reasonable. But in general, medical professionals, especially in pediatric medicine, really do want to help. Also remember that you will be living on intimate terms with these doctors and nurses for weeks or months. A little diplomacy is in order on everyone's part. Still, you have a right to know everything that seems important to you about your baby's health. If you don't understand the answers you are being given, ask for things to be explained another way. You can ask for a second person to explain things to you, too; after all, sometimes two particular individuals just don't quite click—and it isn't necessarily either one's fault.

Make lists of the questions you want to ask of whomever you choose as your main source or sources of information—it's easy to forget things when you're under stress and nervous. Take notes or record conversations you have with your doctors and nurses. This may help you to remember all that is said and to absorb it later at home in the evening, the next morning, or even in the weeks and months to come. Note-taking also helps immensely if one spouse is not able to be there at an informational session. You may be wondering how your doctor might react to being taped or having notes taken. As a doctor, I am not threatened if a patient wants to tape my instructions. But I'm used to being interviewed by reporters because of the medical research I do. Especially in today's medical-legal environment, some doctors may be a bit nervous around a tape recorder. Explain your request to your doctor and ask his permission before you pull out a notebook or tape recorder. Explain to him or her that you want to tape the conversation because you find it very hard to remember all these new facts, that you're not familiar with medical jargon, and you'd hate to have to come back and bother him or her again with the same questions. It would be an unusual doctor who will not understand and respond positively to that logic!

THE PARENTS' ROLE

Being a parent of a baby in intensive care is a tension-filled role and, as this mother so accurately describes it, often not immediately gratifying:

"One day, they disconnected my son from his respirator and let me hold him. He was still attached to a lot of other things, though. I was afraid to breathe. He was all hooked up. It was not that fulfilling."

Another mother's memory of the first time she held her tiny daughter is very similar:

"I didn't hold Caroline until she was five weeks old and off the respirator. The nurses asked, 'Do you want to hold her?' And I said, 'No, no . . . ,' but they talked me into it. The next day I had the worst stiff neck—I had sat with her, rigid, for a half hour. I didn't breathe the whole time. *I* needed the oxygen! They said, 'Look at your baby.' But I couldn't. All I could look at were the monitors.''

There are just too many things that conspire to come between you and your baby right now. I will not mislead you and claim that you can turn this into the instant euphoria you frequently feel in the early weeks of getting to know your full-term infant. This was a feeling I remembered from Danielle and will always feel deprived of with Ashley. This is a real and heartfelt loss. But those early days and weeks in the NICU are a beginning to your relationship with your baby. If you find a place amid the wires and medical commotion for being simply, seriously, and completely a *parent,* the joys will come after the anxieties begin to be resolved. For now, this is a love that makes your heart ache, but the bond that will form will be quite awe-inspiring.

We've spent almost the entire chapter telling you about the possible medical problems your baby might face and how your doctors might handle these medical situations. Through all this, I've stressed the role you might play as a parent of a sick child. You do have an important role, even though it may seem like one that is physically removed from your baby; that role is acting as the baby's advocate and thinking of his developmental, physical, and emotional needs. Is he getting appropriate care with minimal pain? Is he getting periods of decreased stimulation and perhaps even darkness? What is he being fed? Is he getting some pleasant stimulation? Is he having consistent caregiving and contacts that are not just related to medical care? Seeing to all of this is your job as a parent, although the nurses and doctors may do much of it if you do not.

Bear in mind that because each baby has a different personality, some nurses will get along better with your baby than others will. You might notice that one nurse may not pay a great deal of attention to your baby while another always makes a big fuss over him. Likewise, one nurse might calm your baby down, another might irritate him. Obviously, the nurses should do their best to treat each child with the same attention and care, but they are human and probably aren't even aware when they show their favorites special attention. One of my anxieties whenever I left Ashley alone in the nursery was how much affectionate attention she might receive in my absence. Although she was born at a "good" weight for a premie, she subsequently lost a great deal of weight and frankly looked like a starvation victim. She was definitely not "cute," like a term baby, nor like some of the chubbier or developmentally more mature and responsive premies. Oh, I could tell she was a sweetie, but who would have the time to notice this in my absence? The nurses would always fuss over how cute Danielle was when she would come in to see her sister and I wanted to tell them, "Can't you see that look hiding in Ashley? Please take the time and get to know her."

But nurses and doctors in an NICU simply do not have a great deal of free time. You, the parents, are the only people whom your baby will be certain of seeing from day to day. You are certainly the only ones who can form a long-term bond with him, something that every baby needs to lead a healthy and happy life. Both parents can and should spend time with the baby—even if you can't pick your baby up. Take turns watching your other children; get babysitters some of the time.

By touching and stroking your premie infant, talking to him, making eye contact, and letting him get to know that you are a stable person in his life, your parent-child bond will begin to grow. Your touch can and will make a difference in the health and emotional well-being of your baby. Remember— your gentle touch might even relieve some of your baby's pain. Your role is to counteract, as much as possible, the negative sensations of the NICU, where there is no day/night cycle, the noise level is high and constant, and there are multiple and changing caregivers. Do not overstimulate; do one thing at a time. Otherwise you are just stressing the poor little thing more. Remember all of your baby's senses, too. As we mentioned in the last chapter, when visiting your baby in the NICU, you might want to wear the same perfume, aftershave, or soap so that the baby will learn to recognize your smell; bring in recorded audiotapes to be played when you cannot be there. The baby will come to recognize your voice, your smell, your face, and your touch. As you spend more and more time with your baby, you will begin to see him respond to you. Don't be discouraged if at first your baby seems to pay no attention to you. He needs time to sort out all the input of the NICU and time to connect your voice, smell, and touch with the idea of "Mommy" or "Daddy." Always think in terms of "one stimulation at a time"; if you're rubbing, don't make eye contact; if you're talking, don't rub. Try not to overload your already sensorially overloaded premie. The NICU is not an ideal setting for a newborn, especially an immature newborn—this is certainly no womb! No one knows what effect this kind of environment has on a premie's long-term development. Do your best to counteract all the NICU stimuli, not just now, but in the months and years to come.

To make the baby seem more like yours, you should talk with the medical staff about some things you can do to personalize your corner of the NICU. You might ask, for example, if your baby can wear clothes. You should realize, though, that the answer at this point may be no. The doctors and nurses may need to see and observe every square inch of your baby's body, and they may need to get at your baby quickly for emergency care. Still, a tiny bow or small toy may be allowed and can make visiting the NICU a little more personal and cheerful. If your baby wears a diaper, decorate it with a colorful Mickey Mouse sticker, or hearts and stars, so he seems just that much more "dressed." Psychologically, this can give you a real lift.

If you wish to give your baby breast milk, you should immediately speak with the staff about the possibility and practical details of doing so. As long as your baby is taking feedings orally or even by nasogastric tube, you can supply your own expressed breast milk for him. (For more details on breastfeeding and expressing, see Chapter 7.) Try to arrange to be at the hospital for feeding times. Even if your baby is being tube-fed, you can often hold him during a feeding, so he starts to associate your smell and appearance with the happy feeling of a full tummy.

When you can't be with your baby in the NICU, feel free to call and check up on him. Get the phone number from the nurses and ask them for the best time to call. Then do it. Don't feel awkward. Even though they're busy, the medical staff understands your situation and should be pleased you are calling. The nurses are usually wonderful about this; they are sincerely pleased that parents call.

Finally, don't overlook your own health and medical needs and the needs of the rest of the family. Mothers, especially, may ignore their own medical needs in trying to keep up with the needs of the family in this crisis. Remember that you are still recovering from pregnancy and delivery. Your body is trying to produce milk for the baby, and at the same time you are under a great deal of stress. You should realize that when the baby does come home at last, you'll need to be in good shape and not a run-down wreck. Dads and supporting family should provide moms with extra care and support, although dads don't have an easy time of it either, between working, holding down the fort, and getting to know their premie. Do not forget the needs of your other children. Moms and dads should discuss priorities, distribute responsibilities, and talk to each other about this; try to explain things to the other children as much as their developmental level allows. (See Chapter 8 for more on siblings.) People can recover from fatigue and anxiety, but feelings of anger, hurt, resentment, and failure, caused by a lack of communication or support within the family, don't go away quite as readily. Do the best you both can

at balancing premie parenthood, other children, and work responsibilities—and then absolve yourself and your spouse from
feelings of failure.

DIFFICULT DECISIONS

When your child was first admitted to the NICU, you
were most likely asked to sign a blanket consent form, agreeing
to any and all medical procedures for your baby. Basically, this
consent form gives the hospital the right to perform "routine
care" of your premature baby. But you have not signed away
all your parental rights with regard to your baby's health. You
will still, most likely, be asked to sign another consent form if
your baby needs special surgery or any unusual medical treatment. You will then sign an "informed consent form" that
will list the possible complications of the procedure. Speak with
your neonatologist about the risks and benefits of the procedure
before you sign.

Rarely, the situation is such that parents may decide they
prefer not to have their baby treated. This is obviously an
agonizing decision but one that you, as a parent, have the
right to make, in conjunction with the medical team caring for
your child. Very infrequently, there will be a difference of
opinion between parents and the medical team. A doctor may
want to be aggressive in trying to save the life of a baby who
parents believe should be allowed to die. In situations like these,
there is always some recourse for the parents. Parents might
ask for a second opinion if they do not believe in following this
neonatologist's course of action. Every hospital also has an ad-
visory board or committee to help deal with situations like
these. The committees are made up of medical personnel,
sometimes a parent, an ethicist, and often one or more cler-
gymen. The board will consider the situation and make a recommendation. If parents disagree, they can resubmit their case
for consideration and the board may change its mind. There
are no absolutes in situations like these. No one can say for

sure which decision is right and which is wrong. There are so many variables, and they demand that unquestionably difficult decisions be made. Although it is quite rare, cases that cannot be resolved by hospitals and parents may, sadly, end up in court.

Use the resources available to you. Speak with the hospital social workers, doctors, the clergy, other parents, and family members to help make your way through difficult moral and medical decisions.

6. The Intermediate-Care Nursery

Your baby may go straight from the delivery room to the intermediate-care nursery, or he may have spent some time in the NICU first before "graduating" to intermediate care. Your response to the intermediate-care unit may vary depending on the route your baby took to get here.

GOING FROM THE NICU TO INTERMEDIATE CARE

For the parent whose child has moved to intermediate care from the NICU, the feeling is usually triumphant:

"When Emily was moved from NICU to intermediate care, that was the happiest day of our lives! She was seventeen days old. For the move, the nurses dressed her in some little clothes, and for the first time she looked like a real baby! Once she was in intermediate care, we could give her bottles, bring in outfits for her to wear. Fifteen days later she left the hospital."

GOING STRAIGHT FROM THE DELIVERY ROOM TO THE INTERMEDIATE-CARE NURSERY

Alternatively, if your child was sent directly from the delivery room to the intermediate-care unit, you may be just about as overwhelmed by this nursery as you would have been by the NICU. Your child is, after all, very small and immature and, sadly, very much at risk for problems. If you look back at Chapter 5, you may feel relieved that your baby is not as sick as the premature infants in the NICU. Part of you may also feel guilty that you're so upset about your child's condition when there are children sicker than yours. One premie mom reports that this guilt was a reason she was so anxious to get her baby home, away from the other parents and their premies. She says:

"You definitely get survivor's guilt. Your total focus is on your own baby. Then you see a malformed baby or a baby dying next to her. Or one day you bounce in, saying, 'I think I'll give her a bath today,' and run into a couple bursting out of the doors, sobbing. It's no good. No one can share your joy. You just have to get out of there and get home with your baby."

As much as is possible, try not to feel guilty that your child is doing well when others may not be. You have a right to your feelings. The smallest health problems will certainly upset you, even though you are at the same time thankful things aren't worse. Besides, your baby's problems aren't really small yet!

The problems of a premature baby in intermediate care are related to immaturity but do not require as much technology or the number of personnel available in the NICU. In general, the NICU handles pulmonary, heart, and acute neurological problems while the intermediate-care nursery is equipped to handle feeding problems, apnea, bradycardia, temperature control, infections, and jaundice. Since these latter problems also affect babies in the NICU, they were covered in the last chapter. Please refer there for details that are missing here.

Like the NICU, the intermediate-care nursery is not always a pleasant place and not the best setting for any baby's development. There are still monitors and noise, no day/night cycles, and changing caretakers. As parents, you have an important role in providing continuity, love, and gentle, positive stimulation.

As we mentioned in the previous chapter, touching, talking, rocking, and the like should be done with care. Even though intermediate care signals the fact that your child isn't critically ill, a lot of stimulation can still overload his system right now. So, go ahead and talk to or touch your baby—but try not to do too much at once. Otherwise, you may get a negative reaction—your baby may retreat from the very stimulation you were hoping he'd enjoy. And this may make you feel as if you're just no good at parenting. Once again, he is not acting the way you expect a baby to act and your feelings may be hurt. You may feel that nothing you do can make your baby happy, so why try. It can be very frustrating, but when you do get a response, all the frustration will be forgotten in the joy of the moment. Your importance as a parent will become clear the first time your baby reacts to you—when the feel of your hand on his arm calms him, when your baby smiles at you, when his little hand grabs your finger, when he turns toward you to hear your voice, when he first takes a real feeding from you, when he looks at a toy with interest. When he does respond, you will, perhaps for the first time, truly feel like a *real* parent of a *real* baby. That time will come sooner than you think.

EQUIPMENT

The following equipment, described in Chapter 5, is often also used for babies in the intermediate-care nursery. We suggest you refer to the last chapter and to Chapter 3 to read about these pieces of equipment and why they are used.

Bili lights
Monitors, especially for apnea and bradycardia
Intravenous lines
Catheters
Nasogastric tubes
Oxygen hoods

Most babies in this nursery will be in isolettes, as opposed to the warming trays described in Chapter 5. An isolette is basically a large, clear plastic box. The isolette keeps the baby warm. Some isolettes have portholes through which you can reach the baby without having to open the side of the isolette (opening quickly lets the heat out); all isolettes have one side that lifts up in some way. The temperature in an isolette is maintained in the same way as the open radiant warmer and can be set to change automatically as the baby's temperature changes or can be held stable. To minimize heat loss, you may be asked to touch and handle your baby through the isolette's portholes. But you will also be able to take your baby out of the isolette more and more often the bigger and healthier he gets.

Babies who are almost ready to go home will be moved to regular hospital bassinets. Before babies are discharged they must be able to maintain their body temperature without the help of an isolette. This is indeed quite a graduation and is usually made with the help of (often improvised) warm caps, cloths, mittens, and booties, to minimize the baby's heat loss. It's nice to have some clothing bought and ready in preparation for this graduation, since the improvised clothes, though actually kind of cute, do make the babies look a bit like mini-ature "street people."

ROUTINE TESTS, PROCEDURES, AND EVALUATIONS

The following day-to-day tests or procedures were dis-cussed in Chapters 3 and 5, but are also done frequently in the intermediate-care nursery:

Weighing
Blood tests, drawn from a vein or by a heel stick
Transfusions
X rays
Sonograms (ultrasound)

In addition, however, a lot of screening tests will be given to your child in the intermediate-care nursery, often more than once. If your baby was moved here from the NICU, these may be tests you have seen administered before or they may be tests that were put off until now because there were other, more important life-saving issues to be concerned with back then. Also, a baby in intermediate care is in more stable condition and less stressed than a baby in the NICU and therefore will respond better to these basic tests of his abilities.

Hearing, sight, and development will be tested. You may not be told about these tests in advance and simply arrive to find them being administered. The technician may not explain what he is doing but just go about his business as if it had nothing to do with you. This testing is fairly routine and doesn't mean anything is wrong, but the purpose of the test should be explained to you. Do not expect the technician to give you the results of the test, however. As I have said before, the techni-cian's job and expertise are in giving the test, not reading it. Sight, hearing, and development will be tested again and again. Premies respond so differently from day to day, even from

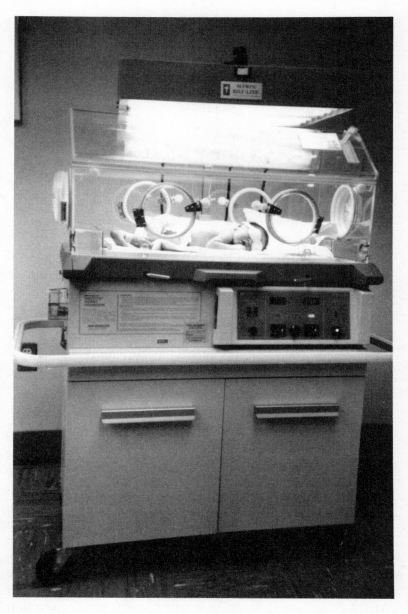

A baby being treated for jaundice rests under the bright bili lights in his isolette.

hour to hour, that tests often have to be retaken. The results very much depend on how awake the premie is and his general condition at the time of the test. A baby can appear grossly abnormal if tested at the wrong time but actually be perfectly all right. That is why these tests are often repeated or done over an extended period of time.

HOLDING AND DRESSING YOUR PREMIE

The first time you hold your child will be a happy moment, but you may feel as tense as you are elated. Congratulations! Parenting has blossomed from simply being able to watch, whisper, and stroke. You can cradle your child, talk, touch, and make eye contact. But remember to limit your urge to do everything at once. Too many different types of stimulation at once can still upset your baby. This rule of thumb is particularly important when and if you attempt to breastfeed. Breastfeeding and milk production will probably become big issues for you now. See Chapter 7 for more on this subject.

The more you hold your child and the more he begins to respond the way you expect a baby to respond, the more immediately fulfilling your role as a parent will become for you. Now is definitely a time to bring in clothes, little knit caps, booties, small toys, hair bows. All these items make your baby seem more like an individual—both to you and to the medical staff. Many stores now carry clothing in premie sizes. Some major manufacturers such as Carter's make premie-sized clothing. Doll clothes also work, but buying them for your child can be demoralizing. There are also a few mail-order houses that offer premie clothing and accessories, but keep in mind that these will be useful only if they deliver fast. Find out for certain, because your baby will be growing quicker than you can imagine. Here are two mail-order companies you can try. The first, Oh So Small, is run by a woman who comes from four generations of premies herself:

Oh So Small
c/o Jo Anne Bock
6432 Pacific Avenue
Tacoma, Washington 98408
(Send fifty cents for a catalogue)

Early Arrivals
3875 Telegraph Road
Suite A, #150
Ventura, California 93003
805-648-2189
(Gowns, sleepers, jogging suits, tops and bottoms)

FEEDING ISSUES

At first, your baby may not have received any oral feedings, but instead was fed through a peripheral or central line. You cannot really be the one to decide when your baby is ready to have food in his stomach—or whether he should get the feedings by tube, bottle, or breast. But you should always be involved in the decisions on *what* should go into his stomach, (i.e., formula or breast milk), and you should be involved in the feedings whenever you are in the nursery. Feeding, be it by tube, bottle, or breast, is an extremely important time for both a baby and his parents. One of the few pluses to tube and bottle feeding is that dads can be as involved as moms. Dads should take full advantage of this situation to get to know their premies, and moms should enjoy these breaks. Do not be intimidated if the nurses are more successful than you are at feeding your infant. They've had lots of practice—and besides, that's not what parenting is about. But if you notice that one particular nurse is very successful with your child, watch her and ask her for tips; she'll likely be flattered. Reassure yourself that all of this day-to-day care is nothing more than learned skills.

For preterm babies, four types of milk are available:

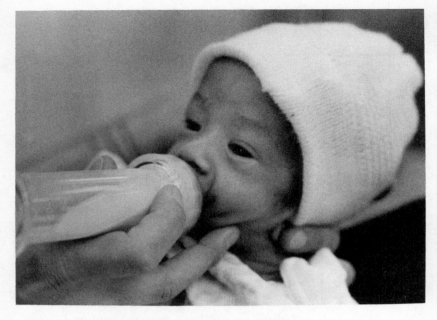

One plus to bottle feeding is that Dad can be involved.

1. Regular infant formula, soy-based or cow's-milk–based
2. Preterm formula
3. Your expressed breast milk
4. Breast milk from a "milk bank"

Most physicians agree that the milk from a premie's own mother is best for him. This is certainly true in terms of preventing infection. Breast milk is an amazing substance; the elements in your breast milk change with your baby's growth and needs. Because of this variability in breast milk, there is some debate as to whether breast milk obtained from mothers of full-term infants (which is gotten from a milk bank) has adequate nutrients for a premie infant. It is unclear whether banked milk might need to be supplemented with some of the substances that are missing or if some premie formulas would be better nutritionally. *Your* breast milk is ideal for your baby; however, it may not be very easy for you to obtain a good supply of it for him. (See Chapter 7 for advice on this.) If, for whatever reason, your baby is placed on formula, you should ask about the formula: what is it and what is in it? You should know what formulas are available and how your baby's doctors are deciding what and when to feed your child.

In the beginning, a preterm baby needs to be fed relatively large concentrations of proteins, certain fats, and minerals, more than what is available in regular formula or full-term breast milk. For this reason, preterm formula is specially made to have a higher protein and mineral content. Breast milk from the mother of a preterm baby also has a similarly high protein and mineral content. Preterm milk is higher in protein and minerals than full-term breast milk. Preterm breast milk is also high in calories (74 calories per 100 ml), but preterm formula is formulated to be higher still (80 calories per 100 ml). Surprisingly, however, preterm babies do not necessarily gain weight faster on a high-calorie formula when compared to babies on premie mom's breast milk; weight gain depends on calories *absorbed* by the gastrointestinal tract, not just on what is put into it. Breast milk is frequently better absorbed and better tolerated than formula, especially in infants who have been ill or who have had bowel problems.

Many of your medications will go into your breast milk; some medications will even be concentrated in breast milk. For example, aspirin, some antibiotics, some sedatives, some anti-seizure medications, alcohol, and some vitamins are all passed from your body into your breast milk. So ask your neonatologist if it is all right to take a certain medicine while expressing your milk or breastfeeding your premie. Also, your baby may be taken off breast milk for a few days if his bilirubin levels are increased. (See Chapter 5.) This is because some of the fats in human milk can interfere in an indirect way with the removal of bilirubin from the body. It is not certain that the baby must be taken off breast milk, but it is better to be safe than sorry. After a few days off breast milk, it is almost always possible to put the baby back on without any further problems.

Banked breast milk is expressed human breast milk donated by full-term mothers, usually women who have been lactating for several weeks or months. It contains less protein and fewer minerals than preterm milk. Donors to breast-milk banks should be screened for infections that may be transmitted through breast milk; double-check that your milk bank does this. Also, more and more banks are pasteurizing their breast milk, just to be sure it is safe. Breast milk in banks is stored frozen. Both the pasteurization process and freezing destroy all the immune cells in it; this is unfortunate, since these cells help prevent infection in your baby's intestines. However, these processes do not destroy other substances in breast milk that also protect your baby from infection. Unfortunately, many cities don't have breast-milk banks; mine—Atlanta—does not, for example. In addition, some breast-milk banks that now exist are closing. These banks are nonprofit, voluntary enterprises and are becoming increasingly concerned about legal liability issues.

Both preterm and full-term breast milk is low in iron. As noted earlier, a full-term newborn has iron stores in his body that will last him up to six months; this is not the case for the premie, whose iron stores will last only one to three months. Thus, a premie will soon need iron supplementation, either as medicinal "drops" or in iron-fortified formulas. Premies also need supplementation with several vitamins. Some of these will be given by vein or by injection into a muscle in the first few days of life; later, they can be given just like iron, as either medicinal "drops" (often coming in combination with iron, so you can give them all at once) or in readily available fortified formulas. For example, to prevent rickets, a bone disorder caused primarily by a calcium deficiency, the premature infant needs to receive vitamin D supplementation. The following chart gives you a general comparison of the nutrients in various formulas and breast milk. Remember, though, that breast-milk content will vary somewhat from one person to another and from day to day in the same person. Breast milk has lower concentrations of many minerals and vitamins than do formulas. In spite of this, babies do not have clinical deficiencies

CONTENT OF VARIOUS FORMULAS
AND BREAST MILK*

	REGULAR (FULL-TERM) FORMULA	PRETERM FORMULA	PRETERM BREAST MILK	MATURE BREAST MILK
Calories (per 100 ml)	67	81	67–75	67–75
Protein (g/100 ml)	1.5	1.6–2.4	2.7	1.1
Fat (g/100 ml)	2.7–3.7	3.8–4.5	2.9	3.8
Folic acid (μg/100 ml)	3.2–10.0	10.0	†	5.2
Vitamin A (μg/100 ml)	61	96	†	60
Vitamin D (μg/100 ml)	1.0	1.3	†	0.01
Vitamin E (μg/100 ml)	600	1.5	†	350

*Data collated from a number of sources.
†Vitamin content of preterm breast milk does not differ significantly from mature breast milk.

because they are on breast milk; the vitamins and minerals that are in breast milk appear to be very well absorbed through babies' intestines to their bodies.

A separate decision to be made is the method of feeding: can your baby drink from a bottle or breastfeed, or will a tube have to be inserted through his mouth or nose so that the milk can run straight into his stomach? Using medical terms, the decision is between oral feedings and orogastric or nasogastric feedings. A flexible plastic tube, known as a gavage tube, is inserted either through the baby's mouth (orogastric) or through the baby's nose (nasogastric) and into the stomach. The tube may be left in place continuously or taken out and replaced intermittently. In theory, premies who do not yet have a gag reflex might not find this tube uncomfortable if left in place. The repeated removal and insertion of this tube can cause distress and lead to bradycardia and apnea. Tube-fed babies are often given nipple tops or pacifiers to suck on while being fed, so that they can learn to associate sucking with feeding. These sucking babies also may gain more weight than babies who aren't given anything to suck on during feedings. If your baby can suck, you may wonder why gavage feeding is being used. There are a number of reasons. First, even premies who suck well still may not be able to coordinate safely their sucking, swallowing, and breathing so that they do these in the right order. A mistake can be quite serious, since it can mean aspiration of milk into the lungs, causing pneumonia. Second, feeding uses up a lot of energy for a premie; this energy might be better spent on growth for now. Third, a young premie will often take more formula by gastric feeding, simply because he tires out so quickly when he feeds by mouth. (Certainly Ashley's weight gain slowed precipitously when we switched from tube to bottle feeding, and again slowed when we switched to breast.)

Initially, your baby may receive supplemental nutrition into a peripheral or central vein through an intravenous line. Once the baby is receiving enough calories through gavage or oral feeding, the IV feedings will be discontinued. A healthy preterm baby will probably begin gavage feedings within two hours after birth. The baby may be given sugar water through the gavage tube for up to the first twenty-four hours. Then either diluted premie formula or diluted expressed breast milk would be given for a day or two, followed by full-strength premie formula or expressed breast milk. Some premies, though, will be started on full-strength premature formula or breast

milk immediately after birth. The timing and volume of feedings will be based on what your baby's stomach can absorb
comfortably at a time. Before each gavage feeding, the stomach
contents will be drawn back gently through the tube, to see if
any milk from the last feeding remains in the stomach. If some
does, less may be given at this feeding. If your baby can absorb
very small amounts at a time, the interval between feedings
may be decreased. Your baby may even be fed in continuous
drips through the tube. This is done by dripping the milk or
formula down the gavage tube through an intravenous line,
pump, and tubing. In general, the goal will be to increase the
amount of milk your baby receives at one time and to increase
the intervals between feedings—just as you will be doing yourself when you bring the baby home. If at any time there is
concern about the possibility of necrotizing enterocolitis (see
Chapter 3), all feedings will be temporarily stopped and the
baby may again go through the advancement routine described
above before returning to full-strength feedings.

Premies are not "demand" feeders; they will not tell you
that they are hungry. So feedings for now will be given on a
standard schedule, determined as described above. After feedings, the infant may fall asleep and/or have episodes of apnea.
This may mean that the feedings were a little too stimulating
or tiring. As your baby matures, this will be less and less often
the case. With increasing maturity, he may be at his most alert
immediately after feedings. As his feeding patterns mature, so
will his sleep patterns. It will take time, and the nursery routine
and lighting do not help, but eventually your premie will eat
and sleep in a pattern that is more conducive to a restful life
for you and the rest of the family. Again, be patient and have
faith; things will get better.

Even if your baby cannot yet feed directly at the breast,
keep an eye to the future. If breastfeeding is your goal, you
had best be working on it from the very beginning. A premie
mom's milk supply is often small at best, and early stimulation
is essential to increase production. Besides, your premie could
use that breast milk right now, not just later. So talk *immediately*

to the nurses and doctors about it and read the next chapter. Find out how the hospital wants you to bring in your expressed milk, whether they have containers they would like you to use or whether you should buy and sterilize your own, where in the nursery it is stored, how you should store and label it at home, and in what volumes it should be stored. (Your milk is precious stuff! If the nurses discard the milk they don't use at a single feeding, put just enough for one feeding into each container—and remember, that amount will be increasing rapidly.)

You should also ask about breast pumps and how to use them. The hospital staff may not think to tell you or may think that you already know—so ask! Manual pumps can be frustrating and slow for many moms, although they proved best for me with Ashley. Hospitals often have electric pumps available for use there. These can also be rented for home use from your hospital or local pharmacy. Hospitals may also have lists of places where you can buy electric pumps, but these are very expensive. (See Chapter 7 for a list of some electric pumps available for purchase or rental.) Rental certainly will be worth it if you plan on pumping every one to four hours for the next few months and can afford the rental fee; your baby's health insurance may cover this.

Even if your baby is not developmentally able to breast-feed, I strongly recommend that you put your baby to the breast if he is clinically stable. It is a wonderful feeling and will help your milk come in as nothing else can. Ask to use the breastfeeding room; virtually all nurseries now have them. Swaddle your infant, to minimize undue stimulation, and put him to your breast—no rocking or talking right now. Let your baby concentrate on one thing at a time. If he even turns his head to the breast (a rooting reflex), consider yourself successful. One or two sucks . . . terrific! A coordinated suck and swallow are incredible. Most of all, just enjoy having body contact with him in a setting of peace and privacy. Lower your expectations. If you're too hopeful, nothing will go right and you'll be crushed. Putting your baby to the breast at this stage is really to help you feel more like a mom, to give your baby and yourself time for close physical contact, to help increase your milk flow, and to remind you that all this pumping will eventually lead to a breastfeeding baby. (Read Chapter 7 for more on how to build and maintain your milk supply and begin successful breastfeeding.)

Weight gain is carefully monitored in the hospital and can seem at times like the determining factor in your baby's life. Often intermediate-care nurseries have rules that only babies of a certain weight (usually around five pounds) can be discharged. Almost all newborns will lose 5 to 10 percent of their body weight in the first few days after birth. Preterm infants may lose even more weight because their bodies have a higher water content than do those of term infants. This initial weight loss is normal and does not mean that there is anything wrong with your baby. After the first few days, your premie will start to gain weight, probably at the rate of about fifteen grams a day, and should regain original birth weight by three weeks of age. All this weighing and this somewhat arbitrary weight goal may make your child's weight gain seem extremely important. Of course it is, but it is not more important than his clinical status and it is not more important than other areas of development.

What will be done if the physicians think your baby may not be gaining weight fast enough? If you breastfeed, your baby may be weighed after every feeding to see how much milk was taken. This can make you tense and nervous about your milk production, but try to take it easy. This is not a test. Babies who are not gaining weight at an adequate rate (always a judgment call on the part of your doctor) may be given supplementary nutrition by vein for a while, just like very sick premies in the NICU. This will be stopped as soon as weight gain improves.

LONG-TERM OUTLOOK

Now that your infant is visibly growing a little stronger each week, you will probably have a great urge to put him through your own personal series of tests and try to sort out the long-term outlook. Please try not to do this. You will just exhaust him and worry yourself. Unless he has severe and obvious handicaps, it is simply too soon to sort out the long-term outlook. But this is a good time to begin asking questions. This may be the first time the medical staff discusses the possibility of less obvious congenital defects and their implications. In fact, you may not even know that certain medical tests have been done until the doctors go over the results with you. Why do the doctors wait so long before talking about these topics with you? Usually because they are too busy worrying about life-and-death situations or do not want to discuss the defects until they themselves know more about them. When you discuss long-term issues with your physicians, remember to make lists of the questions you want to ask and keep notes or record your meetings. (See Chapter 5 for more on this.) For more specifics about the long-term problems some premies and their families may face, see Chapters 9, 10, 12, and 13.

FINANCIAL ARRANGEMENTS

Now that your baby is in intermediate care, you and your husband should take the time to sort out financial arrangements. Hospitals have a host of people who are being paid to help you with this. It is easier to get financial advice from the hospital financial department while your baby is in the hospital for two reasons. First, financial personnel may be more responsive while the baby is still "theirs." Second, their offices are just downstairs or down the hall. It is a lot easier for you to walk there from the nursery in person than to drive there in your car after the baby is home. This personal contact will probably be more effective than a less personal telephone call.

Use all of the hospital's financial networks. Don't forget the social service department; they may be the most compassionate. Hospital, and sometimes home, care of a premie can be extremely expensive. Financial worries add even more stress to an already intensely stressful time. Often, this financial burden is felt more by the father than the mother. Not wanting to trouble her further, he may keep the hospital bills to himself for a time. These worries should be shared, but one person should probably take over primary responsibility. Unfortunately, in our society, financial institutions may be more responsive to a male. Bill and I certainly found that personnel at financial institutions were often more responsive to a male voice on the phone. Maybe this will change with time but for now take it into account when you decide who should deal with the finances. Besides, Mom may have more than her share of the childcare, especially if she is breast-pumping or -feeding, so it is not unreasonable for Dad to take on this onerous task. Most important, remember that these mounting bills don't have to be paid immediately. Most institutions and people will try to be understanding, but the form letters can be downright nasty, even if the hospital or your insurance company is the one in error, not you. It may be hard for you to put up with all the bureaucracy without losing your temper.

Many parents are shocked by the cost of premie care. As one mother notes:

"I remember the first time that Paul thought about the hospital bill and he said, 'Gee, I'll bet it's about $500 a day!' Well, I saw the bill later and it was already up to $25,000! Luckily, the complete hospital bill was paid for by our insurance. I handled all the finances and it wasn't that bad. We ended up spending about $1,000 of our own money, for things like the monitor, which wasn't completely covered."

Another parent said the final bill was $250,000!

Even families who have insurance coverage often end up needing assistance with these bills. Insurance often pays only 80 percent of the costs, leaving the parents to find a way to cover the other 20 percent on their own. Given the size of the bill for premie care at most hospitals, this 20 percent can be an overwhelming amount for many people. The first thing you should do is to find out exactly what your insurance plan covers and how claims must be processed. The sooner claims are mailed in, the cleaner and easier the whole process should be for you. And if forms are filled out correctly the first time, there will be less time wasted on bureaucratic entanglements. Unfortunately, there is not a lot of organized assistance available to people who are having trouble making up the difference between the actual bill and what the insurance company will pay.

Premature babies often come at a time in people's lives when they can least afford it—couples who are young, just married, just buying homes, and just starting out will have the most difficult time facing these insurmountable costs. Sometimes, couples find out that their insurance will not cover what they thought it would. If, for example, you or your husband switched jobs and/or got a new insurance plan recently, your pregnancy and your child's birth may not be covered. If you were already pregnant at the time coverage began, it is considered a preexisting condition and the insurance company will not pay. This happens to many young couples whose lives are more apt to be in a state of flux as they switch jobs and move to new towns.

Donna Carson, director of social work for Emory Regional Perinatal Center in Georgia, says there *are* places you can turn for help if, for whatever reason, you are having trouble paying your hospital bills. She suggests you begin with the hospital social worker and with the business office at the hospital. Then contact your local health department and/or department of human resources for information on services and financial help available to you.

Some families will qualify for Medicaid, a government-assisted plan for medical coverage that is based on a family's income. Even if your income is such that you would not normally qualify for Medicaid, you may be able to in this special circumstance if you have a high-risk infant and a hospital bill of $20,000 or more. The plan is called Medical Assistance Only and may help pay some of the hospital bill. Check with your local department of family and children's services. Unfortunately, Medicaid often covers very little of the bill, sometimes as little as $1,800. If parents are unable to pay the rest, this means that the hospital must suffer the loss. Many public hospitals will accept patients who don't have insurance, knowing that they will never be able to get the whole bill paid. Some private hospitals, however, are less benevolent and will not take patients who do not have insurance coverage.

Luckily, many hospitals are willing to be flexible about payment schedules. They may allow parents to pay over a number of months or even years, at a rate that suits their financial abilities. In other cases, however, certain hospitals have been known to insist on immediate and full payment of the bill, even if it means that the family must sell home and car to meet the payment. If this happens to you, you may want to consult a lawyer or the Legal Aid Society for advice. You might also try some of the other financial-assistance outlets mentioned below.

For children with long-term problems, such as chronic lung disease or blindness, parents may want to apply for Supplemental Security Income (SSI), administered by the Social Security Administration. Parents should also apply for SSI if their child must stay in the hospital for three months or longer. This financial assistance is based totally on the child's medical needs. If the application is approved, it will help even those parents who are insured to pay the balance of the bill not covered by insurance. The earlier you apply the better, because, if accepted, benefits are retroactive to ninety days before the date of the original application. This program sometimes also covers special medical equipment, at-home nursing care, and ongoing therapy. It also covers medical bills for a terminally ill child. Call your local Social Security office for information. (*Note:* If your application is turned down the first time, and this is common, reapply for reconsideration. It is very often accepted the second time, according to Donna Carson.)

Many states have a children's medical services office. Often, these offices can help you financially. Your local health department will know of them. To apply, you need a referral from a physician. A children's medical services office helps children with ongoing problems or those in need of special surgeries. It may pay for a large portion of the hospital bill and outpatient services, if the child qualifies. Rules, regulations, and qualifications vary from state to state and region to region.

Try to get as much of the financial and insurance paperwork as possible squared away now. You won't want it all hanging over your head while trying to deal with a premie newly home.

7.

The Three B's:
Bonding, Breastfeeding, and Being There

Parents of premature babies have often been called premature parents. This title is very apt. The mother of a full-term infant experiences emotional, physical, and hormonal changes in the last trimester of pregnancy that a premie mom never gets to experience. Instead, both parents of premies are thrown into roles that at first don't seem real, especially in the NICU or intermediate-care hospital setting.

Why does that lost trimester make such a difference? At the beginning of the third trimester, both parents usually experience last-minute doubts about their preparedness for parenthood. They may moan about how their life as a couple will never be the same again, wonder about what they have gotten themselves into, and question their practical abilities at handling a baby. They may grieve for their lost independence and solitude. Slowly, however, through the physical changes in the soon-to-be-mom, conversations, nursery preparation, childbirth classes, and lists of baby names, expectant parents begin to see themselves as ready for this new role. They come to realize that, yes, a baby really is about to enter their lives. At the beginning of the third trimester, the pregnant woman often thinks about herself: how she feels, what labor will be like for her, how she will cope with the delivery. The baby seems distant, almost secondary. By the end of the pregnancy, however, most women feel that they have had enough of being pregnant and are ready to face labor and delivery. They have also usually come to grips with the realities of parenthood and want to meet that little person they've been talking to and been kicked by.

Premature parents, having missed this last phase of pregnancy, do not have an image of themselves as parents and often do not feel ready to take on the responsibilities of caring for a baby. You may worry that any last-minute feelings of fear or doubt about parenthood have somehow caused this horrible thing to happen, that maybe you didn't want the baby enough. Having a baby thrust upon you too soon by nature, you may both resent the child and believe the child must resent you. Instead of having positive feelings upon seeing your child for the first time, you may experience fear, shock, and other negative emotions.

Most experts believe that premature parents adjust to the prematurity in a fairly predictable pattern: first by grieving over their lost pregnancy, then by grieving over the loss of their imagined Gerber baby, and finally by adjusting to their situation, to their real baby, and to their role as parents. Through this process they are able to begin to form a healthy relationship with their child.

What is this magical thing called "bonding"? In its most rigid interpretation, bonding is thought to be a process that occurs in the first few hours after delivery. For ideal bonding, the baby would be placed on the mother's tummy right after birth and then put to the breast and allowed to nurse. Mother and baby would cuddle and make eye contact. Dad might give the baby a warm bath, and *voilà*, bonding has occurred! If this is bonding, then premature parents undeniably cannot experience it. But this concept of bonding is based on animal studies and very superficial human observational studies. Most researchers, including those who first described this "bonding" process, feel that the above scenario is too narrow and simplistic to explain the growing feelings, emotions, and attachments that develop between human infants and their parents. Real attachment comes from the days and nights spent at your newborn's side, stroking his arm, getting to know him as a unique individual, growing with him. Attachment occurs over the lifetime of a relationship. It is the emotion that develops as we get up at night with our children, enjoy the cute or insightful things they say and do, see the better sides of ourselves in them. And it is also the feeling our children come to have for us, as they learn to trust us, love us, rely on us, idolize us (when they're young), and forgive us (when they're old).

You may have read about studies showing that premature children are at increased risk of being abused by their parents. (In fact, I've conducted and published some of these studies.) There is an association between prematurity and being abused, but you must keep in mind two things. First, the association is a weak one: relatively few premature children are abused and few abused children were premies. Second, the relationship is not necessarily one of cause and effect; it may just be that the same people are at risk for both. Let's give a specific example: young parents from stressful, low-income environments who have little emotional or financial support are at increased risk of both preterm delivery and abusing their children.

Being removed from your child for weeks or months while he is in the hospital could impair your longer-term interactions with your baby. But this will not necessarily be the case—and *not* if you interact with him as a parent right from the start, even in the NICU and intermediate-care nursery. Twenty years ago, parents were purposely excluded from NICUs and intermediate-care units. Now doctors and nurses appreciate the importance of premies' being with their parents, especially in these stressful settings. These weeks as a hospital-based parent will not provide you with the joyful memories that you would have if your child were a full-term newborn, but they will provide you with a strong foundation for your future relationship with your baby.

Let me give you a personal example of how this early parenting can lead to strong, lasting bonds. We brought Ashley home from the hospital very early and gave her "intermediate care" here. I literally could not leave her side for very long. My husband, Bill, would joke that Ashley was growing from my arm (and before I could pick her up, it seemed my arm was attached to her mattress). This image was more appropriate than he realized. She may have left my body early, but she still had a need for close care and I had a strong emotional, as well as medical, need to be near her. As a pediatrician, I have had other premie parents express this same intense urge for physical closeness and contact with their premie:

"We have a closeness. I sometimes feel we are the same soul. We walked the streets of hell together. There is something about our relationship that I can't put into words."

A father talks about his strong attachment to his now six-year-old premie in relation to his other children:

"I don't think I show favoritism but so help me, she's so precious. I think it's a question of loving so much more what you almost lost!"

The need and desire to be close can be fulfilled by parenting your baby from the time he is born, even if he is in the NICU or intermediate-care unit. The long-term rewards of this attachment are great. Quite commonly these feelings of intense closeness, of oneness, remain long after infancy. I often think that this may be the payback for never having had the normal joys—the breastfeeding, rocking, holding, and cuddling—you have with a full-term newborn from the time of birth.

Undeniably, there are a great many impediments to attachment between a premie and a parent. Perhaps the first and most severe impediment is fear—fear that you will lose your baby, fear of becoming attached to a baby who will die. This is usually resolved in the very first days or weeks.

As one mother of an infant born at twenty-eight weeks gestation describes it:

"A few hours after Grant was born, we went to see him

in the nursery. They told me what he would look like—that he would be strapped down with his arms and legs spread out, but nothing they said could have prepared me for that first sight. I was shocked, scared, and sad. There aren't words to describe how I felt. We only stayed a few minutes and then went back to my room. Initially I had just been so happy that my baby was alive but I didn't realize he was that sick until I saw him. Then, I was afraid to love Grant because I thought he might die. I tried to act like I was accepting—if something happened, well, that's that. This feeling lasted only about half a day! Very soon, I began to think that, no matter what, that baby was my firstborn. For better or worse he would always be my firstborn, whether he left the earth that night or not. I realized that the only thing my husband and I had to give him was love, and if he were to die, at least he would die knowing how much we loved him.''

Besides fear of death, the very practical issue of physical separation from your baby is an impediment to bonding. There are strict medical limitations on the amount of physical contact you can have. If your baby is moved to a faraway hospital with intensive-care facilities, you may not see him for days after birth, while you recover in the hospital where you delivered. The father is often the first parent to see the baby, spend time with him, touch him, and maybe even hold him. This often puts fathers in the unique position of being physically closer to the premie than they would be to a full-term baby. It can also occasionally make the mother feel even more left out, although rationally she may agree that her husband should be with the baby and not with her.

Even if both parents have immediate contact with their baby, the contact is often severely limited by the child's medical condition. Cuddling him may be impossible, picking him up may not be allowed, even touching him may be difficult. As a doctor, I often see parents who are afraid to touch their premature babies at first. This is not surprising. The tubes and lines and monitors all seem to be in the way, the baby seems so fragile. Parents may worry that if they touch anything they may knock out a catheter, cause an alarm to go off, or hurt their baby. Don't worry! Your baby's doctors and nurses will guide you until you are comfortable. If you follow your doctor's advice, you can't physically hurt your baby by touching him. Your goal as a parent is to give your baby comfort, and the only way you can do this right now is through gentle touching, talking, and the like. As long as you adjust your activities to your baby's developmental and clinical state, your touch can do your premie only good.

Most parents whose babies I have cared for seem to sense this intuitively. This mother explains how her presence and touch helped her baby:

"Once, the doctor was about to do a heel-stick blood test on my baby and suggested that I might want to leave the nursery for a moment. I agreed and was on my way out when I heard my baby screaming. I ran back and the doctor asked, 'What are you doing? I thought you were going to leave.' I said, 'I can't leave, my baby's crying.' So I stayed and my baby calmed right down.''

Touching can begin to seem too limited very soon. You may want desperately to be able to hold and hug the baby, sing songs, make eye contact, bounce, tickle, and kiss. These things come in time but obviously not soon enough. The first time you hold your baby will certainly be a joyous moment but he may still be attached to monitors and the time allowed with him may be short. This can be extremely frustrating:

"My husband, Eric, got to hold Grant before I did. I had given birth to Grant while visiting my mother in Florida, ten and a half hours away from our home in Little Rock, Arkansas. About a week after he was born, my husband had to return to Little Rock for his job. Before he left, the nurses took Grant out and let Eric hold him. He was one week old. I wasn't allowed to hold Grant until another week had passed. Until then, I would sit alongside his warming tray and touch him. He didn't wear diapers, but I got to change the little pads under him. We were told that Grant wouldn't know whether we were there or not but I think he did, right from the beginning. I felt like he was responding to me. If I talked to him, or stroked him, he seemed to calm down. I was so happy when they finally let me hold him.''

I would suggest that you go ahead and take photos of your baby—tubes, monitors, and all! At first, you may feel it is out of place to start snapping photos of your baby before he is 100 percent out of the woods, but these are pictures you will want to have and keep. Even from week to week in the nursery, these pictures can help you see the changes and improvements in your baby's size and appearance. When you see him every day you do not notice these little developments, and you may wonder whether your baby is really growing.

Once you are past some of these obstacles to getting to know your baby, you will find a very tiny person with his own

A concerned parent watches her baby through the plastic walls of an isolette.

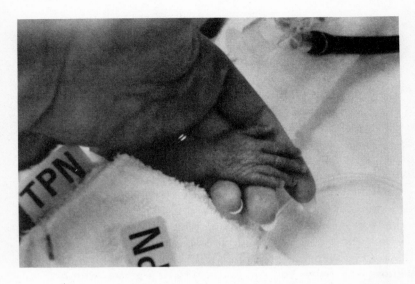

Grace, at ten days, weighing two pounds five ounces, rests her little hand in her mother's.

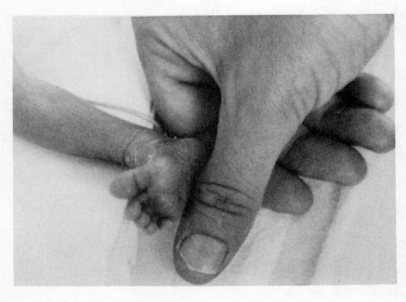

Twin brother Matthew's foot is smaller than his dad's thumb.

Grace and Matthew today, at age three and a half.

unique personality. Every premie I have ever cared for as a doctor has had his own distinct ways. As a mother, I can tell you firsthand that Ashley's personality has in many ways remained the same since birth—smiling, sweet, and eager to please, but with an iron determination to do the very thing that may hurt her most, and not hurt anyone else. I sometimes joke that she was born prematurely simply because she wanted to come out and she wasn't going to let anybody tell her any differently. From the start, she has taught us the hardest lesson of parenthood: that children have to make their own mistakes!

Some of the things that normally draw us to our newborns are exaggerated in a premie—the helplessness, the small size, the vulnerability, the dependency. At the same time, because their needs are exaggerated, parents of premature babies can feel incompetent and, when they see the nurses in charge of their baby's care, even superfluous. You are *not* in the way. The medical staff *cannot* do a better job of parenting your baby. A few intriguing studies of parents of hospitalized premies in the hospital have shown that there is no correlation between the parents' own negative assessment of their practical skills and their actual skills, compared to other moms or to the nursing staff. *Do not* feel inferior. Parenting is your job. Let's just review some of the basic points of how to parent a hospitalized premie:

1.   A parent's role is not to give medical care. A parent should not fight with the medical staff or alienate them. That doesn't help you and that doesn't help your premie.

2.   A parent's role is to try to counteract some of the sensory onslaught by being there for the baby as an early, stable, and soothing influence in his life.

3.   Avoid the urge to test your baby. Can he see? Can he hear? Is he awake? Does he have any brain function? (Of course he does—he knows that you're bothering him!) If you give him a test, he'll probably fail it (you would, too, in that setting), and you'll make yourself needlessly worried and anxious.

4.   If, during your visit, your baby becomes agitated, don't chastise yourself. Just sit back and look, if that's all your baby can handle at that moment. Later, you can try to interact with him again.

5.   Get to know your baby's body, his reflexes, his moods. You may begin to be aware of his alert times, when he wants and needs to feel your touch or hear your voice, and when he just wants to be left alone.

6.   Remember that at this point your baby can concentrate on only one sense at a time. If you rub, do it lightly, in one place, and don't talk. If you talk, don't touch. Overstressing your baby is counterproductive. You want to make him feel good, not bombard him with even more negative stimuli.

7.   If you have decided to wear the same scent (soap,

perfume, aftershave) each time you visit your baby, just sit beside him when you first come in. Let him sniff and realize you're there before you say or do anything.

8.   Leave something in the isolette or on the warming tray that is lightly scented with the fragrance you've chosen. (If you have been pumping your milk, you might leave a used breast pad with the baby. The scent of your milk can be very comforting.)

9.   If you sense that your baby is in pain, rub him gently elsewhere, or talk to him softly, to distract him from the pain.

10.   Look into your baby's eyes, but don't expect to make prolonged eye contact. Turn your gaze away when your baby looks back at you and let your baby study your face unchallenged. Often, the premie needs to be the initiator here. He will make eye contact with you when he's ready.

11.   Try to arrange your visits when your baby is most alert. If you can't be there for an alert time (sometimes he may be most alert in the middle of the night), arrange for the nurse to play a tape of your voice at that time.

12.   Bring in small stuffed toys, clothes, bows. They will do wonders for your morale and eventually for your baby's as well.

13.   Take photos. Share some of them with your family.

14.   Try handling the feedings yourself, whether tube or bottle. Bottle-feeding a premie is a learned art. In the beginning, watch and see which nurses are best at feeding your baby. Copy their attitude and movements when you try to bottle-feed. Swaddle the baby, so his own movements don't distract him from the task at hand. Don't worry if things don't go well at first. Getting a premie to drink from a bottle is not easy, especially while you're tense.

15.   Get involved with your baby's nutrition. If he is on formula, find out which one and how much he is drinking. Ask about breast milk instead of formula, if this interests you. Find out the doctor's plans for advancing the diet.

16.   Stay in close contact with all the doctors and nurses on whom your baby's care depends. If you see the neonatolo-

gist in the nursery, but he's busy, and you have questions, ask him if you can make an appointment to speak with him about these things.

17. If you are concerned about your baby's medical care, speak to your baby's doctor. Do not fight with him, but discuss the issue. Do not let it go without speaking up and voicing your concerns.

18. If you don't understand your doctor's explanations, ask him if he could explain it a different way or could suggest someone else who might also be able to talk with you and explain it, using a slightly different approach or using examples that might make it clearer to you. Your baby is getting very sophisticated medical care, so you needn't be afraid to ask about things or admit that you don't understand how something works.

BREAST MILK

Many moms want to breastfeed their premies even in the face of many obstacles. It is a major challenge, but gives you a wonderful feeling of doing something of tangible benefit to your baby. Your breast milk is in many ways the best food for your baby, although premie formulas also do the important job of nourishing quite nicely. You may cling to the notion of breastfeeding as being the "only thing" you can do for your baby, especially if you feel responsible for somehow "failing" him by going into early labor. But if breastfeeding isn't a viable option for you or if it just doesn't work out, remember that there is a lot more to parenting than supplying nourishment. And you—and Dad—can have a physically close and loving interaction with your premie while feeding with a bottle. After all, you may well be using a bottle even for your breast milk at first. Obviously, I am giving you some mixed messages here, but there is no single answer for everyone and I don't want to lead you to think there is. I breastfed Ashley, but that doesn't make breastfeeding the right choice for you. Other mothers have told me it was not right for them.

As one mother describes it:

"I tried to breastfeed my daughter but it didn't work out. It was very, very frustrating. I pumped for two and a half months. It was too hard. I had no energy. I was emotionally and physically drained, and pumping my milk only added to that. I did it because I thought breast milk was best for my baby. But if I had to do it over again, I wouldn't even try."

Let's look first at some of the obstacles to successful breastfeeding, so that you know what you are up against. Remember, as you read on, that each of these obstacles can be overcome—I fed Ashley breast milk by tube for four weeks, by bottle for three weeks, and by breast for seven more months—and also remember that the obstacles may not be as great for some moms as for others. I well remember how much I envied one premie mom with an apparently limitless milk supply, while I would pump for an hour and a half to get enough for each two-hour feeding. Most premie moms are more like me than the woman I envied. Because your pregnancy ended early, your hormones are not yet primed for milk production. In addition, you have a baby who is too immature to suck and swallow, so your two main stimuli to establishing a milk supply simply aren't there—hormones and physical "priming." Normally, breastfeeding can begin right after delivery, when the baby is first put to his mother's breast; you can even manually pump some milk in the last few weeks of a full-term pregnancy. Unfortunately, in a premature birth, it would not be safe to hold your baby to the breast to try this, nor would it likely be very productive. Without some surrogate for the stimulation of a breastfeeding baby, your milk supply will not come in. Nature is set up so that mother and baby keep in perfect balance—the mother makes as much or as little milk as the baby seems to need and want at each feeding. This is why when a baby begins to lose interest in breastfeeding, the milk supply rapidly declines and ceases.

If you want to produce milk for your baby's use now or

plan to breastfeed your baby later, you will have to learn how to express milk and how to keep up your milk supply. You are also likely to need a few spare tricks up your sleeve. We'll give you some here. Your baby's nurses and doctors will likely be eager to help but may be remarkably uninformed. Your best source of information is an experienced premie mom, if you can find one, and the rare experienced nurse or physician with a special interest in premie breastfeeding. When Ashley was born, the nurses and other moms thought I was a breastfeeding expert of sorts. (I had published papers and done some research on the scientific side of breast milk and I had effortlessly breastfed Danielle, my full-term first child.) So the nurses sent premie moms to me with their questions. It was an awful feeling. Here I was failing miserably at producing milk myself and other frightened, exhausted women were coming to me for advice—a pathetic case of the blind leading the blind. But experience does teach, and now I think that I could get milk out of a stone. So don't panic; there are ways to get that milk out.

You may find, however, that your husband and family are not being terribly supportive of your attempts to lactate. Your husband may find it torture to watch your seemingly hopeless endeavors; he may feel that you've been through enough and should let yourself alone. Your children may not have a clue as to what on earth you are doing. At first it may intrigue them, but then they'll wish Mommy would spend those few short hours at home with them instead of a pump. Your mother, perhaps a source of support in other ways, may not have breastfed you and may be unconvinced by today's pro-breastfeeding arguments. She may tell you to leave the feedings to the doctors, not to "knock yourself out" by trying to breastfeed, or she may try to convince you that your baby will gain more weight on formula. Remember that you are *her* baby and her goal is to protect you as much as yours is to protect your premie. It is very important for these folks to support your efforts. I was very lucky: Bill was totally understanding, Danielle never tired of jabbering away to me while I pumped, and my mother took pride in another mark of her daughter's virtue—I could even breastfeed! You need this kind of support. If you don't have it, see if a sympathetic nurse or doctor will have a talk with your family and help them to mend their ways.

Your own body also can stand in the way of successful lactation. Physical and emotional exhaustion can be a real obstacle to effective breastfeeding. Stress and fatigue can decrease your milk supply and make pumping or nursing more frustrating. To top it off, you may not be drinking enough fluids. Fluid intake is extremely important for adequate milk production. I always settled down to the pump with a cup of warm milk. It became a way of telling my body to get going, while it also kept up my fluid intake.

Even after breastfeeding has begun on a regular basis, there can be frustrations. A baby who is a poor nurser can make you feel that every feeding is a battle. Furthermore, once your baby is receiving milk straight from the breast, there is no way to count the ounces you are giving him. Your worries about how much milk he is getting and how much weight he gains can put a damper on the joys of nursing. Some women actually express their milk into a bottle and then bottle-feed, just so they can see the ounces empty into their babies. Others use scales and weigh the baby before and after feedings. While this may seem like a good idea at first, it eventually becomes nerve-racking and counterproductive. The tension of this constant "testing" can decrease your milk supply and make nursing even more difficult. Also, a baby who has been bottle-fed may always feel more comfortable with the bottle and not switch easily to the breast. Sucking from the breast is harder work for the baby than drinking from a bottle.

This mother had many of these obstacles in her way:

"I think to nurse a premie is so hard. If you have another child—no way! It's a continuous, round-the-clock job! If nothing else, I'd like to tell other mothers that it is very difficult to do. I was so depressed. I had all this milk stockpiled. I didn't get a chance to try breastfeeding the baby until the day before he left the hospital. They put me in a room with other people and just a screen around me. He latched on and at first I thought maybe we could do this. But at home I was so obsessed with the baby's weight gain, I just couldn't do it.''

To avoid some of the frustrations mentioned above, you will want to learn as much as you can about breastfeeding and about expressing your milk until your baby is ready to breast-feed. Take advantage of any special breastfeeding instruction the hospital has to offer you—books, videotapes, classes—and of any nurses, doctors, or other moms with special breastfeeding/pumping skills. Ask specifically for information on how to express milk and how to breastfeed a premature baby.

So far, we have been talking about lactation and breast-feeding as if they were two sides to the same coin, but they are really very different arts. Your first goals will almost certainly be to initiate lactation and to produce, through pumping (expressing), an adequate milk supply for your premie. Only when this is accomplished and your premie, for his part, is improving can you both move on to the fine art of breastfeeding. Let's handle each of these skills in turn.

EXPRESSING BREAST MILK

Expressing milk manually, even with a pump, is far more difficult than nursing a baby. A full-term healthy infant, for example, can usually empty a breast of milk within five minutes. Pumping, especially for a premie mom and most especially in the beginning, may take you an hour to do what your baby will eventually do in a few minutes. Pumping is in part more difficult because your baby really is more clever at getting milk out efficiently than a pump. Pumping is also more difficult because you are missing the emotional and hormonal stimuli that contact with your baby would bring on—bring on so strongly that it can be shocking at first. We really are not in complete control of our bodies! Sometimes just hearing your baby cry or seeing him can help the milk to ''come in'' and start to flow. So it may be helpful to look at a picture of your baby, or think of your baby while expressing. These are good things to do when you are pumping at home. You may also want to try having your premie nearby, if he is stable enough, when you are pumping in the hospital. This is something that your husband could help you with; he could hold the baby for you while you pump, or hold the collection jar in place while you hold your baby.

Understanding how breast milk is made may also be of some help to you as you learn to express it. Breasts are composed of glandular tissue surrounded by muscles and fat. The fat and muscles determine the size and shape of your breast and have nothing to do with milk production. No matter how flat-chested you are, you can still breastfeed successfully. As you and your husband almost certainly noticed, your breasts began to change in preparation for lactation back in the early stages of your pregnancy. You also probably noticed that they were tender and swollen. If your pregnancy lasted long enough, you may have even begun to leak a little colostrum in your third trimester, before the baby was born. (This leaking is normal and has nothing to do with the premature ending of your pregnancy.) Colostrum is a clear "milk," rich in nutrients and antibodies, meant for the baby the first few days after delivery.

Stimulation or suction of the breasts causes the brain to release a hormone called prolactin, which stimulates active milk production by the glandular tissue in the breasts. The more stimulation the breasts receive (i.e., the longer the baby sucks or the more frequently the breasts are emptied), the more milk a woman will produce. Even a woman who has been given a drug to stop lactation or who has let her milk supply dwindle can usually bring the milk back by starting on a program of frequent feedings or pumping before her milk supply is completely gone. Some women who have let their milk supply dry up entirely can stimulate relactation the same way, but it is not easy. So if you decide not to breastfeed at first and then change your mind, there is a chance you can still breastfeed, if you are determined and persevere.

When you are ready to breastfeed, contractile cells squeeze the milk down into the milk ducts inside your breasts. Milk builds up in a collection area behind your nipple, then passes out through tiny openings in your nipple. This milk-producing and squeezing action is known as the "let-down" reflex. It is a sign that the milk is ready to flow. You may feel it as a tingling sensation or an uncomfortable pressure in your breasts. The let-down reflex is caused by the hormone oxytocin, released by the anterior hypothalamus of the brain in response to the stimulations mentioned above (sucking, pumping, psychological stimulation).

Getting your milk to flow is the basis of successful breast-feeding. As a premie mom, you may have to really work to succeed at this first essential step. Let's start with the basics, none of which is simple for a premie mom visiting her child in the hospital and possibly caring for the others at home. First of all, make sure you continue to eat a high-quality diet, just as you did when you were pregnant. You will need to be well nourished in order to pass the proper nutrients along to your baby. Second, your fluid intake (water, juice, milk) should be at least two quarts a day. Caffeine and alcohol should be consumed in limited quantities only, since they are passed to the infant through the milk. Incidentally, two studies suggest that there is some truth to the old wives' tale that drinking beer helps milk production. Other alcohol does not help. Furthermore, it does not appear to be the alcohol in beer that causes milk production to increase: both alcoholic and nonalcoholic beer induce prolactin release and stimulate milk production. Breastfeeding mothers should not smoke; nicotine lowers the amount of milk produced. Third, try to get some rest. As we mentioned earlier, fatigue is a common spoiler of breastfeeding success. If possible, make time for naps during the day.

Breastfeeding moms are supposed to wear a supportive, well-fitting nursing bra. Some women get by with a regular bra, a few with no bra at all, but the support of a bra should make you feel more comfortable and possibly prevent breasts from sagging. (When I had Danielle, the obstetric nurse actually had the nerve to demand to inspect my bra, so I went braless just to torment her. At home, though, I did follow this advice.)

Try to develop a ritual associated with expressing your milk, such as having a glass of milk, hot chocolate, or decaffeinated tea. We aren't that different from Pavlov's dogs; performing the ritual may soon be the only stimulant you need to bring on your let-down reflex. A warm bath before expressing and hot washcloths placed on your breasts can be a big help as well. Before you try to express, you may also want to call the nursery to talk about your baby, or look at a picture of him. If calls to the nursery make you nervous and tense, though, don't do this. Likewise, if a picture of your baby upsets you, try a baby shot of one of your other children or a baby shot of a niece or nephew, if you have no other children. If you can, have a support person give you a back rub. Try making a recording of a crying and/or cooing baby and listen to it while you pump.

When more heroic efforts are called for, be creative and try to control your inhibitions. For example, if you have a friend with a nursing baby, and both of you are healthy and feel comfortable with this plan, you could nurse her baby once a day to help increase your milk supply. (You and the baby should be checked over and have some tests done by your respective doctors first.) A hungry, nursing baby is very effective in stimulating your milk production. I'll bring up another idea with some embarrassment, but force back family modesty in the hopes of helping you out. A husband can be very good at stimulating milk production by sucking the milk from your breasts. What your husband does is remarkably similar to what a baby does, and this can sometimes produce milk when all seems hopeless. Of course, for a project like this one, your mate must be willing and the two of you must feel comfortable with the idea. Neither one of you is likely to find this plan erotic, but it really can make a difference. Your husband can also manually massage your breasts and express your milk for you. (Don't forget to collect it!) This may work out surprisingly better than when you try to do it yourself. To massage the breasts and "prime" them for expression, husbands can use the heel of their hands, beginning at the chest wall and pushing down and outward toward the nipple.

Remember that the most efficient ways of pumping and expressing vary from woman to woman and from baby to baby. My first daughter, Danielle, was a good eater. While at work, though, I used a cylinder pump with great success. Ashley, of course, could not breastfeed at first and no technique of pumping came easily. Eventually I found that hand-expressing without a pump produced the most milk for me, although this is not the case for most premie moms. I also used an electric pump to stimulate my milk production and to free up one hand to use for other things while I pumped. Early on, you may spend a lot of time pumping and it can be a godsend to have at least one hand free to do something else. The message here is to try a lot of different techniques and use what works for you. Talk with other mothers of premies about methods they've tried and found successful. You may pick up a new tip that makes all the difference for you.

When all else fails, you can also ask your doctor about a prescription for a drug called oxytocin, which you would take as a nose spray. Oxytocin, as mentioned earlier, is a hormone that is made by the anterior hypothalamus in the brain; it stimulates the let-down reflex and breast-milk ejection. If you are having a lot of difficulty getting your milk to flow, this may be a solution. I somewhat regret not trying it.

HOW TO HAND-EXPRESS MILK

If you express your milk by hand, you are using the oldest, simplest, and most portable of techniques. Some women find hand expression more comfortable and less cumbersome than using pumps. To express milk by hand, first wash your hands with warm water and soap. Then find a quiet place and relax for a minute with any or all the relaxation techniques we discussed above. Place one hand on your breast, with four fingers supporting the bottom of the breast and the thumb placed on top, just behind the areola (the dark area surrounding the nipple). Press in toward your chest, then gently press thumb and fingers together to squeeze out the milk. Move your hand around all the breast tissue behind the areola to express milk from all the ducts. The milk that comes out is sterile, but your skin, even if clean, is not. So have your milk drip directly into a sterile container and then save it in the refrigerator or freezer. Milk itself is remarkably good at preventing bacteria from growing, even up to eight hours at room temperature, but you certainly don't want to take any chances with your premie's health. Date the container (day and time), even if you will be using it at home, and label it with your name if you will be bringing it into the hospital. (See below for more on how to store expressed breast milk.)

CHOOSING A PUMP

If hand-expressing is not for you, get to know mechanical pumps. There are many brands and types available for your use, ranging from the manual to the electric. Many pharmacies now have electric pumps for rent. Your baby's insurance may cover at least part of the rental. Hospitals also have them available for use, at least in-house. Try one out at the hospital before you rent. Battery-run pumps are available for purchase and are less expensive than the electric pumps, but many moms find the suction and the power produced unacceptable, especially after they have tried an electrical (wall-plug) pump. Non-electrical, hand-held pumps are less expensive and readily available from drugstores, discount stores, or children's specialty stores. You can choose among various brands of cylinder and bulb pumps. Cylinder pumps create suction when you slide the two cylinders back and forth. Bulb pumps work by creating suction when you squeeze and release the bulb. Most mothers find cylinder pumps more efficient and less messy than bulb pumps. The milk drips into the lower part of the cylinder as you pump.

To be effective, it is important that you have a good suction where your skin and the pump come together; a little dampness on your skin or water around the rim of the pump should help with this. The pump rim should be close against the skin on all sides; there cannot be any air leakage. Be sure that the rubber flange on a cylinder pump is in good shape, or there will be air leakage around it and you will have poor suction; flanges can be bought separately by writing to your pump's manufacturer. (My pump has lasted five years and has

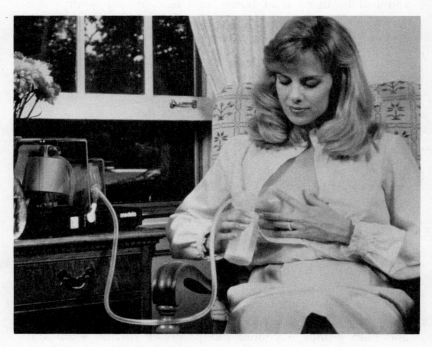

An electric breast pump is a good choice for some.

been loaned to friends when I wasn't using it, with the only change being a new flange as a gift to each one using it.)

You may find it useful to massage your breast for a minute before pumping, and a couple of times during pumping, to stimulate milk flow toward the areola. Remember that any part of your pump that might come in contact with your breast milk must be sterilized before each pumping session.

While I don't advocate one brand of pump over another, you might try one of these two companies if you want to use an electric pump but are having trouble finding one:

> *The Egnell Breast Pump*
> *Egnell, Inc.*
> *765 Industrial Drive*
> *Cary, Illinois 60013*
> *800–323–8750*
>
> *The Medela Breastpump*
> *Medela, Inc.*
> *6711 Sands Road*
> *P.O. Box 386*
> *Crystal, Illinois 60014*
> *800–435–8316*

Note: Electric pumps cost $800 and up to buy, so if you want to use an electric pump, you'll probably want to rent one instead. Call the above manufacturers and they will give you information on the closest rental location. Most often, electric breasts pumps are available for rental (for $30 to $60 a month) from pharmacies, medical-supply stores, and La Leche League chapters. Find out whether or not the rental of a pump is covered by your insurance company and under what circumstances.

STORING EXPRESSED
BREAST MILK

Find out in advance how your baby's nursery handles breast-milk transport, storage, and feeding. What kinds of containers are acceptable? How do the nurses and doctors want containers to be sterilized? Do they have specific containers they will give you to use? Do they allow you to use plastic nurser bags? How do they want you to store your milk? How do they want you to mark it? How do they want you to transport it to the hospital? On ice? Frozen? Where do they store the breast milk? Do they discard any milk left over from a given container if the baby doesn't take it all at one feeding? Two feedings? If so, divide your precious milk into appropriate portions—and remember that as your baby grows, the amount he will be taking at each feeding will quickly increase. Does your hospital test the expressed breast milk you bring in for its bacteria count?

Your milk is probably so hard to make that you'll want to be sure it's used, so check with the hospital on all these issues. When possible, pump your milk at the hospital so it can be used when fresh.

Let's go through some general storage rules:

1.   Always collect breast milk under sterile conditions, as described above.

2.   Refrigerate, freeze, or use breast milk immediately.

3.   Refrigerated breast milk should be used within twenty-four hours.

4.   When kept in your refrigerator's freezer section, breast milk can be kept for up to two weeks. In a deep freezer, breast milk can be stored for up to three months.

5.   In general, it is best not to add new breast milk to old. But if for some reason you have to pool the milk, the new milk must be refrigerated first. Expressed breast milk is warm; if added to frozen breast milk, it will cause the frozen supply to begin defrosting.

6. Once breast milk is defrosted, do not refreeze it. Thawing and refreezing of breast milk can cause the protein in the milk to break down and can increase the risk of contamination.

7. To use frozen breast milk, thaw it in the refrigerator and then bring it up to room temperature before feeding. Breast milk may separate when stored and needs to be mixed before using. You can warm breast milk by either putting the bottle in hot tap water for about ten minutes or microwaving for five to thirty seconds (every microwave differs). Microwaving is the twentieth century's gift to parents, but be careful. Some physicians advise against any microwaving because there is a real tendency to overheat when you microwave. Also, microwaving causes "hot spots," areas of very hot breast milk within cooler milk. I am not so negative about using the microwave, as long as you don't overheat, and you mix the milk well (don't shake it!) and check the temperature before you give it to the baby. Tube feeding is no different from bottle feeding—if the milk is too hot it will harm your infant. Heating milk at normal temperatures will not harm the immune properties of the milk.

8. The immune cells in breast milk will not survive storage for more than a few days of freezing. That is one reason why fresh breast milk is always best. But storage and freezing will not damage most of the many other immune elements in breast milk. Overheating will destroy immune elements, as well as damage the protein in breast milk; warming will not, so be careful.

STERILIZING

Any part of your pump setup that comes in contact with your breast or your breast milk must be sterilized before you can use it again. If you are pumping in the hospital, there will be a sterilizer available for your use. Ask a nurse to show you where it is and how to use it. Your hospital's staff may want to give you specific instructions on how to sterilize the equipment if you are pumping at home for use at the hospital, but the following will do the job. Place all equipment, containers, and lids, plus a pair of tongs, in a pot of cold water. Prop the tongs against the side of the pot so that you'll be able to get them out later without touching the water. Put the pot on the stove and heat to boiling. Boil for fifteen or twenty minutes. Turn off the heat and let the pot cool. Retrieve the tongs and use them to lift the sterilized equipment, containers, and lids out of the pot, placing them on clean paper towels to dry. Keep your sterilized containers closed with sterilized lids.

An alternate method would be to place all items in a colander, submerged in cold water in a large pot. Heat and boil for fifteen to twenty minutes. When the water is cool, remove the colander and allow the utensils to drip dry. If you need to use the equipment quickly, you can remove it after the full boiling time and let it air-cool.

FEEDING DIRECTLY FROM THE BREAST

You lucky, successful soul, to have graduated to breast-feeding! Of course, this means that now that you may have mastered the fine art of pumping, you have a totally different, equally fine art to learn: breastfeeding a premie. First and foremost, do not be shy about asking nurses (again, go for the ones who have been around for some time and have the experience) and other moms (in and out of the hospital) for advice. Ask for hands-on advice; it may be embarrassing, but it is worth it. Having someone show you is a hundred times better than anything you can read. Also ask if the hospital has a teaching video you can watch on this topic. In addition, keep these tips in mind:

1.   Try to feed your baby only when he is awake and alert.

2.   Do not overstimulate him. Do not rock, sing, or try

Try different positions when breastfeeding to find the one best for you.

to make eye contact with your baby when you're breastfeeding. That's just too much for him now. His goal is to eat.

3.   Swaddle your baby, to help him limit his own movements, which can distract him from the activity at hand.

4.   Ask the nurse to help you position the baby. Try a few different positions to discover which is best for you. You may also want to try a nipple shield or a breast shield that might make premie feeding a little easier. Ask the nurse to show you how to use it and try it out.

5.   Make sure one of the baby's cheeks is touching your breast; you may want to rub your finger or nipple gently against that cheek. Your baby will, you hope, "root," or search for the nipple with his mouth and take hold of it. A newborn's reflex is to turn toward whatever touches his cheek. So don't try to push his face toward the breast or he may turn away, toward your hand.

6.   You may want to depress your baby's chin and tongue

before putting him to your nipple, to position his throat and mouth most effectively.

7. Try to get him to take as much of the areola, the dark area around the nipple, into his mouth as he can. This is the part of the breast he must suck on to get milk. If he has only your nipple in his mouth, he won't get much milk and your nipple may become very sore.

8. You may want to press in your breast where your baby's nose is, to leave a clear breathing passage for him and to make sure he can breathe easily while sucking, but don't get in his way or you'll just frustrate him. Feeding is hard enough work for him without your interference adding to his difficulties!

9. Lower your expectations. If you're too hopeful, nothing will go right and you'll both be crushed. Your baby has been through a lot and is not accustomed to breastfeeding. Don't expect him to be a champion eater right away. Likewise, especially if this is your first baby, don't think breastfeeding comes naturally, especially for a mother of a premie. It is an acquired skill that takes practice—something you really won't get enough of while your baby's in the hospital. Right now, just enjoy the closeness of being alone with your baby and putting him to your breast. As the days and weeks go by, however, feedings should become easier and more pleasurable for you both.

10. In the beginning, the purpose of breastfeeding is not for your baby to gain weight; you are simply trying to establish a new method of feeding. Feeding from the breast takes a lot more energy than being tube- or even bottle-fed. Eventually, your baby will gain weight while being solely breastfed, but right now he will probably need supplemental feedings by tube or bottle. Tube feedings may not be the most comfortable way to eat, but they do not involve any activity on the baby's part. Breastfeeding, on the other hand, is an active process and burns up calories.

11. Even if breastfeeding is not yet contributing a lot from a nutritional standpoint, you are accomplishing a number of

things by doing it. You are getting physically close to your baby, skin to skin, which is very comforting for both of you. You are also getting emotionally close to your baby in this process. And you are helping to stimulate your breast milk production. You are taking important first steps toward eventually moving your baby from that uncomfortable feeding tube or bottle on to a warm, tasty breast.

Now that we have covered some of the intimate issues between you and your baby, in the next chapter we will look at how the special situation of having a premie affects the rest of your family—and how their reactions to all it entails affect you and your premie child.

8.   Family Matters

The premature birth of a child can be extremely traumatic for the entire family, not just the parents. This is a family nightmare and can be dealt with best as a family. If there are other children, helping them to handle this event and the upheaval that occurs in the weeks that follow places a major additional burden on already strained parents. You, as parents, are in a very real way the center of your children's existence and you have a major responsibility during this time, not just to your premie but to your other children as well. Your own parents may supply you with much needed support, but it is equally possible that they will be overwhelmed by this event and unable to do anything but add to your negative emotions. And during this family nightmare, life goes on for others, despite the fact that your personal world is falling apart. This mother is a case in point. She says:

"Grant was born unexpectedly a few days before my sister's wedding. I was supposed to be in the wedding party. Everyone told me not to do it. I was physically exhausted. But I got out of the hospital in time and so was in the wedding. My sister really appreciated the fact that I did that. But at the same time everyone was really worried about me and the baby.''

This kind of devotion is certainly above and beyond the call of duty and the energy of many new premie parents. But other demands on your time and energy must be met if the immediate family is to survive intact. These demands include those of your other children, your spouse, and, if there is any remaining energy, your own parents, siblings, and close friends. In this chapter we will discuss these needs and demands. I will not pretend that there are pat answers, since answers depend upon each of you individually, the interactions within your family, and the practical limitations of your situation.

SIBLINGS' REACTIONS

For the children in your family, the birth of a premie can be an extremely traumatic event. First of all, an older sibling may have had little or no advance warning that a baby was on its way, or what a baby would mean to his life. Some parents like to put off any serious discussion of the new family member until the last trimester, so it's possible that the new baby was born before he was even mentioned. Even if an older child was aware that ''Mommy had a baby in her tummy'' and that a ''new brother or sister'' was on the way, he would probably not be aware that the baby would mean major changes in his own life. There may have been no time to switch a firstborn child from his crib to a bed before the arrival of the new user of the crib. The child may have had no time to see or get used to the arrival of baby equipment or baby clothes.

Second, the birth of a premature baby causes a disruption in the usual family routines and in the way the family acts and reacts. Perhaps most upsetting for the premie's siblings is the separation they feel from their mother and father. Because parents have to spend so much time at the hospital, concentrating on the baby or worrying about bills and phone calls from the hospital when at home, a sibling can feel left out and forgotten. Too young to be able to help his parents or to be included in any significant way, he can only stand by and wait, something most children are not very good at doing. The older child is also separated from his young brother or sister and doesn't know whom to blame for the fact that the baby is "here" but has not yet arrived at home.

To complicate his life further, your older child will be suddenly subjected to the reality of illness and even death. Visits to the hospital are frightening to all of us, but more so to a child. The medical equipment surrounding the baby either won't seem to bother him at all or will frighten him even more than it would an adult, depending on his age and personality. Most children associate death with old age, with little bearing on their own lives; a common train of questioning is: "Is Granddad old? Is he going to die?" Seeing a seriously sick child—especially a brother or sister, with whom he may identify—can raise concerns about his own vulnerability. He can also sense his parents' anxiety, sadness, and fear. Small children identify strongly with their parents and certainly see us as their all-powerful protectors, so a child's level of anxiety will reflect our own and will increase in proportion to that of his parents. Seeing his parents frightened and helpless is a scary revelation for a child who previously considered his parents invincible.

Different children will express and deal with this stress and their fears in different ways, depending upon their individual personality, age, level of understanding, and relationship with each of their parents. In general, an older child (age six and up) will be able to understand more, but, at the same time, he may find it harder to adjust to the birth of any new baby, premature or not. A toddler will try to understand what is happening but will probably misinterpret much of what goes on. He may, for example, believe that this baby's illness is somehow his fault or that he is being punished for something. A younger child, such as a one-year-old, will probably not understand anything about the birth. He will only feel intensely the separation from his mother and be unable to fathom why she's away. He may respond with anger and even very real depression. Whatever your child's age, he may well respond to this situation by rejecting you during those few precious moments you can spend with him; he literally is pushing away the very persons he most desperately wants.

A major factor in our family's decision to provide Ashley with intermediate-nursery care at home was Danielle's response to the hospital setting and our feelings about what was best for the family as a unit. We tried to make Danielle comfortable in the hospital setting, but realized that this was unsuccessful when Daddy joked that she could "stay in the hospital overnight with Mommy" and she became hysterical. We constantly felt torn between our two children and their needs: both of us wanted to be with both children during every possible moment. We were profoundly lucky that we had the medical training needed to care for Ashley at home; it was best for all of us. Ashley received the parenting care that I strongly feel makes all the difference in the world for a premie; Danielle was a wonderful assistant and got to know her little sister intimately; Brandy, our dog, got herself another baby (though this one frightened her a bit), and we all were together. The only cost was a couple of months with little sleep and several moments of great anxiety. Needless to say, I'd do it again. My mother believes that my husband and I were meant to be pediatricians so that we would be ready for this situation; who am I to say she is wrong?

Unfortunately, I cannot give you a crash course in pediatrics, so you cannot take your premie home when he leaves intensive care for intermediate care. Nor, for that matter, would this necessarily be the best solution for your particular family anyway. But there are many ways that you can help your other children adjust to the birth of a premature brother or sister. Spend energy and thought, no matter how tired and worried you are, assessing how the situation is affecting each of your other children. Then try out some of these suggestions, designed to help you cope during those early weeks, when your premie is still in the hospital:

1.   No matter what his outward reaction, your older child is going through a hard time right now. Even if he expresses his anxiety through anger and rejection of you or of his premature sibling, he is in pain and he needs you. You may believe your child is being selfish and petty, especially when your premie has real problems, but children are by nature selfish, and your older child is facing real problems as well. If he seems to be taking it all extremely well, don't consider him one less worry. Look deeper. Is he having trouble sleeping? Is he regressing developmentally? Very often, if a child feels he caused the situation, he will be on his best behavior outwardly but will be torturing himself with guilt inside.

2.   Try not to divide parents between children—for example, giving the father sole responsibility for the older children and leaving Mom in charge of the premie. This arrangement is not going to be satisfying to either parent in the long run. Nor will it satisfy a child who is being deprived of one parent's attention. Instead, share the hospital and home responsibilities.

3.   Set aside some special time for each of your children. This should be uninterrupted time, meant for each of them alone. It may not be long and it may not be possible to do it every day, but it should be their time and you should find space for it in those early weeks, at least every few days.

4.   Each day give all the children an update on the premie and the day's events at the hospital; take into account each child's level of development and understanding. Bring pictures home. Make your baby seem real to them—and real in relation to each of them, their life, looks, personality, etc. In this way you can also gradually get them ready for the baby's eventual homecoming and make them eager to get to know their new sibling.

5.   When you are at the hospital visiting your baby, call home and talk to your kids. Toddlers, especially, do not have

a good sense of the passage of time and would rather hear from you periodically than know only that you'll be "home by three." Whatever you do, never promise to be home at a certain time. They will be on pins and needles waiting for you and, worst of all, they will be crushed if you are late.

6. As much as you can during the day, stop to talk to your children, hold them, hug them.

7. *Do* take your children to the hospital for visits, and do this as much as possible. Before you take them into the NICU, assuming they are allowed in, explain to them what they will see. They will want to see this "mythical" baby and be assured that he is real. You may want to wait until your premie seems a little more stable (for example, you may want to wait until he's off the respirator); this decision depends upon you and the personalities of each of your children. Most nurseries have windows that the children can stand at and look through. Some hospitals may even allow closer contact under certain circumstances. Even if they are allowed only to look at the baby through a glass window, prepare your children for some of the machinery, and for the size of the baby. Explain and point things out while you're there as well. Do not let them feel alone there, even for a second. Point things out about their baby; let them touch and talk to him. Talk again after you leave about their thoughts, fears, concerns, and plans for their baby once he's home.

8. Let them express their negative feelings. It's okay for them to say what they feel: "That baby is making Mommy sad" or "The baby is taking Mommy away." Let them know that negative feelings toward the baby are normal but at the same time emphasize that they will soon get to know and like the new baby and that, no matter how they feel, they must always be gentle with the baby.

9. Your toddler may not tell you in words how he is feeling. He may instead show signs of being upset—having nightmares or temper tantrums, regressing in toilet training, clinging to you, ignoring you. Be tuned in to these signals. He may not be telling you how he feels in words, but he *is* getting

his message across. Respond to his anxiety, not just in words but also in action. Knowing what's causing these temporary behavioral problems can give you a jump on dealing with them.

10.   Think about how you will handle it if your child sees you cry. It's really impossible to hide your fears over an extended period. I tried not to cry in front of Danielle but did not always succeed. Sometimes Danielle asked if I had been crying. I was honest and told her yes, and then would try to explain why. I told her I was worried about her little sister, Ashley, and that I was also very tired. I told her that when grown-ups are tired and worried, they sometimes cry. I can't tell you how to handle a similar situation with your own children but I can tell you that you need to find a way that's right for your family; you can't simply ignore the situation.

11.   If your baby should die or leave the hospital with permanent and severe handicaps, your other children will grieve along with you. They will also feel guilty and wonder what they did to make this happen. Children may also fear that the same thing will happen to them or believe that it should have happened to them instead of the baby. Don't forget them in your own grief. Don't think that just because they don't talk about it and appear to be coping well, they are. They need your help.

We all make mistakes, and if you make some with your other children during this time, don't feel that these cannot be corrected with time. But with extra effort and some ingenuity (difficult to muster when you're exhausted), you'll be able to avoid many mistakes and to find ways to show your children that you still care for them even when you can't be with them physically.

Once it's time to take your baby home, your older children will need to be prepared anew. You can expect some new issues and problems to surface, just as the hospital-related ones disappear. Under the best circumstances, many things can affect an older child's response to the arrival of the long-awaited baby. An older sibling's outlook on this particular event will depend in part on how long the baby was hospitalized, how often the sibling was allowed to visit, how the hospitalization was handled by the family, and what the baby's health is upon release from the hospital. Both a child's personality and his fundamental characteristics, such as gender and age, will play a role in the relationship that develops between siblings. For example, a four-year-old girl may easily take on the role of "Mommy" with her younger brother or sister. A six-year-old boy, however, might not understand how to act around a baby who can't do anything yet, who may still be quite fragile, and who may even be attached to a monitor that gives off startling noises. All children feel some rivalry and jealousy toward their siblings; these feelings tend to wax and wane throughout life. The fact of your baby's prematurity might heighten, or lessen, these feelings at the time you bring your premie home from the hospital.

For example, Danielle was very protective of Ashley and touchingly affectionate and supportive to me during the first months of Ashley's life. Danielle is very observant, so certainly her reaction was a response to Ashley's obvious vulnerability and fragility. This response was almost too good to be true and worried me a bit, but once Ashley became older and stronger and began to crawl, steal Danielle's toys, and get attention for her antics, Danielle began to view Ashley as more of a threat and a normal amount of sibling rivalry reared its ugly but healthy head.

This endearing protectiveness on the part of a toddler for his premie sibling is certainly not unique to Danielle. A mom describes her older son's reaction to his premie brother this way:

"My four-year-old went into the NICU and saw his brother all hooked up to the machines. I wanted him to see the baby that way so he'd know that he would have to be gentle with him at home. It worked because he's been pretty cautious. In fact, when I'm shoving food into the baby's mouth, trying to get him to eat, my son will say, 'No, Mom, he's not ready for that.' "

The role and level of involvement of a sibling in the care

of his premature brother or sister depends on the older child's age, personality, interests, and maturity, as well as your premie's health. Certainly, even toddlers should be allowed to touch the baby. If the infant is stable, they should also be allowed to hold the baby on their laps, under supervision, of course. Ask your older child what he would like to do with and for the baby. Talk about the kinds of things you can do with a baby (e.g., hold his hand, kiss him) and what you can't do (try to play ball with him, pull on an arm, poke at a face, pinch). If a mature child of school age wants to help you feed, bathe, or clothe the baby, for heaven's sake accept the help—but supervise the child. Do not give a sibling too much responsibility. Verbal interaction between your older child and the baby should also be encouraged. Let your child spend as much time as he likes with you as you care for the baby. Sing, read, and talk to both of them at once. Try also to reserve some time alone for him, without the baby present. If your older child appears to want no part of the new baby, don't push. But keep him near you, perhaps playing in the same room as you and the baby. This will give the child time to adjust to the new baby at a distance, without having to interact directly.

To prepare a child for a baby's homecoming, you'll want to do some planning and rearranging ahead of time. Try not to associate changing rooms or giving up the crib too closely with the baby's arrival. Instead, while the baby is still in the hospital, try to ease your older child into some of the changes that will have to be made to accommodate the new baby. He didn't have the prebirth time in which to adjust, but he does have the hospital time. If your child feels too insecure to make certain switches at this time, you can probably put them off a little longer. For example, if a child resists the idea of giving up his crib for a bed, don't push. A crib is a very personal possession and some children don't part with it too easily. Instead, make arrangements for the baby to sleep in a cradle, travel crib, or bassinet at first. A premie can often sleep comfortably in a bassinet until six months of age. During this time, you can work on moving your older child from the crib to the bed. Once he moves to the bed, it may help to paint the crib or change the bumpers to make it feel less like his and more like a new and different crib. If you've thought about moving your older child out of his room into another, think again. This may be too upsetting and not worth the trouble. Does it really need to be done right now?

More likely, both your older child and your premie will have to share a room. Under routine conditions, asking children to share a room is a reasonable request. The siblings have to get used to sharing. With a premature baby, sharing a room is still a reasonable request but sometimes has to be modified a bit. If the premie is on a monitor or wakes up frequently, this may wake or upset the sibling with whom he shares a room. In this situation, you may have to wait a while before the two can happily coexist in one room. Instead, the premie may need to be close to you or be kept in a separate room.

Although having other children at home means extra work, more strain, and additional worries, it is also worth counting your blessings. One premie mom says it extremely well:

"All the time my baby was in the hospital, I knew that if, God forbid, anything should happen to him, I was going home to two kids. The other first-time mothers would go home to nothing."

MOTHERS

As a premie mom, you have an incredible balancing act to perform, since your role has been and will be central to the well-being of your premie, your family, and your marriage. In addition, if you have chosen to breastfeed, most of the premie's care will inevitably fall into your lap. All of this responsibility comes at a time when you're stressed, exhausted, and insecure. The situation is eased if the family attempts to be both emotionally and practically supportive. (This point will come up again and again in this chapter.) While moms are critical in both the in-hospital and the home parenting of a premie, they cannot do it alone. The entire family must be involved in a premie's in-hospital life, and both parents must meet the responsibilities of taking a premie home, fitting him into the family structure, and fulfilling the baby's great practical and developmental needs—without losing sight of the other family members' needs as well.

In addition to these family and social stresses, many, if not a majority of, premie moms today must face the stress of their outside-the-home employment. You may well have had to take unpaid maternity leave, adding to the family's financial burden. For a variety of reasons, you may feel pressured to return to work as soon as possible. There may be little understanding on the part of employers that a premie at home requires even more work than one in hospital. Furthermore, the amount of maternity leave allowed is generally determined by the mother's state of health, not the baby's. So a mom faces the possibility of having to return to work because *she* has recovered from pregnancy and delivery, although her baby is still anything but stable. I was in this position and deeply regret that I did not share my anxiety with my obstetrician, who probably would have written for an extension of my leave. I'm also sorry I did not extend my leave by taking vacation time or leave without pay. Instead, I succumbed to pressures to return and went back to work before Ashley was even off a monitor, and only two weeks after she was finally able to feed at the breast. I realize now that my fatigue was in large part the source of this irrational decision; since you are also likely to be exhausted, try to learn from my experience. Remember that your state of exhaustion is part of your own health status; share this information (and your premie's needs) with your obstetrician when he or she is writing to your employer about how much maternity leave you need. Unless your salary is desperately needed by your family, do not let your employer make you feel guilty about staying home. Jobs will come and go and an employer's commitment to you is limited at best.

Your child's infancy comes just once—and the outcome of it will last a lifetime.

FATHERS

Dad's involvement with his premature son or daughter may be very different from what it would have been had the baby been born on time. As we mentioned earlier, the father often becomes the baby's "advocate" early on. Some men may feel relatively at ease in the high-tech atmosphere of an NICU; they may feel more in control in this setting than their wives do. Many women find it helpful that their husbands do not perceive the NICU as quite as alien an environment as they do. Some come to depend on their husbands a great deal because of this. One father who rightly refers to himself as "old broad shoulders" explains how he became the major go-between linking his wife and the hospital:

"The doctors would call me and tell me what was happening. Then I would explain it to Nancy. I was more gentle. I didn't sugarcoat but I always injected some hope; the doctors *couldn't* do that. I was more political about it. That way Nancy kept her sanity. She stayed terrified for six months. That was killing me as much as anything."

Dad may be the first to see the baby, the first person to see the baby smile. In the beginning, Mom may not have been physically able to be in the nursery as much as Dad was. If your baby wasn't able to feed at the breast, Dad may have become actively involved in bottle feeding or tube feeding. So for many reasons, a premie and his dad may have a very close relationship early on, forming long-lasting bonds. One mother says her husband and daughter have a very special closeness still. She describes it this way:

"My husband, Paul, was in the nursery with Emily from the very beginning. Emily is totally a daddy's girl. I think they'll be even closer than Paul and Ansley, our second child, born on time. After Ansley's birth, Emily said that Ansley would have to get another daddy. Paul is all hers.''

For some moms, it may be difficult to accept this early closeness between premie and dad without some jealousy, especially because of the guilt they may be feeling about their early delivery. Other moms are thrilled to see their husbands so involved from the beginning, whether or not they themselves can be. Often, the balance of closeness may shift somewhat when the baby goes home, since by then the baby may be breastfeeding, the husband is probably at work full-time, and the premie is now cared for primarily by the mother, at least for the first few months. The father now may be the one to feel some resentment, in having to give up some of the closeness of the past months. It is a shame for Dad to lose this hard-earned intimacy; certainly he should try consciously to minimize the loss.

One problem that may arise because of father-premie closeness is that other children in the family may envy the unique place the premie has in Dad's heart. It's best if the father tries to use the experience of closeness he had or has with his premature baby to try to get similarly close to his other children. He should make an effort to spend time alone with each child, getting to know each of them as individuals, and should avoid comparing them to his premature child. This is especially important in instances where the premie may have long-term problems or disabilities. As discussed above, that situation places continuing stress upon the marriage and the family, and almost certainly creates feelings of guilt and resentment in the other children—guilt because they are normal and resentment because the family's activities and structure may come to center on the disabled child.

It is also possible that a new premie father (or mother) may initially withdraw from his premie, rather than move into a parenting role. There are a plethora of reasons for this reaction, from guilt to fear, grief, disbelief, and an unwillingness to accept the idea that one's child could be less than perfect.

This places unnecessary additional stress on the other spouse and on the rest of the family. If this does not pass quickly, it is important that the parents receive outside help in sorting out these issues. A parent who sees his baby as "defective" or a "failure," or a husband who blames his wife for their premie's problems, will cause permanent scars not just to himself and his premie but to the whole family as well.

While moms in general have more than their share of child responsibilities, in these early weeks and months it is usually the dads who must face the added burden of balancing job and family responsibilities. When the baby was in the hospital, the father may have received heartfelt sympathy from his co-workers and boss, and was probably given either some leave or some flexibility in his work hours. Unfortunately, once the baby comes home, Dad is usually expected to return to the grind of "business as usual"—and may even be under increasing pressure to perform and make up for time taken off during the baby's time in hospital. Of course, this is a ludicrous state of affairs! Caring for a new premature baby at home is exhausting for the whole family, Father included, and family stress continues well after discharge from the hospital. Dad may in fact need time off even more now, and certainly could use less pressure at work. But this is rarely understood, and family security demands that Dad respond to job demands. Sadly, even Dad may not give himself a break; he may be convinced that a man should be able to handle it all. One father explains how his work suffered:

"I had my own business, running a pet shop. I ended up losing it because I wasn't at the shop much. I just could not pay attention. I couldn't keep my mind on business. Any profits I had went to pay for trips to the hospital, 120 miles a way."

As with all the family problems we are discussing, there are no miracle answers to Dad's stressful situation. But it is important that Dad let the rest of the family know about these pressures. Otherwise, how can Mom and the children realize that Dad needs sympathy and support, too? Because society does not often make allowances for fatherhood, Dad may have to think about and ask for the special treatment he wants and deserves.

HUSBAND/WIFE RELATIONSHIP

A husband and wife may react differently to their premie and the problems he is having. To make it even more complicated, the reactions the two of you are having will change rapidly in the first few hours, days, weeks, and months of your premie's life. Let's face it: it's unusual for two people to be at the same emotional stage in their response to a crisis, so try to be patient with your spouse. Not being in sync can sometimes work to your mutual benefit, because it may create a supportive balance to the "team response" (Dad's depressed when Mom sees reason for hope, Mom's in tears while Dad is comforting, etc.). Unfortunately, at other times, it can cause deep scars, because neither spouse can understand why the other is acting a certain way and neither is getting the support they both desperately need. One scenario might be as follows: The father may feel very close to the premature baby but his wife may be distant, because of her own health, feelings of guilt, concerns about the other children, or fear for her premie's chances of a healthy survival. In a situation like this one, the father may become angry and pull away from his wife, wondering, "How could any mother not love our poor, unfortunate baby?" She may, in her turn, resent his rejection when she is very much in need of support and, in addition, be jealous of his closeness with her baby. The opposite scenario could just as easily take place. The father may pull away and throw himself into other activities: paying the hospital bill, caring for the home, spending time with an older child, devoting himself to his job. The mother may well interpret this as anger toward her for her "failure" or even as a rejection of the baby as being "defective."

What a mess—and a sick baby to boot! No wonder even the best of marriages will have trouble making it all the way through a crisis like this. Indeed, many marriages are ruined by children's medical disasters. It is unlikely that even yours will conquer premie parenthood without snags, disagreements, and hurt feelings. One mother describes how she felt:

"I'm sure it was a big strain on my husband but he didn't show it. I said to my mother one day, 'He's not showing any emotion. He has no feelings.' My mother just said, 'What do you want him to do? Sit around and cry? What good would that do you?' I think he was just trying hard not to do or say anything to upset me."

The key here is for Dad and Mom to talk with each other frequently, no matter how exhausted they are. This is of course easier said than done, since emotions run deep, are difficult to express, and may not even be fully understood. Also, it's very hard to talk at a time when you are feeling hurt, angry, and isolated. But remember that this is important not just for your marriage, but also for your premie's well-being. Anger, guilt, fault-finding, and assumptions about each other's feelings will be carried over to both your premie and your future life as a family. Your baby will certainly sense any tensions you might have when you are at his side; these stresses will then affect your interactions with him. This is not giving him "positive stimulation"! Furthermore, while there is no doubt that the birth of a premature baby is particularly stressful for the husband/wife relationship, the stress will only worsen if it appears that the premie may have major or lasting problems.

Talk to each other and accept your differing views. Frequently, you and your husband are too tired to try to sort out your own feelings, let alone each other's! Take your time. Try to talk before issues escalate into fights. You will probably find that your perceptions and feelings are very different. You may never agree, but you might be more sympathetic about each other's needs if you hear them expressed.

If things are really in emotional disarray, see a counselor

now about this. The hospital may well have someone on staff who can help you both; if not, the hospital staff should be able to refer you to an appropriately trained and experienced therapist who can see you right away. Or ask your neonatologist, pediatrician, or hospital social worker for the names of several therapists who have worked with premie parents and/or parents of children with chronic diseases or cancer. Don't delay too long if you need professional help. Your marriage may not be able to mend on its own.

On the bright side, however, the experience of premature parenting sometimes brings a couple closer together. You and your husband are working together toward one goal—the health and well-being of your child. But after the baby is home and through his difficulties, this marital closeness may be replaced by complacency. You are both exhausted and need some recovery time. Accept this, but don't let the complacency go on too long or you'll lose the closeness you've gained.

SINGLE PARENTS

Single parenthood means more work, more fatigue, and a greater risk of isolation. Make every effort to reach out to others—friends and relatives. Extend your network to include church and social service workers, if necessary. I have frequently seen young mothers enlist the help of their mothers. These young grandmothers are often able to nurture and care for both the new mother and her baby. Most important, get all the help and advice you can from the hospital social services department, *before* your baby comes home from the hospital. You may be pleasantly surprised with the amount of assistance that is available to you. But setting things up often takes time, so get started right away.

GRANDPARENTS

Having your own parents' support during the early months of your premie's life can be a godsend, but do not be surprised if they cannot give it at first. My own mother, with whom I am very close, could not come to see us right away when Ashley was born. But I could tell even over the phone that she was not handling Ashley's prematurity well. This became very apparent when Ashley was about a week old: I was talking about Ashley and my mother asked who Ashley was! Until then, I had avoided telling Mom much about Ashley's problems and had purposely not sent her any pictures. That day I sent her some photos—the least shocking I could find, of course. It worked wonders! She became very involved and wanted daily updates on Ashley's status. She even went a little overboard, announcing that Ashley should never wear Danielle's hand-me-down clothes because our premie had suffered enough! In retrospect I realize that until I sent those photos, all my mother could feel was the pain and worry in my voice, so she was trying to protect herself, and me, from the reality of Ashley's birth. Once she saw Ashley's photos, she could shift some of her sympathy from her daughter to her now-very-real granddaughter.

If your parents seem unsupportive when you need them most, try to be patient and remember that there may be a number of reasons for their attitude:

1. They come from a generation in which prematurity signaled almost certain death (or, at the very least, serious long-term disability).
2. They may be more worried about *their* baby than your baby and may even feel some anger at your premie for causing you sadness and stress.
3. The possibility of your baby's death (real or imagined) may remind them of their own mortality.
4. They may feel guilty that the baby is facing possible death rather than they, who have already lived a full life.

5.   They may feel even more awkward than you in the high-tech environment of today's hospital intensive-care units.
6.   They are uncertain about what you need or want from them.
7.   Since they come from a generation in which people frequently "put their faith" in their doctors and did not become involved with medical decisions, they may not understand why you are so involved in the care of a child who is already being taken care of by a knowledgeable medical staff. They may not support you when you question your baby's doctors or challenge some aspect of hospital policy. They may also have trouble understanding a father's desire to take time off from work, be with the baby, and be a part of the baby's parental care.

While it helps to understand their reasons for being distant, their lack of support will still hurt. If this unsupportiveness is coupled with suggestions that you somehow brought the premature labor on yourself, a serious strain may be put on your relationship with your parents or in-laws. About all you can do is try to educate them, if you have the energy. Tell them about prematurity. Show them literature, so they know the premature birth was no one's "fault." If they live nearby, bring them to visit the baby in the hospital and then at home. Ask your neonatologist to take time to talk with them about their grandchild. If they don't live nearby, send photos. Sending pictures to very close friends and relatives is a good idea, even though they might not be the most flattering pictures you will ever take of your child. They often work wonders, getting the person more directly involved with your baby. See if grandparents can arrange a trip to see you and the baby. If all this fails and they continue to create even more anxiety for you, politely tell them that you love them but simply do not have the energy to see or speak to them until your baby is better, and let the chips fall where they may.

As the baby matures and your parents feel more secure

about his survival, they may suddenly become more involved. They may begin to enjoy this little baby as their newest grandchild. But accept the fact that grandparents may not be very good at handling the irritability, crying, and fussiness that are often a part of the first year of prematurity. They may not have as much patience—and have refined their memories of your own childhood to match their ideal more closely. They may view many characteristics related to an immature nervous system as being part of your baby's essential personality, rather than as a result of his prematurity. If so, do not push their interaction with your premie; they may just be in for a pleasant surprise in the years to come.

YOUR SIBLINGS, OTHER FAMILY, AND FRIENDS

It is extremely difficult to predict which people among those you feel close to—and those you had thought of only as acquaintances—will come through for you in this crisis. Feelings may be hurt or you may be surprised and deeply touched. Often, help may be withheld because of fears or uncertainty about whether or not getting involved would invade the family's privacy. On the other hand, help may be offered because a similar experience has made someone aware of what you must be going through. Just remember to take any help that is offered and don't let your pride keep you from making it known that you need help.

One mother explains how difficult it is to predict who will be best able to provide support and help:

"Because my husband had to be away during the week (his job was ten hours away from the hospital the baby was in), I asked the hospital if I could have another support person with me in the NICU instead. They would not normally allow this but because I was alone, they agreed. I chose my sister because I thought she'd be better at this than my mother. The first day I brought my sister in with me to the nursery, I thought she was standing right next to me and I turned to her to say something but she was gone. She was standing across the room, hyperventilating. She didn't react well at all. So the next time I brought my mom with me. She handled it much better. She was really strong. The first time she saw Grant, she was so pleased with the way the baby looked—he looked bigger and better than she had imagined after all she had heard!"

Friends and acquaintances can be great support persons, as described by this mother:

"When I came home from the hospital, I knew I would be coming home to an empty house. But there were all my neighbors. They'd made me a big Italian meal. There were flowers, posters. Just no baby. They did the same thing all over again the day Jonathan came home from the hospital."

Unfortunately, friends may not realize how much help they can be. They might hang back, unsure of their role. They may have many inhibitions. They may be afraid to talk with you about your baby. They may not know whether to call or send flowers when the baby is first born. Those who do visit may see you and the baby in the hospital and not realize you need even more help and support once the baby is at home. Often, they assume everything is back to normal when the baby is home. Friends may even think you want time alone to rest and be with your baby.

In fact, though, you may feel most isolated when your baby comes home. Make yourself call at least a few people. Keep in touch with the outside world. Suggest that you could really use some help now that the baby is home. Be specific: ask them to pick up some groceries for you, drive you and the baby to the pediatrician, come over and help you clean up the house. Sometimes, if you ask for a specific favor, friends are better able to respond. At least they know what they can do for you.

SUPPORT GROUPS

Many parents of premature babies decide to join parent groups made up of other parents of premature babies. If you feel comfortable with this idea, these groups can be good information sources and provide plenty of emotional support as well. Each parent, though, must decide whether a group setting is appropriate. Many mothers I have spoken with feel that formal support groups are not for them.

One premie mom explains why she felt uncomfortable with the idea:

"I had heard about parent support groups and talked to my gynecologist about them. He said he didn't believe in them and thought that all people did there was sit around and cry about their problems. I didn't want to do that. I didn't want to hear about other people's problems and know about all the bad things that could happen."

Another mother felt quite differently about support groups:

"The parents you meet at the hospital are just focusing on their own babies. I didn't find that we interacted too much. Instead, I went to a premie parents' support group. I became pretty active. The group is not real big but it helped. When I first had Emily, I felt like I was the only one in the world who had had a premature baby! Then you go to a meeting and see the other parents and they all have the same problems you do. Now that my daughter is three, though, I find that I'm losing interest in the group."

Although this mom felt that a support group helped her, she found some other ongoing premie groups less positive experiences for her, in light of her daughter's continuing difficulties. She explains:

"At the hospital where Emily was born they have annual reunions for the premies and their parents. It's a nice idea but it's always very, very upsetting for me when I take her. All the other kids seem fine but Emily, because of her mild CP [cerebral palsy], can't walk more than twenty-five feet yet. It just seems like she's the only one with an ongoing problem and that upsets me. This year, I think I'll send my husband with Emily."

Yet another mother found that the parents she met right there at the hospital were a comforting group:

"All the parents in the nursery were concerned about one another. We'd talk. I'd be worried with them when something went wrong, excited for them when they got to take their baby home. Even the fathers seemed to cling to one another. I tried to stay in touch with some afterwards but they didn't really need me anymore."

For further information on parent support groups, ask your neonatologist, pediatrician, or nurses, or contact Parent Care, an umbrella organization for parenting groups: University of Utah Medical Center, Room 2A210, 50 North Medical Drive, Salt Lake City, Utah 84112, 801-581-5323.

If you wish to start a group (assuming you have that kind of energy!), write for a copy of "Organizing Support Programs for Parents of Premature Infants" to: Center for Parenting Studies, Wheelock College, 200 The Riverway, Boston, Massachusetts 02215.

Or write for a booklet called "Guide for Organizing Parent Support Groups" from: The March of Dimes, 303 South Broadway, Tarrytown, New York 10591.

9. Graduation Day –
Taking Your Baby Home

This is the moment you've been waiting for—your baby can come home at last. Happy as you are at this news, you may also be frightened by it. The day is a long time coming but when it arrives you might feel unprepared. When your premie was born, you wished for a baby you could take home with you right away. Now, after weeks of hospital care, you may feel nervous about the idea of caring for your baby without medical help. When the actual day (or night before) comes, these feelings of insecurity may overwhelm you even if you have been chomping at the bit for weeks. Because of this ambivalence (believe me, I felt it, too!), the decision on when your baby should come home should be made jointly with the medical staff. Don't let them push you too hard either way, but don't be overwhelmed by either your own cockiness or your own insecurities.

You're probably ready to bring your baby home if you're irritated by the staff's involvement in the care of your child, or if you're eager in spite of the monitors, medicines, assorted equipment, and instructions that may accompany him. Let the doctors know about your feelings. If you feel unprepared for your baby's homecoming tell them why. At the opposite end of the spectrum, if you want to take your baby home earlier than they might think best, explain your reasoning. They may not be fully aware of outside factors in your decision and you, in turn, may not fully understand the medical situation and its implications. Disagreements should be discussed openly. You should certainly never take your baby out "against medical advice," since you would never forgive yourself if something happened; on the other hand, I have never known a parent who wished to do this.

My husband and I brought Ashley home quite early, before she was able to bottle- or breastfeed, and certainly long before she had reached some "magical" weight. We did, however, pass the temperature-control test, with the assistance of booties, cap, mittens, blankets, and Atlanta's July heat. The major reason our neonatologist supported our decision was that we were two pediatricians fairly experienced in intensive-care medicine and Ashley was "stable" in the intermediate-care sense of that word. Because of our training, we felt comfortable gavage-feeding her at home and dealing with monitors, premie instability, and endless crises. Many people would not be able to deal with all of this, although I do think parents can deal with more of these things than many medical providers realize; in fact, many premies now come home with monitors and even oxygen. But admittedly, even the rare visitor to our home those first months looked at us a little oddly, seeing our tiny Ashley propped up in her infant seat with tubes and wires sticking out and monitors going off, as we sat around her making conversation, as if nothing were out of the ordinary.

DO YOU FEEL READY TO TAKE YOUR BABY HOME?

Let's run through a checklist of questions you should ask yourselves, and answer (with the help of your neonatologists and nurses), before you bring your baby home.

1. If your baby is coming home with some ongoing medical problems, do you feel comfortable handling potential medical complications? Do you understand what you have been told about your baby's problems? Have you ever had any courses in CPR (cardiopulmonary resuscitation) or first aid? (If your baby comes home on the monitor, you will be required to take a one-hour CPR lesson; a first-aid class would be useful for *any* parent.)

2. Do you have anyone at home who can help you to care for your premie, and for your other children? Do you have a good support system you can call upon? Are there grandparents, other relatives, or friends who are willing and able to help out in this situation?

3. Can Dad take any more time off work right now to be home the first week or two?

4. If you have other children, you may be anxious to get your premie home so that you'll all be together. Do you feel that you will be able to handle your premie while dealing with the other kids?

5. Have you seen and tried every aspect of your child's care, from temperature-taking and diaper-changing to responding to an apneic episode and handling medications?

6. Are you close to a hospital with pediatric facilities or an emergency pediatric clinic, in the unlikely event that a medical problem should arise?

7. Do you feel that you have recovered physically from the birth?

8. Do you feel you have adapted psychologically to the realities of having given birth prematurely?

9. Do you and the hospital staff feel you are adequately prepared to take your baby home?

10. Have you firmed up all your hospital financial matters as much as you possibly can, while you have the hospital financial and social services personnel readily available? Do you have some names to call for help when there are billing errors, financial crises, and the like after your baby comes home?

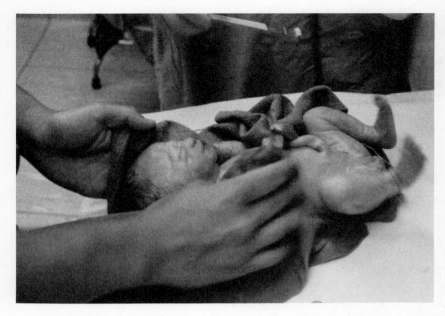

Ashley at birth.

If you have at least thought through each of these questions, can answer "yes" to the majority, and have the agreement of your premie's physician, it is probably time for your premie to go home.

The hospital staff will have been preparing you all along, bit by bit, for taking your baby home. You should become more and more involved in your baby's day-to-day care as the time for discharge draws nearer. Nurses will show you how to feed, hold, burp, change, and bathe your baby, among other things. If they do not think to do this, ask them to go over it all with you. Once you are home, you yourself will find the best ways to perform these tasks, given your particular lifestyle and your particular baby, but at least you'll have been taught the basic steps.

Unusual or extraordinary baby care should be gone over carefully before discharge. Your baby's health may depend on your ability to follow these instructions to the letter.

Ask the nurses to help you plan for the baby's discharge

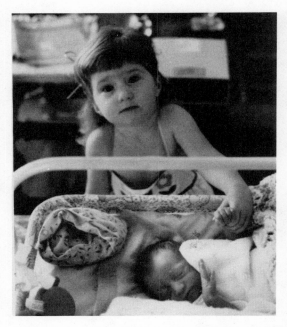

Ashley at six weeks with her two-year-old sister, Danielle.

in a way that will minimize disruption of your premie's feeding and medication routine. Otherwise you will be paying the price for days after!

Make sure that you have telephone numbers of doctors to call for advice or in case of an emergency. Be sure to know where you should bring your baby when a medical problem arises. If your baby is taking any medications, the medical staff should show you how to give the medication and they should watch you do it by yourself. In medical school, the old line is "see one, do one, teach one." This really is the best way to learn. So watch the nurse, do it yourself, then teach your husband, mother, whomever! Remember to ask the doctor or nurse the following questions about each medication and write down or record the answers.

- How often should the medication be given?
- Must it be given at the same time each day?
- Can the medication be given with food?

Three-year-old Ashley with Mom.

Three-year-old Ashley and five-year-old Danielle with Mom and Dad.

- If not, how soon after or before eating can the medication be given? (Theophylline, for example, frequently given to premies with apnea and bradycardia, can badly upset the baby's stomach. Given too close to a feeding, theophylline may interfere with the absorption of the food and may upset the baby's digestion enough to cause him to vomit.)
- What exactly is the medicine for?
- What possible side effects or reactions can there be? Which ones are serious enough that the doctor should be called and/or the medicine not given?
- Will the dose have to be increased as the baby grows? If so, how?
- When is the baby likely to stop needing this medication?
- Relative to those given other premies, how big a dose is this?
- How can the baby's various medicines interact?
- What would be the result if the medication were not given?
- When should the doctor be called?

Do not take the baby home until you understand the answers to all these questions about each medicine, and do not go home until you have each medicine and a prescription for more in hand. Write down the name of each drug and all the instructions relating to its use.

Sometimes, one or more nights before discharge, one or both parents are allowed to stay overnight at the hospital and room in with their baby. The parents will be solely responsible for all care during this time . . . but help is just down the hall. This can be extremely reassuring: performing the high-wire act of full premie parenthood with a safety net under you. You'll go home knowing that you've already made it through one day "on your own." If your hospital doesn't offer this routinely, ask if rooming-in for a day could be arranged, what it would cost, and if any of it would be covered by medical insurance. I didn't think to ask about rooming-in with Ashley before discharge but, even with my medical background, would have appreciated the opportunity. Other mothers I know of did take advantage of rooming-in and found it helpful. One mother describes it this way:

"We spent the night with Eric in the hospital before his discharge. He was finally ours! We didn't know what to do with him. We did not sleep at all that night, even though we knew there were nurses just down the hall. The next night, our first night at home with Eric, was much better. He finally felt like our baby. He slept in our room that night. I could hear him grunting and scooting around—it kept waking me up. After that, we put him in his own room and I found I could sleep better."

The anxiety of those first few nights at home alone with your child can be exhausting. One father describes the sleepless nights of worry when his daughter finally came home after six months in the hospital:

"I used to know how many breaths per minute were normal for her and I would lie awake looking at my watch, counting the number of breaths all night long."

A MONITOR AT HOME

Premies are now frequently discharged while still on an apnea/bradycardia monitor. Before discharge, any parent whose baby is coming home on a monitor must receive CPR training. Be sure that at least two of your baby's primary caretakers receive this instruction and that they feel comfortable using it. It is rarely needed, but there is no point in having a monitor if you don't know what to do in the event that it goes off and you cannot arouse your baby with stimulation.

If the alarm goes off and the baby is breathing and resting comfortably, then just reset it. If the baby is gray or you can't tell if he is breathing, touch him gently. If this isn't enough to rouse him, tap toes and hands. You have already been through much of this in the hospital, but will be amazed at how much you bother him this way that first insecure week at home! After a while, you will both relax more. If tapping does not arouse him (a very rare circumstance), tap a little harder, if necessary, but never so hard that you cause redness or a bruise. In the unlikely event that the baby still cannot be roused, use CPR and call for an ambulance. One mother explains how hard it was to be calm about the monitor in the beginning:

"I was told that if the monitor went off, I should wait ten seconds before doing anything to see if the baby would bring herself back. The first time it went off, I ran into her room, counting one–one thousand, two–one thousand. I got to three and said, 'Screw the doctor!' and roused her—she was blue. I asked him later if he would really wait and count to ten if it were his child. He said, 'I see your point.' "

The most commonly used monitors have electrodes that go under the baby's armpits. The electrode wires attach to a small machine that stays at the side of the crib. The electrodes are kept in place by a spongy belt wrapped around the chest and connected with Velcro. As the baby grows the belt must be changed. In the winter, this belt doesn't seem to bother infants too much because they have a lot of clothes on anyway, but in the summer, they may find it unpleasant because it's bulky and hot. The area around the belt must be kept clean. The belt should be removed for cleaning also. Keep all the electrodes and connections clean with alcohol or the monitor may register many false alarms. If you are having a lot of false alarms and cleaning doesn't help, have the company renting you the equipment come out and check it or replace it; humidity may make a machine give many false alarms and nothing can be done at your home to fix it. Be sure you have at least two of all these pieces of equipment (except the monitor itself, of course).

Here's a mom whose feelings about her son's monitor seem fairly typical:

"When they sent Eric home with us he weighed four pounds six ounces. He was a normal little newborn except for the heart monitor and the fact that we had to bring him into the hospital every three months for ultrasound. The monitor went off a number of times when we first got Eric home, so a sleep study was done in our home one night. He hasn't had any alarms in the past six weeks but we still use the monitor. I think we'll continue to use the monitor until after he has had all his DPT shots. Sometimes I joke that he'll be going to school attached to a monitor, though!''

It is not clear in many cases whether a monitor is really necessary; studies have not shown that it affects mortality rates in premies, or that premies are at higher risk of sudden infant death syndrome, or SIDS. Often it is used as a crutch by both medical personnel and parents. One mother admits it was nothing more than a crutch for her but says that if she had to do it again, she would still use the monitor:

''The doctors did not want to send Matthew home on a monitor because they said he had no apnea. But I said no. I wanted the monitor. It was on my personal insistence that they finally signed for it.''

The monitor is certainly called for, however, in certain situations—for example, when a family has previously had a child who died of SIDS.

If your baby is sent home on a monitor, you will probably develop a love/hate relationship with this machine. At first, no matter how many times it goes off, you'll be grateful that it's there. When it stops going off, you'll probably be convinced that the monitor's broken! As your baby stabilizes and matures and as you become more secure, you'll probably want to kick it if it ever does go off, especially because it's often a false alarm.

Here's one mother's story of many false alarms:

''The second night at home, Emily's monitor went off constantly! Every time we went in she was fine. We thought it might be the monitor, but then again, it might have been Emily. We were up all night. Finally, we called the hospital and they told us to put some water on the leads to get them to stick better. Then we found out that the monitor had a company phone number on it and you could call them with questions as well. Emily was on a monitor for eight months. The last two months, it went off very few times. When she came off it, we were very ready.''

Your baby's readiness to come off the monitor will be judged on the basis of ''sleep studies,'' which can be done right in your home and brought to your neonatologist to read. These studies measure the maturity of your infant's sleep patterns, thus assessing in a crude way his neurological maturity as well. Ashley had many sleep studies and it was quite a while before she stopped ''failing'' the test.

BILI LIGHTS AT HOME

Premies with mild hyperbilirubinemia, who are doing well in every other respect, sometimes can be given phototherapy at home; this is not as difficult as it may sound. The same sort of bilirubin lights you saw in the hospital would be delivered to your home on a rental basis; controls would be set for you and you would be told how and when to give the phototherapy. We'll just summarize the instructions here. Remember to keep the eyes patched whenever your baby is under the lights—they can burn the retina, just as a sunlamp can. Keep your baby uncovered (with the possible exception of diapering him), so that the light can reach his skin. Be sure that your baby gets lots of fluid—breast milk and/or formula, plus water and/or glucose water. The lights can dry the baby out and bilirubin levels will climb if your baby gets dehydrated.

If your baby is having phototherapy at home, you'll have to bring him in for a blood test every day so that your doctor can check the level of bilirubin in his blood. The blood tests can be done at home if you are willing and able to draw blood (usually by a heel stick). Sometimes the hospital can arrange for someone to come to your house to draw blood. If not, your baby's nurses can teach you to do a heel prick; this way you could avoid taking the baby out of your home. The blood sample, however, would still have to be taken to a lab or physician

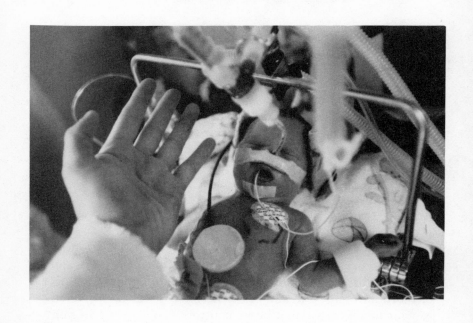

Emily: as a newborn, at eight months, and at three years.

for the results to be read. One note of caution: it may be emotionally difficult for you to do a heel prick on your own baby; do not be embarrassed about it or try to force yourself to overcome it. But if you do feel capable and comfortable doing it, here is some advice. Warm the heel first by wrapping it for about five minutes with a warm, wet washcloth. Clean the skin with alcohol; do not use Vaseline. Insert a fresh needle or stilette each time. Puncture quickly and do not puncture deeply. Collect the blood into tubes as instructed. Hold the heel until bleeding stops.

There's a possibility that if your baby is jaundiced, you will be asked to stop breastfeeding for a few days. This will give doctors a chance to see whether some of the fatty components of breast milk are interfering with the elimination of the bilirubin. This can feel like yet another setback to your attempts at breastfeeding but it will be for only a few days and you can pump your milk during that time (to keep up your production) and use it later. Be sure to save your expressed breast milk for future use! Even though your baby can't have it right now, it will be useful to have on hand later if you want to go out or sleep through one of your baby's feedings.

OXYGEN USE AT HOME

If your baby was on a ventilator for a long time and has residual lung damage, or if he has one of several heart defects, he may need supplemental oxygen at home, constantly or occasionally. You may be sent home with small oxygen tanks for this purpose. Oxygen can be given through a mask, hood, or nasal prongs. Keep cigarettes, heat, and flames away from the tanks and away from the baby when oxygen is in use. Also, if your child has residual lung problems, keep him away from cigarette smoke and try to be especially careful about his avoiding people with colds. Oxygen therapy will not last forever; your child will outgrow any need for supplementary oxygen, if not in the next months, certainly in the next year or so. Lung tissue continues to grow until age six. What appears to be extensive lung damage is likely to correct itself over the next few years. Heart defects can usually be surgically repaired once the child has grown a bit.

TUBE FEEDING

It is becoming less frequent for a premie to be kept in the hospital until he reaches some magic weight for discharge. But if he is still getting most of his calories through tube feeding, usually because he is not yet strong enough to get all the calories from breast or bottle feeding, you may wonder when you will finally get him home. As I mentioned before, even tube feeding can be done at home, if you are very eager and your neonatologist feels it would be safe. We did it with Ashley and

I don't believe it's too difficult for some brave and careful parents to learn, even if you do not have medical training—if you want to make the effort, if you are willing to accept the responsibility, and if your neonatologist feels comfortable about it. The nurses must work with you one-on-one to teach you the technique, but I'll summarize it here.

A small plastic tube is slipped through your baby's mouth, down the esophagus, and into his stomach. Before inserting it, you would first measure the correct amount of tube by holding it against the baby's chest to find out about how far down it would have to go to reach his stomach. The next step is critical and can really be taught only in person: once the tube is down, you must very, very gently blow a little air into the tube, while listening to the chest or stomach with a stethoscope. This way you can check to make sure the tube is in the stomach—and didn't end up down the wrong tube and into the lungs. The sound of air going into the stomach is distinctive; the sound of it going into the lungs is very different and very dangerous. Once you've heard the difference, it is difficult to confuse the two. NEVER, NEVER put formula down that tube unless you are certain that the end of it is in the stomach and not in the tube to the lungs! If you're not sure, pull it out and put it down again. (It will almost always naturally go down the esophagus to the stomach, unless the baby happens to cough or gag at the wrong time.) If you are certain that the end of the tube is in the stomach, connect the tube to a syringe, suspend the syringe above the crib, and pour the correct amount of milk into the syringe. The tube should be taped in place around the baby's mouth and at his cheek, even if you are going to remove it right after the feeding. The tape prevents your baby from purposely or accidentally pulling the tube out. (Your baby won't like this tube any more than you do and as he matures he will become increasingly good at dislodging it.) It may be a good idea to tie your baby's arms down, but I just could not bring myself to do this, so I would hold Ashley's hands instead. This didn't give me much freedom to do anything during feedings, though! As your premie becomes increasingly clever, he may also burp air into the line and you will notice that the contents of the syringe are not going down. Remove this air from the line by pushing the syringe down ever so slightly—push the liquid down by about one mark (1 cc). As a rule of thumb, the better your baby gets at thwarting your gavage-feeding attempts, the closer he is to being bottle- or breastfed. Try offering the baby a bottle or your breast occasionally; you may be pleasantly surprised. When you first switch from gavage feedings to breast or bottle, don't be disappointed by an initial weight loss. Now your premie is using energy to eat; also, he may tire and thus not eat as much as when he was being tube-fed. And if you are breastfeeding, your baby may need supplementary bottles—breast feeding is more work for your baby than bottle feeding.

Your child may be sent home with more complicated ongoing problems than those covered here. See Chapter 12 for information on ongoing medical problems you'll have to deal with at home, including the care of colostomies, tracheostomies, and shunts.

ROUTINE CHILDCARE

Bringing home any baby is anxiety-provoking. Bringing home a premie is an especially anxious time. If you expect everything to be slightly slower and a little harder with a premie, you will likely handle problems more comfortably. Keep in mind that it will take time for you and your premie to adjust. As in any new relationship, adjustments must be made by everyone—including your baby, who is now in a very different environment from the one he has known so far. Depend on your support system—friends and relatives *and* a doctor (either the neonatologist or a pediatrician whom you can call or see).

Feeding.   You should discuss feeding schedules with your doctor. Does your doctor advise "demand" or scheduled feedings for your infant? (Your premie may yet be too immature to demand-feed.) If scheduled, should the feedings be every two hours? Every three? Every four? Should you wake the baby to feed him if he sleeps more than four hours at a stretch? In general, I see no problem in allowing a premie to sleep for six- to eight-hour periods at night if his weight and weight gain are good.

Weight gain. This is the bane of many premie parents' existence. Weight gain seems to take forever. In the hospital, you probably saw your baby lose his birth weight and dip way down, only to slowly, slowly climb back up toward his original weight. Getting back to birth weight can take up to a month. You've seen your baby weighed as many as three times a day. Naturally, weight is on your mind! But if your infant is developing well in other ways, and especially if your pediatrician is not worried, you should try not to dwell on the fact that your baby is small for his age.

Infection. It's true that your baby has a slightly greater chance of infection than a term baby, but try not to overprotect the baby to the point of isolation. Your baby's immune system is not on a par with a term baby's yet, and it's easier for him to catch colds or get other infections. Even a full-term baby's immune system takes years to mature. Still, it's okay to allow members of the immediate family to come in contact with the baby, if they are well. Keeping siblings away only deepens sibling rivalry and jealousy. But if a sibling or someone else in the house becomes ill, that person should keep his distance. If Mom or Dad gets sick, it can be difficult or impossible for them to distance themselves from the baby. If you get sick, keep these tips in mind: wash your hands both after coughing or sneezing and before touching your baby; don't breathe or cough into the baby's face; don't share eating utensils with the baby; minimize kissing. You might wear a surgical mask while having close contact with the baby, for extra protection, but this borders on the excessive. In general, the baby should be kept away from shopping malls and other crowded places during that first month or two. Outsiders, especially sick ones, should not be allowed to have close contact with the baby during his first month home. Obviously, the baby's general health and continued growth will eventually temper these suggestions.

Bathing.   Giving your baby that first bath may seem frightening but it's not too hard to do. The stimulation of a bath won't hurt your premie (even if he doesn't seem to be enjoying himself too much), but if you're worried about how he'll handle it, you can stick to sponge baths for now. During a sponge bath, you uncover only one part of the body at a time, thereby keeping the rest of the body warm and dry. If you believe your baby is ready for a full bath, you have your choice of the tub, the sink, or a countertop plastic baby bath. The tub is the hardest because it's the biggest and difficult for you to reach without kneeling and bending. The sink is fine for a premie, but you may feel even safer with a molded plastic baby bath. Inside the baby bath, for extra security and ease, you can place a large sponge, about the length of the baby and contoured specifically to fit a baby's body. (Many tubs are now made with this sponge attached.) The sponge can't slip and it supports the baby so you can take your hands off him for a second if you have to. Here's how to give a bath:

1.   Turn up the house's heat if necessary; make sure the room is 76 to 80 degrees Fahrenheit.

2.   Get out *everything* that you might need so you don't have to run for anything. Line up next to the tub the towels, soap, shampoo, fresh diaper, and clean clothes, including socks or booties and clean monitor equipment.

3.   Test the bath water. It should be warm, not hot or cold. Feel the water with your wrist or elbow for the best temperature gauge.

4.   Take off the baby's monitor. Don't be nervous about this time off the monitor. You're watching the baby and would

certainly be able to see any breathing problems. Besides, a bath is very stimulating.

5.   Skip the soap the first few times. A soapy baby is too slippery to handle until you're feeling like a pro!

6.   To put the baby into the tub, place your arm under his neck and gently grip his shoulder with your hand. Use your other hand to hold him at the ankles. Move carefully and slowly, keeping the baby's body close to your own as you gently dip him into the water. If you move too quickly, the combination of the sudden movement and the cool air on his skin will frighten him.

7.   Do not let go of the baby, even if you are using a shallow baby bath. The water may make him feel calm or it may upset him. In either case, the touch of your hands securely on him will keep him feeling safe.

8.   Keep the bath short.

9.   Have a towel ready. You might even want to put it over your shoulder, tuck it into your shirt, or tie it around your neck. Then all you have to do is pick the baby up, hold him to your chest, and wrap. Dry the baby gently but thoroughly.

10.   Dress the baby right away, after reattaching the monitor leads.

11.   Let your baby rest now. This was quite an event for him!

Dressing.   Dressing your baby need not be a chore. Dress your baby like any baby. Make sure he is warm but not too hot. If he is cold, maintaining body heat will use a lot of his energy and you don't want that to happen. But because he doesn't have a very good temperature-control system yet, being hot is just as bad—he can't adjust to that either. In general, keeping your baby at a comfortable 73 to 80 degrees is fine.

You will almost certainly want to buy some premie clothes for your baby because regular baby clothes will be too large. Happily, a lot of department stores now carry premie sizes. If you are having trouble finding the clothes you want, though, call or write one of the mail-order houses listed on page 93. Don't buy too many premie outfits! Four to six outfits will suffice; you will be amazed at how quickly your premie grows! When purchasing clothes, opt for easy-care outfits that are simple to get on your baby. Snaps are preferable to ties. A snap-front T-shirt is easier than an envelope-neck T-shirt when your baby has monitor leads. Clothes with snap crotches or nighties with drawstring bottoms make diaper changes quicker. There's no need to take off an entire outfit just to get to a dirty diaper. If there's any way you can afford it, get a washer and dryer installed in your home, if you don't already have them. With a premie in the house you'll be doing lots of laundry, and you won't want to be running to the Laundromat all the time!

For diapers, either cloth ones or disposables are fine. I used cloth for sentimental reasons; also, these are much cheaper. Cost might be a real issue if you have a premie. However, disposables are more convenient and using them takes less time than using and washing cloth diapers. You can buy premie-sized cloth diapers in some stores and through mail-order houses, but you can also fold or cut regular ones to fit. Buy premie-sized disposables through specialty children's stores, your hospital pharmacy, or your neighborhood pharmacy. Call first to find out if a place has them in stock or will order them for you.

Bowel movements.   Parents frequently ask me, as a pediatrician, about "normal" bowel movements for babies. I tell them not to be surprised at how much energy your premie puts into pooping! This is sometimes a premie's top priority—even over eating. Attempting to move his bowels can cause him to waste a good deal of energy and can stress him at times. But there is nothing you can do about this, so just be understanding. With time, his priorities will change. Also, do not be concerned by frequent pooping by such a little baby. As long as his bowel patterns do not change, he is urinating well, and his skin is soft and pink, everything is fine.

Crying.   This can drive a parent crazy and there's something about a premie's cry that's different from a term baby's. When you first bring your premie home, he will probably vocalize less than term infants do. As he grows and matures developmentally, you may find that he seems to cry more than the average baby and that his cry sounds different from a term baby's. Several studies have shown that a premie's cry elicits more anxiety in an adult than a term baby's cry, even when the adult is not the parent. Still, no one knows what makes a premie's cries sound different to us. If your premie cries a lot, it can be extremely frustrating—it's always hard to tell exactly why he's crying and what you're supposed to do about it.

Crying, of course, adds to the stress of an already stressful parenting role. Try to remind yourself that you and your baby will get better and better at communicating with each other over time and that your baby will eventually cry less frequently. Meanwhile, follow any clues you may have to find out the source of the problem. Check all the usual things: Is the diaper soiled? Is the baby hungry? Does the baby want to be in a different position? Does he need to be burped? Is he tired? If he is inconsolable or his cries are escalating in frequency, you may want to check with your doctor about a possible medical problem. If medical problems are ruled out and your baby is still a crier, you might just be overstimulating him. Go back to one stimulus at a time, and milder stimulations at that (soften your voice, hold without rocking, perhaps just have him near you).

CHOOSING A PEDIATRICIAN

Having been surrounded by doctors and nurses since your baby was born, you'll probably be very choosy about a pediatrician for your child. Because you and your child have been through so much already, you will need to find a compatible and sympathetic pediatrician who understands *your* situation. Finding just the right pediatrician takes time, but it is well worth it in the long run. You *must* choose a pediatrician before your baby leaves the hospital.

There are several ways to get the names of pediatricians. You can ask your neonatologist for the names of one or two pediatricians who frequently care for premies. Or you can contact your local medical association and ask for the names of board-certified pediatricians in your area who have a special interest in premies. (This method is a blind one and thus not ideal.) You can also ask your friends for recommendations. Your friends can judge only whether or not they personally like a particular physician and find him or her sympathetic or responsive. They can also tell you how available the doctor is, how expensive, how easy to talk to. They may not be good judges of a doctor's medical skills, especially if their children haven't had any problems more serious than ear infections, but interpersonal skills and availability are important in a pediatrician.

Call about three of the pediatricians whose names you have obtained and ask for interviews. Usually there will be no charge for this; we pediatricians really are the most understanding of doctors! Be honest when you call. Tell the secretary that the appointment is for a precare interview and that you are calling several pediatricians to whom you were referred.

When you meet with each pediatrician, have a list of questions, either in your mind or written down, that you wish to go over with him or her. These might include:

1. Where did you train, at what medical school? Where did you do your internship, your residency?

2. Was your training all in pediatrics? Are you board-certified in pediatrics? (In other words, has the doctor actually taken and passed the pediatric board exams?) These pediatric boards are not the same as medical boards, which any doctor

in any sort of medical practice had to take; pediatric boards are additional, specialty tests. A doctor may call himself a pediatrician because he sees children; this does not mean that he is board-certified as one. Also, these tests cannot be completed until a doctor has practiced medicine for at least a specific number of years, so a "pediatrician" may not be fully "boarded" yet. (When my husband and I interviewed pediatricians, one told us he had passed his boards. Only when we asked specifically, "Do you mean your pediatric boards?" did he reply, "Well, no." You would think he would have known better than to try to mislead two pediatricians who had themselves passed the pediatric boards, but you never can tell!)

3. How long have you been in practice?

4. Who are your partners? Which one of you sees the baby on routine visits? When he is sick during office hours?

5. How do you handle night calls or emergency calls after office hours?

6. How do you handle hospital admissions? At which hospitals do you have admitting privileges?

7. Do you charge for telephone-call consultations? Do you have specific hours when you will accept calls with questions on general topics that might not require an office visit?

8. What do you charge for office visits? Routine immunizations?

9. Specific questions important to you, such as "Are any of your other patients premies?" or "When do you believe a premie catches up with a term baby?" or "How do you feel about breastfeeding?" These sorts of questions may give you important clues as to how *simpático* this doctor is.

When deciding among the pediatricians you interviewed, you'll also need to ask yourself some practical questions:

1. Is the doctor's office close enough to you?

2. Is the hospital where the doctor has admitting privileges close enough to you? Does it have a good reputation?

3. Was the waiting room crowded?

4.   Do sick (contagious) children come at a different time or sit in a different part of the waiting room so they don't infect children there for checkups?

5.   Did the doctor seem willing to answer your questions? Did you find the answers satisfactory?

6.   Are the nurses and secretaries pleasant?

7.   Do you feel you have a good rapport with this doctor? Would you feel comfortable or uncomfortable calling him or her with a question or problem? Do his or her views on child-rearing issues mesh well with yours?

Once you have chosen a pediatrician, you should set up a schedule of office visits during these early months of your baby's life, so that you have regular appointments for well-baby checkups and immunizations. Your baby can and should receive vaccinations at the same time as a full-term child: at two months, four months, six months, fifteen months, and eighteen months or two years. Interestingly, a premie's ability to respond to these vaccinations at age two months is comparable to that of a full-term baby at two months.

Remember that if your relationship with your pediatrician is not working out, it is totally reasonable to find a new one. But don't "doctor-shop"; it's time-consuming and leads to having no one know your baby well.

10. Early Development

Now that you are home and think you have put prematurity behind you, you may find yourself wondering, "Why isn't my baby like other babies?" At first it may bother you that he doesn't seem to cry much. Then you may be worried because it seems that he's always crying—and always irritable. As more times goes by, you may be worried because he's still so small—or because he doesn't talk yet. I know parents often find it difficult to relax about developmental milestones, especially in the early years. For this reason, we have put together in this chapter a guide to early development, which suggests appropriate interactions, toys, and activities for the premature baby from birth through thirty months corrected age.

Your endless anxieties during the first few years (and often beyond) really boil down to: "Is my baby progressing normally? Will he be normal?" These questions can be difficult to answer on the basis of current research. After all, no two premies are alike, any more than any two other children are alike. There is no single, set-in-stone premie personality or premie development pattern. As I've repeatedly emphasized, though, premature babies *are* developmentally different from full-term babies. It is routine pediatric practice to evaluate a premie according to age counting from his expected, rather than his actual, birth date, until he is about two or three years old. For example, if your baby was born two months prematurely and is now three months old, he actually has a developmental age of only one month. Most pediatricians will tell you that developmentally you should not count this premie's first two months of life any more than you would count a full-term infant's last two months in the womb. Imagine, then, that the time your baby spent in the hospital was like time he should have spent in the womb. Adjust his "age" to make allowances for this. This obviously gives your premie a bit of a break in terms of what is expected of him developmentally, which is certainly appropriate. It does not, however, additionally take into account the experiences, setbacks, adverse stimulation, and adversities he may have experienced in the hospital. Research has only begun to look into the long-term developmental effects of all this; nothing has yet been done about discovering its more subtle, lasting effects.

So it's a good idea to remind yourself that your parental expectations should be tempered, especially during the first year or two of your premie's life, even on into the early teens, if necessary. If your baby was or is still sick, then development may lag further behind even this basic rule of thumb.

Now let's go through the developmental outline that follows, which is geared for premies during the early years. Unfortunately, there are as yet no standard guides specifically for premies, so these are just adaptations of guides for full-term children. Remember to use your baby's corrected age as you read on. Most important, bear in mind that there will be a wide range among babies, whether preterm or not, as to when they are ready for the various activities mentioned. You will find that your baby will achieve "readiness" in a startlingly sudden way, so don't push, but check periodically to see if he is ready (in other words, interested). Furthermore, remember that even corrected age may not be quite right for your baby, given his premie experiences and complications. Learn to follow along in response to your child's cues to what he is ready for. In this way, you can avoid some of the negative connotations of classifying your baby as being "behind" or trying to "catch up." Your premie is not behind. He is just right for who he is and how he was born.

Zero to six months after the due date. Right from the beginning, your baby had a personality of his own. You saw it in the way he reacted to various nurses or procedures in the NICU; you'll see it in his sleep cycles, in the way he reacts to feeding, in his restlessness or calmness, and the times he cries. Each premie has his own personality and will develop at his own speed and in his own pattern, just as every full-term child will. One father whose daughter was born weighing one pound thirteen ounces explains how quickly he and the medical staff came to see his daughter's unique personality:

"She's a fighter. She used to clench her little fists in the hospital. You couldn't keep her down. She just has an attitude of positiveness, such a pleasant personality. Anyone that has had anything to do with her always comments on this."

For many mothers and fathers, however, premies do not seem so pleasant in the early months and parenting can be difficult. One mother explains:

"He's not placid. He never was. He's probably not that much different from other kids but I've always had the attitude that it has been harder for me than for other moms."

Of course, even parents of some full-term infants experience difficulties and face unusually hard times due to colic, sleep problems, and such. Still, a lot of premie parents feel that, at least in the first year, their child is crankier or more sensitive than other children. Is this related to prematurity? Almost certainly the answer is "At least in part." This "crankiness," however, is not your child's *personality*. It is due to an immature nervous system coupled with the negative impact the hospital environment may have had. These effects and this immaturity will not go away overnight. Ashley, for example, was not the easiest of personalities in her first nine months or so of life. I didn't really notice this at first, since I both knew her well enough to see her good features and was so concerned about her well-being that I didn't care if she was cranky. But I did notice that other people's reactions to her were quite different. Bill's parents, for example, would ask: "Does she always cry like this? Does it ever stop?" If you can just put up with those early months without getting a negative attitude yourself—and, equally important, without becoming overly protective of your premie—you can look forward to a time when the grandparents and everyone else will forget they ever found your child's disposition disappointing. Certainly this is the case with Ashley, who is now a delightful child. You, too, can someday smile to yourself about the fickle nature of adults' memories and affections, if you just don't give up on your premie now.

I must stress that saying premies may be cranky in the first months or even years of life is not the same as saying there is a "premie personality." In one comparative study involving ninety-eight preterm and eighty-nine full-term infants at twelve months postterm, the two groups did not differ in overall temperament type. It is certainly possible, however, that your baby's early experiences in the hospital can color his personality and development, just as many other experiences will shape him. For example, there is increasing evidence that the stresses of the NICU may have some effect on development.

Premie babies frequently have a narrow "stimulation window": it can be harder to attract and keep their attention, but too much stimulation may cause them simply to withdraw. It is unclear whether some of this may be related to hospital events or medical complications rather than to prematurity per se. For example, in one study of premies who were no longer in the hospital, those suffering from respiratory-distress syndrome were found to be less adaptable and more likely to withdraw from new stimulation than other premies. You will never be able to determine just how or to what degree your own baby has been affected by being born early or spending time in an intensive-care nursery, although parents may worry about this almost obsessively in the first few years of their baby's life.

Says one mother of a four-year-old:

"When I think about it—the lights and noises of the hospital—I always felt it would have an effect on him. He's very attached to me; very cautious. I think it's plausible that this has something to do with his prematurity. So when it comes to something like separation, I still give him the benefit of the doubt. He's even behind his corrected age when it comes to that. He's very temperamental."

During the early months of a premie's life, periods of alertness are short and infrequent. Interaction with your baby will not be as rewarding as you may expect it to be. Your baby may not be very responsive to your attempts to play or cuddle. Don't worry about this—it will change as your child matures. Here is how one mother described the early months with her son when interaction was difficult:

"He seemed a mystery to me. I didn't know what he was feeling. He slept a lot at first and I was glad. He was unresponsive for a long time. I could see other babies were much more responsive. Timmy had a very prolonged infancy. I remember the first thing he responded to—a face on a rattle. He liked that."

Although they all grow into very different individuals, premies do have some shared characteristics in the first few months of life. These characteristics are related to the premie's immature nervous system, body characteristics, and, as discussed, possibly the time spent in the hospital, which was anything but conducive to development. Your goal, as a premie parent, should be to recognize these temporary, shared characteristics for what they are and not mislead yourself into thinking that these are your premie's own permanent personality traits. The trick is to get to know your individual child hiding just beneath the premie façade.

For now it may be necessary to back off a bit, to avoid overstimulating your baby. If you respond by trying harder to stimulate him and get his attention, your baby will likely retreat further. This does not mean ignore him; just try milder, simpler stimulations. By three or four months past due date, he will be spending more and more time awake, will look at the world around him, and will show more of an interest in toys and activities. All the energy he has had to expend on eating, digesting, and growing will finally be spent elsewhere— on getting to know the world around him.

As a newborn, he will probably be more interested in your face than in any toy. Your baby will love to study your face, especially if you are eight to ten inches in front of him. This "focal distance" will increase in the early months of life. He will also be attracted by bright colors. Try hanging a bright mobile over his crib; offer colored stuffed toys and rattles. You'll soon see him trying to follow some of these objects with his eyes; practice this with him. Begin with one toy or activity at a time and increase the intensity of "playing," as indicated by your baby's response and increasing maturity. Later in this period, he will become interested in his own hands—looking at them and playing with them—and then discover that he can reach out and touch things. One of the things he will especially enjoy exploring with his hands is your face. Hand discovery, however, often takes longer for premature babies than term babies. As one mother reports:

"As a baby, my daughter wasn't flexed [like a term baby]. A baby needs to have her hands in front of her face to find them and play with them. Her hands weren't there. She was slower to work with her hands, clumsier with them later."

Touching, rocking, and fondling your baby are all extremely important activities that should not be forgotten. Toys, mobiles, and music can never take the place of your presence and touch. Most important, talk and sing to your baby, even as you go on about your other work. Take him with you around the house so you'll both have some company, and take his siblings, too. Brothers and sisters can be very clever at sensing a baby's stage of development and interacting with him constructively, if sibling rivalry doesn't get in the way.

Right now he can show you only a glimmer of what he is to become, but he is constantly observing and learning and growing, even though you can't always see it happening. Be-

tween birth and six months corrected age, your premie is concentrating on getting bigger and stronger. As his muscles
continue to develop he will gain more and more control over
his body movements.

In the beginning, you'll need to support his head; his neck
and shoulder muscles will be too weak to hold it up until about
one to two months after he passes his due date. But he will be
practicing this skill from the time he's about six weeks past his
due date. To help him perfect this ability, let the baby lie on
his tummy and he'll try to hold his head up briefly. Put the
baby on a blanket on the floor and get down at his level. He
will try to lift his head to see your face. As the months go on
and he gets stronger shoulder, back, and neck muscles, he will
be able to lift his head and chest off the ground. At about five
months after his due date, he may be able to push himself up
on his arms and really look around. Sitting up takes balance,
strength, and coordination. You should begin to see some good
attempts at maintaining a sitting-up position by the time your
baby is six months past his due date, but keep plenty of soft
pillows around him to cushion his landings!

Until he can sit up, your baby will enjoy being held and
being propped up in a baby seat. Roll some receiving blankets
up and place them around the baby's head to help prop him
up, or buy one of the head rolls now available for the same
purpose.

From the very beginning, your baby has attempted to
communicate with you. In the NICU, this communication may
have been very subtle. It was probably a long time before you
heard what is considered the earliest form of communication—
crying. Until then, you probably communicated through eye
contact and touch, and by noting changes in your premie's disposition as he reacted to stimuli he liked or didn't like. As I
mentioned in the last chapter, many people believe that there
is something different and more stressful about a premie's cry
and insist that it must be higher pitched. In a parent's case,
part of this reaction may be due to the fact that you are tired,
already stressed, and on pins and needles about any signals of

distress sent by your baby! Because the cries produce more anxiety in you than normal, you may perceive your baby as having a "cranky" personality. Knowing that this will pass may not make the baby's grumpy hours any easier on you. But remember—this is not your baby's true personality and things will improve as your baby matures.

One mother talks about the early days at home with her premie son:

"I think premies are hypersensitive to stimuli. I would put Timmy in the stroller and we would walk around. I'd go into a store and he'd wake up and start screaming. The change unsettled him. It seemed I could only be somewhere a few minutes before he'd start to cry. I became wary, anticipating this reaction. His crying really got to me. I never let him cry even for five minutes. I always picked him up immediately. The first three months were an emotionally draining, trying time. I thought it was this way for all new mothers. But recently, I ran into a new mother of a full-term baby and I asked her how things were going. I expected her to say it was horrible but she said everything was wonderful. I remember looking at her and thinking that she didn't seem to be lying."

In these first months, you will begin to tell the difference between some of his cries—some sound angry, some sound as if he's in pain, some let you know he's hungry, others tell you he's tired. No book can tell you how to differentiate among these cries. You come to learn this as you come to know your baby. You also learn how to respond—when to back away and let him go to sleep, when to pick him up. As you become more responsive to him, he will become more responsive to you. When you pick him up, he will stop crying. When he hears you coming, he may stop crying for a moment, expectantly awaiting a bottle or breast or a diaper change. If in the next second he doesn't get that, he may start crying again to let you know he is still waiting and still hungry, wet, bored, or whatever.

By about six weeks past his due date, he should also communicate well with smiles—certainly more welcome than cries!

Before this time, probably since he was first born, you un-
doubtedly noticed many fleeting smiles. Although opinion differs on whether these are "real" smiles, you will certainly know
when you get that first social smile—he will definitely smile
back at *you*. Of course, all babies are different and some seem
more "smiley" than others. One woman whose son was born
three months early and is now five years old says that she
waited a very long time for that first smile. She says, "I don't
know how old he was before he smiled at me. . . . I think he
was eight months old. It was a year before he laughed out
loud."

Sleep/wake cycles are short during the early months. You
may feel that you'll never get any sleep! Some of this may be
determined by feeding schedules. Ashley required feeding every
two to four hours for a number of months, so I had to get up
during the night to feed her; it was over six months before she
and I slept through the night. For other mothers, the sleepless
nights go on even longer.

For one mother of triplets, sleeplessness was a fact of life
for a year and a half. She says:

"My children didn't sleep through the night until they
were eighteen months old. One of them had night terrors and
he would wake screaming, with his eyes wide open, but he was
actually still asleep. You'd have to shake him violently to wake
him. In the beginning, there were feedings every two hours.
The feedings would take an hour, so there was only an hour
between them. I'd feed one, then the next one would cry. I'd
catch a little sleep. It was like that day and night. I really
needed help. It was horrible—what it does to you is horrible.
Now that they're all three and a half, I wonder what it would
be like to have one baby—how easy it could be."

Plan your night's sleep around feeding needs, not your
anxieties. Parents, especially moms, often cannot sleep soundly
if their baby is at their side. Every little grunt, turn, or whim-
per tends to awaken them. There is no need for your premie
to be right next to you; the next room will do just fine. Nor is
a nursery microphone—so popular these days—necessary. If

your premie needs a monitor, he will be on one—and you can easily hear it from the next room. Don't get into a pattern of rising for whimpers or you will be sitting with your premie throughout the night, long after his fragility is a thing of the past.

Six months to nine months after the due date.   Parenting should be starting to get a little easier now . . . and your premie is looking more like the playful little baby you had imagined. At six months corrected age, he's old enough to be less of a worry and less trouble, but he isn't yet old enough to run around and get into things. During this period, your baby will probably become much more entertaining and full of smiles. Now is the time to start letting him have more interactive toys. Try a crib gym or a row of toys that can stretch across a crib, carriage, or baby chair. Your baby will enjoy batting at these toys, especially if they make a noise or beads tumble when he hits them. He will start to learn cause and effect as he hits at objects and makes things happen. Encourage hand-eye coordination. Hold attractive objects within reach. Your baby's goal right now is to reach and grasp those objects he sees in front of him. He may find it tough to accomplish, but once he finally succeeds, he'll be thrilled with his newfound ability.

Remember that premies need more stimulation, but overload more quickly than do full-term babies. Interactions that encourage using motor skills and visual/spatial development are especially important and will have a very real impact on development. But always keep in mind that this must be done through *play*. Your baby will sense if you are anxiously trying to *teach* him some particular skill or if you are secretly testing and rating his abilities. Remember that the games you play with your baby should be fun for the two of you.

Encourage the baby's exploration with his mouth but keep unsafe and small objects away. He learns by mouthing things; oral touch and taste are major senses for him. Choose toys that are colorful and easy to hold, and as teeth begin to develop try teething rings and unbreakable plastic toys that are easy to grab and safe to chew on. You might try out that baby swing, but be a little cautious, since it may overwhelm your premie at first rather than soothe him. I still remember Ashley turning gray her first time in the swing—not much fun!

Nine months to twelve months after the due date. By now, the crankiness I have mentioned as typical for premies under a year old should be disappearing. All premie parents probably feel that some of a child's personality is influenced by prematurity and they are probably right. But at least the neurological immaturity that makes premie babies "fussier" has now passed and their own inimitable personalities are shining through stronger than ever.

At this age, your baby is probably moving into high gear. It's time to babyproof your house, if you haven't already done so; babies at this age want to and will get into everything they can reach or knock over. To keep them safe, put cleaning equipment, medications, and poisons well out of reach, preferably in a locked cabinet. Make sure there are no loose cords hanging from lamps for baby to pull down on his head, cover all electrical outlets with safety guards, move breakables off low shelves. Your baby needs to be able to explore freely and you don't want to spend all day screaming no at him. But now is also the time to begin to set limits; don't wait until he's into the "twos" and wants to do the opposite of what you tell him. If you start setting limits now, many of these "rules" will be second nature to him by the time he's into two-year-old rebellion.

The baby is now able to sit up without support and probably has begun to crawl. Remember that crawling is not as easy as it may seem to you. It takes muscle and brain coordination and control; the baby must use arms and legs in a synchronized fashion. Neurological development in general starts at the top and works down, so your baby will be better at first at using his arms. Leg coordination and strengthening will develop later. This is why you may see that your premie's early attempts at crawling involve pushing himself up with his arms and then dragging his legs after him.

Help him to stand and walk. Most babies love having a taste of walking before they're really ready by holding Mom's and Dad's hands and being helped along. Check out some walkers, if you want to use one and have the space for it. Put a strong child gate at the top of any stairway. Never use a walker near the top of stairs, on carpets or rugs, or where floor level changes. Make sure you choose a sturdy walker, one that doesn't tip easily—babies like to reach over and try to pick things up off the floor while in them.

Continue to encourage hand-eye coordination by putting toys just out of reach and letting your baby go for them. If he is desperate and clearly can't make it to them himself, help him out; don't frustrate him!

Bring out stacking toys, blocks, and shapes, even though thumping, banging, mouthing, and throwing are what he'll be doing for a while rather than building. Destruction is a key word for your baby now. Babies at this age are also suddenly becoming interested in small things as well as large—tiny crumbs, little pieces of lint. Encourage your baby's fine motor skills but be careful about what he puts in his mouth! Let your baby try self-feeding, messy though it is. Give him a cup. Let him pick up small pieces of food with his fingers.

Continue to introduce your child to the world around him. Go out on walks; let the baby crawl or sit outside on the ground. Talk to your baby and encourage his babbling—this is the beginning of speech. Read to him, sing to him, and *speak* to him. Let him explore big colorful books and blocks. Rudimentary memory skills are developing. For example, now he knows that an object that disappears from view still exists. This is why peekaboo becomes such an amusing game for baby right now.

You may notice that your baby is starting to become wary of strangers. This is quite normal at around eight months corrected age and beyond, though the timing of these periods of "stranger anxiety" may be different for your child. Again, each baby is different and some aren't as upset by unfamiliar faces as others are. You may also notice that your baby has very strong opinions of people: he may love your postman but scream at the sight of his great-aunt. Don't be embarrassed when your baby acts "unsociable" with outsiders or acquaintances. Respect his wishes to stay clear for now.

Your baby may have a security object he clings to— perhaps a small bear that has been with him since his days in the isolette or a favorite soft blanket. As he becomes more independent, he may like to have this familiar something to return to . . . especially when feeling tired or in need of comfort. This security may be needed on and off for years; don't be concerned about it—be grateful he has this wonderful crutch.

Twelve months to eighteen months after the due date. Continue all the above activities while encouraging a more organized response to them—sorting, stacking blocks, filling and emptying baskets are all good games at this age.

Although premies are often slower at language development, language skills should be developing now, especially if you have been talking to your premie from the very beginning. Ashley, for example, lagged far behind in her verbal skills; this made me very anxious until a friend who is a developmental psychologist commented: "Why should she talk? Her sister tells you anything Ashley wants!" This did not stop my worries altogether, but sure enough, over a period of about two months, Ashley went from not speaking at all to speaking in compound sentences. You just can't predict what these little buggers will do; that's why they—and the statistics—can drive you crazy!

To help encourage language development, read books with your child; point at pictures and name them. Name things that your baby comes in contact with every day. Your baby's first words will refer to familiar items that are important to his world, such as "bottle."

Encourage more independence now, as improved coordination means he can do more things for himself. You can give him a spoon with dinner and let him attempt to feed himself with it. You can ask him to throw the tissue in the basket or bring a cookie to Daddy in the living room. Independence can make him a little uncertain as well. He wants independence but he wants to know that the old security is there—that you're still there for him.

The things your baby wants to do right now may exceed his abilities and that can cause some frustration. Children this age are persistent, though, and they keep returning to the same problem until they've mastered it. Some babies will have already taken their first steps by now, but do not get worried if your baby is slow to learn walking. Of course, as any parent will tell you, this is easier said than done. Most parents do worry: "I was concerned. He didn't walk until he was nineteen months old," reports one mother of an eight-year-old, born three months early. For her, it was a long wait.

Some babies barely crawl at all and then suddenly walk. Others will crawl for six months before they'll even make an attempt at a step. It depends somewhat on which form of locomotion works best for him. Each baby is different and has different skills and interests. Also, before he can walk your baby must reach a certain level of physical maturity. His skeleton must be strong enough to support his weight, his muscles must be developed enough to be ready to walk, and his coordination must be fine-tuned. Most kids love to push a chair on uncarpeted surfaces, and it gives them the support they need to walk an exciting distance!

As you watch your child's development during this time, you will probably be keeping an eagle eye out for problems to a much greater extent than you might with a term baby. As one mother explains, developmental milestones feel even more crucial to the worried parent of a premature child:

"As a parent of a premie, you look more anxiously for milestones. With my son, born at term, I assumed all was okay. With Caroline [born prematurely], I never made that assumption. I was always alert to things. I didn't shrug them off.''

Perhaps because of this, this woman's daughter was seen every three months during her first two years by a physician, a psychiatrist, and a physical therapist. They found some fine-tuning they wanted to do but basically Caroline never had any problems of serious concern. When small issues arose, therapy and time proved the solution.

''They noticed a laterality, a preference for one side over the other. She would pull to stand on one leg. Physical therapy was recommended. I remember it was held in a big room and I saw a three-year-old there having trouble walking. I wondered, would my daughter have that problem? I asked the therapist, but they don't like to answer,'' says Caroline's mother, emphasizing once again that she couldn't help but worry until each developmental milestone, such as walking, had been passed.

Eighteen months to twenty-four months after the due date. This is a time of intense and exciting development. Your child probably weighs about four times more than he did at birth. A rule of thumb is that at two years of age, children have reached about half their adult height. These figures are very rough, even for full-term infants, and may not have anything to do with your premie.

Your child's attention span very obviously is increasing, coordination is improving, and independence is developing. The nervous system is maturing, allowing for more refined motor skills. Still, don't expect too much too soon. Many parents find that coordination and gross motor skills can be a little slow in coming together. Says one mother:

''When my daughter was in physical therapy, they recommended that I play with her at home the same way. Because she was so premature, she had never been rolled up in a ball [in the womb]. She was all extension and no flexion. I would play with her by bringing her knees up to her chest and curving her shoulders around.''

Good toys for this developmental age include toy telephones, tool chests, toy shopping carts, typewriters, and cash registers, dress-up clothes, and other items that mimic real life and inspire imaginative play. Playing with other children is becoming more important at this age. Children still play alongside more than they do "with" other children, but they seem to enjoy the companionship and being able to observe others at play. They may even mimic one another at play, doing whatever they see other children doing. Having an older sibling or twin can advance this element of development remarkably. For example, Ashley was playing a modified form of hide-and-seek with Danielle by the time she was two years old and in general would try any form of play Danielle wanted to do with her.

Language skills are improving—the children may talk to one another now and not even include you in the conversation! Two-word sentences may be heard, and the child's ability to listen to and understand what you are saying has improved greatly. At this time, you may hear what sounds to you like speech problems—shortened or mispronounced words—but they are normal at this stage in development. Your child may say "ouch" instead of "couch" or "neen" instead of "Vaseline." This is simply immaturity. Try to teach by echoing back the right pronunciation—echo what he said before you answer him, but pronounce it correctly. Don't tell him he is wrong or act as if you're correcting him—calling attention to his mistakes will only frustrate him as he attempts to learn language. And don't make the mistake of talking baby talk back to him, either. Your child needs to hear proper speech so he can learn. If your child is stuttering, this should be ignored for now; do not act impatient. It is very common for toddlers, who are thinking faster than they can form or even find the words, to stutter. Just try to listen patiently. This stage will pass. To increase your child's vocabulary and grasp of the language, it is a good idea to speak to him in simple sentences that he can mimic, such as "Let's eat lunch," "It's time for bed," or "Take your toy."

Major spoilers of the fun you've been having with your toddler are tantrums. Two-year-olds, known for being contradictory, often find that their wishes clash with their parents' orders. When told to do something they don't want to do, such as leave the park where they've been playing, they may respond with a tantrum. This is because they haven't yet found a way to control their anger and frustration and because they can't even explain adequately to you how they feel, because of unfinished language skills. They also may scream and carry on because they see that it works. Bill and I had remarkably benign "terrible-two" years with our girls by following four rules of thumb: (1) we began setting limits long before the twos; (2) we didn't usually give orders—instead, we would give two choices, either of which suited our needs ("Do you want a story or a song now that you're going to bed?"); (3) we never contradicted each other's discipline, even if we disagreed (we would discuss it later); and (4) if all else failed, as quickly as possible we would get to a place where our two-year-old could be safely left "alone" to have a tantrum without an audience, including us. Without exaggeration, each of our girls has had fewer than three full, on-the-floor tantrums all totaled (granted, they are girls). This regimen may or may not be right for you, but in general, two-year-olds need the security of knowing that you will be fair, consistent, loving, and limit-setting.

Twenty-four to thirty months corrected age. According to conventional wisdom, you can now begin to compare your twenty-four-month-old premie with a twenty-four-month-old term baby. For the most part, I believe that you should be lenient and use the corrected age up to age three. Most parents will tell you that at twenty-four months their premies haven't really "caught up" with a term baby yet, and comparison can be very frustrating. I know that Ashley had not "caught up" by age two; by two and a half she had more than "caught up" in some developmental areas, still lagged in others, and was nowhere close to the norms for height and weight. (It was interesting to watch people's reactions to her at this stage; she must have seemed a bit like a wise little elf.) Different premies take different amounts of time to catch up and no premie will "catch up" in every area at the same rate. The amount of time each one takes is not necessarily related to how intelligent he is or will be.

Physical growth slows a bit after twenty-four months. Before, you could have measured and weighed your premie every month and seen impressive changes. Now, you have to wait almost six months to see a difference. Your child gains more inches between his first and second birthdays than between his second and third. At this stage, many parents, even those with term babies, become preoccupied with how tall the child is. Premie parents are often especially concerned because their toddlers are usually shorter and smaller than other children the same age. "Catching up" in height and weight can take a long time, and it is possible that some effects on growth may be permanent, albeit slight. It is very distressing to be told constantly that your child is "below the fifth percentile" in height or weight, which means that about 95 percent of children of his sex and (corrected) age are larger than he is. It is hard not to equate this with a problem or a failure. And it doesn't help when you tell another mother at the playground your child's age and she is visibly startled, as has happened to me. In our society, we often view height with more importance than it deserves. For boys, height and weight are in many ways falsely equated with manliness.

"Daren is all skin and bones," says one mother. "His brother, two years younger, weighs six pounds more than Daren does. Of course, it may just be hereditary. My husband, at six feet two, weighed only 135 when he graduated from high school. With the prematurity, I guess it's a double whammy."

We cannot change the way our society views size, so we must worry about the impact these views will have upon our premies. A small child may learn to view himself as weak and inadequate if parents even unconsciously suggest that bigger is better. Playmates and classmates can aggravate this problem by shunning the smallest of the group, making fun or making him self-conscious. Three- to five-year-olds, whether boys or girls, tend to view a big child as a worthy child. Help your child to a positive self-image by letting him know that you like his body just the way it is, especially because the person inside is so wonderful. Tell him (and tell yourselves!) that he may one day tower over the boys who are now taunting him. Give him a boost by telling him that even though he isn't big on the outside, he *is* big on the inside. One mother says she solved the problem of equating being small with being less important by playing up the amount of courage a premature baby must have in order to survive. She says, "I didn't want Caroline to hear 'small' and think 'weak,' so we'd say, 'You're a tiger, a fighter.'"

Now is an especially important time to explore what things your child might be good at, especially a certain sport, and encourage and support him in developing his skills. If you cannot control your anxiety about size, ask your pediatrician if he might refer you to an endocrinologist (yet another medical specialist!) for an estimation of your premie's potential final height. Your pediatrician may feel it is still too early for this assessment. If you do get an assessment, though, remember that it is a very crude estimate at best. Whatever happens, don't panic. Rather, help your child to achieve his potential, whatever that might be. And remember, the vast majority of premies grow up to be bright, normal, and sometimes tall adults. My husband was born prematurely, was short until just before college, and is now a towering six feet two inches!

With so much early pressure on weight gain, parents may continue to push foods—all kinds, all the time—so that their child will continue to gain weight. The result can be an overweight two-year-old. Don't stuff your child; obesity may commit him to long-term health problems that will cause harm long after you are gone. As a pediatrician, I have encountered many people who believe a fat baby is a cute baby. But in reality, all babies are cute; the goal should be for them to be happy and healthy. Avoid obesity by avoiding bad food habits—don't force your child to clean his plate, don't use sweets as rewards, don't rush your child through his meals. On the opposite side, if your child is "underweight," first ask yourself what you mean by this. If he is equally small in both height and weight and remains at the same percentile over time, he may not necessarily be underweight. If he is developing well in other respects, and his weight is proportionate for his height, I would not worry too much about his being underweight. Ashley is showing us that you cannot force a child to eat; if your premie is like her, try not to torment yourself—and your premie—by trying to push food into him. If your pediatrician finds your premie's growth is declining in comparison to his own past growth, it is time for you and your pediatrician to ask why. Has he been sick lately? Has there been a change in your lives that may have upset him? If so, just give him some time to catch up again. If not, it may be necessary to find out why he is declining from his percentile.

What should you do if you are worried about your premie's development? Ask your pediatrician. If you are both worried, or if you remain anxious in spite of your pediatrician's reassurances, ask your pediatrician if he would arrange a developmental evaluation. These evaluations are usually done by specialists who are well acquainted with the problems of premature children. The specialists who give these tests will be the first to point out to you that the tests are not really very accurate predictors of a young premie's eventual developmental outcome. They will tell you that very young children vary enormously from day to day and from tester to tester in this type of testing. These tests become increasingly accurate as the child gets older—but then so does observation. These tests are very inaccurate if done on children less than three years old. Also, the predictive value of the tests improves if they are repeated over time—for example, at yearly intervals. This will give the tester a better feel for how your child is progressing. Remember that development tends to come in spurts; the result at any one test time might have been very different if done a week or two later.

Language development and vocabulary are still increasing

but you may find that your child's verbal skills lag behind his social skills. It is not clear whether all of this is due to premie neurological immaturity. In some cases it may in part be due to the closeness you have developed with your premie; he may not need to verbalize his needs to you to get them fulfilled. If your child's speech is seriously delayed, however, it may be due to a hearing loss. Ask your pediatrician to have your child's hearing tested if you suspect that this might be a problem.

COMPARISONS: WHY YOU SHOULDN'T MAKE THEM

Every mother secretly or openly tends to compare her child with other children she knows or meets. Is that other child bigger? Taller? Smarter? Faster? The trouble with these comparisons is that someone always loses. If it is your child, you may show him you feel this way, even when you try not to. Remember that all children, but especially premies, develop at their own individual pace. One mother sums up her reaction to playground comparisons and bragging by other mothers this way:

"When someone says to me, 'Hey, my kid can do this and this . . . ,' I say, 'Well, your child was born healthy.' As far as I'm concerned . . . so what if my child is three months behind? It beats the hell out of being dead! Every child goes at a different pace. A premature baby spends so much time just trying to survive. Development comes when the child is physically able to do it."

Different children may concentrate their developmental energies on different areas; one may walk at nine months but not say more than two words until he's two, while another may talk as "early" as fourteen months but not walk until as "late" as fifteen months. Try to let your child develop at his own speed and wait for all his skills to even out and catch up with the rest of the kids his age. Don't push your child to catch up or to try a new skill before he seems ready to do so. Studies show that attempting to teach a child a skill before he's ready to learn it is extremely frustrating, with little gain. Wait instead until he's physically and emotionally ready and he will learn the skill much faster. I know you are anxious to see your child progress and to watch him pass milestones, but try to be patient and let nature take its course. Most important, remember that the greatest gift you can give your premie is supportiveness. Compliment and support him in his own special skills—not necessarily things he is better at than anyone else, but his own personal top skills. This kind of support can have a real impact on both his self-image and his ultimate developmental outcome.

SPOILING

You cannot spoil your baby if spoiling means fulfilling his needs, enjoying his company, cuddling, holding, and loving him. In my pediatric experience, however, I do see a worrisome number of children whose behavior is unnecessarily unpleasant and disruptive. I believe this occurs when parents do not set limits for children, do not discipline them, and do not teach them that living in a family entails responsibilities and thoughtfulness, even on the part of a toddler.

Because of all the problems a premie has had or is having, a parent's anxiety level can be understandably high. You may have more of a tendency to want to help and "baby" this child. One mother now sees that she may have done too much for her son. She says:

"I did so many things for him. So now he always wants me to help him. If something is hard for him, he doesn't want to do it. He gives up and lets me do it."

It can be especially difficult to tell what a premie needs, and you may unwittingly begin placing the needs of your premie unreasonably above those of other persons in the family, including yourself. In the early days, some of this extraordinary attention may be warranted and necessary. If you have other children, keep trying to explain why things have to be this way for now and remind them that the situation will not go on forever. But once the baby is thriving and your pediatrician is giving you a good prognosis, there's no reason to treat this child differently from any of your other children, who should also be having limits set for them. No longer must you jump at every cry, but neither should you ignore the baby or let him "cry it out."

Playing with your premie is *not* spoiling. These children need lots of interactions that encourage motor skills and visual/spatial development. Just don't forget to include the other children and your spouse along the way!

11. Twins and More

Before I went into medicine, I used to find twins and triplets exotic, fascinating, and enviable. I thought it would be wonderful either to be a twin or to have twins. Twinning is unusual, and certainly worthy of wonder. Twins occur in approximately one pregnancy out of every ninety. Triplets are rarer—occurring only once in every 8,000 pregnancies. Once I began to practice medicine and met the mothers of twins and triplets, I quickly realized all was not rosy for the parents. *Being* a twin may be a unique and wonderful experience; *having* twins is usually not as much fun—at least in those first tough years. Having one premie can be very hard, but having two or more at the same time is worse. In this chapter, we'll look at what can be done to make your life a little easier.

One premie causes enough stress, anxiety, and just plain work for two parents. More than one premie is a tough balancing act, but not an uncommon one for parents of premature babies. Among babies weighing less than 2,500 grams, one out of every seven is a twin. As you know, having a multiple pregnancy puts you at risk for premature delivery. So obviously, many, many premie parents before you have coped with multiples—and these parents have survived!

About one out of every three sets of twins are identical twins, meaning they came from the same egg and they look exactly alike. The rest are fraternal, meaning that they were from two separate eggs and may look quite different. No matter how much twins look alike, though, there will always be differences in their personalities and temperaments. Identical twins have different finger- and footprints, and often have different weights and heights as well. Frequently, you can't tell at birth whether twins are fraternal or identical. Even if they are both of the same sex and only one placenta was delivered, twins might not be identical. Sometimes the two placentas may have merged and appear to be one. If your twins are of opposite sexes, however, they are definitely not identical; they are fraternal.

When you first found out that you were carrying multiple fetuses, you may have been shocked. If you had any initial negative feelings, keep in mind that the negative feelings were about the situation, not your children—don't feel guilty. One mother says that when she discovered she was carrying triplets, she panicked.

"I was as white as a ghost. You can't imagine the panic. I thought I'd have to get rid of one. That first night, I couldn't go to sleep. All I could think was, I would have only two arms but three children."

Once they were born, you had more than one little baby to get to know. Premies, in general, are not easy to get to know in the early weeks. Gradually, though, you will see their very separate personalities and abilities come to light. Within days of their birth, your premies will probably show you how very different they are from each other, in terms of both their medical courses and their dispositions. One twin may do well while the other has many setbacks. One child may begin to respond to his parents sooner than the other. These differences can be very confusing emotionally to already stressed premie parents. This unequal balance can naturally lead to some initial differences in the way each parent gets along with the two babies. Do not feel guilty if you begin to feel closer to one twin than the other at first; being aware of this is a first step toward resolving it.

Once they're both home from the hospital, it's hard not to think of "the twins" as a unit, and it can be easy to overlook their uniqueness. You may feel like you have one baby but twice as much work rather than two separate babies. Do not be fooled by their similarities. Each will be very much his own person. Try not to dress them alike, and you may want to avoid giving them rhyming names—these things only add to the confusion between identities. And if you're having trouble telling them apart, try a trick in the beginning, such as painting one toe of one twin with fingernail polish. Later, you should be able to notice subtle differences—one will be taller, have a longer face, more hair, and of course each will develop his own "birth" marks over the first year. If you still have trouble telling them apart once they're old enough to understand, don't let them know. The thought that you don't *really* know who they are can be upsetting to small children. Try not to refer to them as "the twins"; use their names. Ask friends and relatives to do the same.

You may also be concerned about having to spend more time with one twin than the other. Often, the healthier twin is sent home before his brother or sister. You will usually respond more to the twin who responds to you and who comes home first. (Occasionally, however, parents may feel so sorry for the sicker twin that they begin to resent the healthier twin's "luck.") Once your sicker baby begins to get better and spend more time with you, you will become attached just as strongly to him. Until then, try to recognize and deal with your feelings, or seek the help of a counselor. One mother of triplets born prematurely explains how torn parents feel when some of the babies come home from the hospital before their siblings:

"Anytime you have children and have to divide your attention, you feel so guilty. Justin had to stay in the hospital after his brother and sister came home. The ones at home take so much time. You feel guilty neglecting the child who needs you.''

Once at home, one child may be more demanding or crankier and need more feeding, rocking, burping, and general attention. Will the quiet baby feel left out and unloved? Not if you realize this possibility exists and provide him with play interaction, talking, and stimulation. In all families, siblings have to learn to share the limelight, and parents learn to divide their love and attention among the children. Parents will tell you, though, that it *is* a juggling act! Says one mother of multiples:

"Once I had all three at home, things were in mass confusion. They didn't sleep a lot in the beginning. My son David was so emotionally attached to me. I joke that David still has the umbilical cord attached to me. Justin came home with oxygen and a heart monitor. He was in my sight more often than the others. When they were so small, I could handle them all—Justin in a swing with his heart monitor attached, David in the Snugli, Melissa in an infant seat.''

In my experience both as a mother and as a pediatrician, this necessary sharing of attention can be a very positive lesson and experience for children. Children with siblings learn patience and are taught the valuable lesson that the world does not always revolve around them. Twin or triplet premies are especially fortunate in that they have a ready-made close relationship that at times may even tend to exclude their parents and other siblings. They may have their own private language and signals; speech development may be slower because of this. This can be disquieting at times. While twin closeness should not be discouraged, the exclusion of other family members should be. That is not to the twins' benefit, nor to that of the rest of the family.

It is never good to "label" children, and can be especially harmful to twins. Calling one twin "the good one" and the other "the fussy one," or one "shy" and one "outgoing," starts a lifelong cycle that ignores each child's uniqueness and limits your view of your child's whole personality. Equally important, don't foster competition, asking one to "be more like your sister." You will make more problems for yourself than you ever imagined.

BREASTFEEDING TWINS

Don't worry about whether you will have enough milk for two babies. Nature and your body will cleverly provide just enough, by producing more milk to meet the demands of both infants.

"I'm as flat as a pancake but I breastfed my triplets. I was up four bra sizes! I pumped about every two hours and put the milk in bottles. I used an electric pump. Because I had help at home, I could breastfeed one while the others had bottles. At nine months, they were off the breast."

In the beginning, when they are too small or sick to feed at the breast, though, you may have trouble pumping enough milk for more than one child. Try not to give up—every little bit helps. Although your premies may need supplementation with premie formula, your milk can be split among them until they are able to stimulate your milk production by sucking at the breast. At that point, the more time you let them suck at the breast, the more milk your body will make. Although breastfeeding may be difficult at first, you may soon find it more comfortable and less work than bottle feeding—and eliminating work is critical when you have twins! Breastfeeding does not require you to sterilize equipment, measure powders, or wash bottles. Initially, you may have to pump between feedings, then have someone else give the expressed milk in a bottle to one baby while you directly breastfeed the other. If this is the way you handle it in the beginning, make sure you alternate which twin goes to the breast, so that the same one is not always breast- or bottle-fed. You will likely still have to supplement with formula; there is simply no time to pump enough milk for bottle feeding when you have twins. But once the babies are sucking actively, avoid this as much as possible so that your milk production will increase. If you breastfeed both of the children—and you should be able to do this fairly soon—feed them both at the same time and switch breasts between feedings. However, if one is a voracious eater and the other slow and fussy, you may have to switch in mid-feed or even feed them one at a time. The bigger eater of the two will ensure that your milk supply remains adequate.

To nurse two babies at once, try the following "football" position:

1. Find a comfortable chair with good back support and good arm support or prop yourself up on a bed, again with good support.
2. Put one infant to the right breast, with your right hand under his head. His body and legs should extend out, under your arm, rather than across your lap.
3. Place the other infant on the left breast, with your left hand under his head, and his body and legs extending out under your left arm, to your side.
4. Use pillows on each side of you, under their bodies for extra support.

Or you can try breastfeeding two the same way you'd breastfeed one. Place one baby in each arm, with one head at each breast. Cross their feet in your lap. Babies don't seem to mind this slightly squeezed arrangement, but this setup will become uncomfortable for you when the babies get bigger.

Switching breasts can be a little cumbersome when you are working with two babies. If someone is home with you, have them help get you set up and help you switch sides. Use pillows as well, to support your arms, your back, and the children's bodies. Once you find the most comfortable chair and the best way to use pillows, you'll be all set!

BOTTLE FEEDING

Many people do end up using some bottle supplements. If your babies interrupt each other's feeding when you feed them both at the breast at once, you don't really have much of an alternative. You can't be spending the entire day feeding them, and there is not time to pump for supplemental bottles. Also, using formula for a bottle feeding (remember to alternate which baby is breastfed) means that someone else can help out with feedings. If you have chosen to use only formula, you will quickly find that bottle feeding two at once when you're alone can be a chore. If you try to feed one first, the other howls until it's his turn.

To feed two at once you may want to prop each of them up in their infant seats. Sit on the floor between the two seats and give one a bottle with your left hand and the other a bottle with your right. Or prop the bottles and leave both your hands free to help whichever baby has trouble. You can also try propping the bottle for one baby while you hold and feed the other. Switch babies at the next feeding, so that the same one is not always offered the propped bottle. One mother of triplets had feedings down to a science:

"I'd line them all up and prop bottles. A couple of minutes into the feed, one would have to be burped. Then I'd put him down and pick up the next one. Feedings took about an hour."

Bottle propping can be difficult the first few weeks or months, especially if the baby has trouble sucking, can't keep control of the nipple, or knocks the bottle over. As your babies become better at controlling their mouths and arms, things will become much easier.

Make lots of bottles in advance and keep these in the refrigerator. Be sure to make enough in the evening to cover the night feedings, so all you have to do is warm the bottles up. Get a microwave if at all possible! However, be very careful not to overheat the formula and do mix it well and remember to check its temperature before giving it to the babies.

GENERAL FEEDING TIPS

Whether you are breastfeeding, bottle feeding, or both, feeding both your babies at once is usually the most efficient way to do things, and efficiency is the key with twins. Unfortunately, you're not cuddling them during this kind of a feeding, but you can talk and sing to them while they are eating. And you may be making more time in everyone's day for cuddling after the feeding. Burp them "in rotation," first one and then the other, halfway through and at the end.

Do not record intake, unless your pediatrician insists that this is necessary. You do not have the time and energy for this! In general, if your infants are both gaining weight, there is no reason to be keeping records.

When the babies begin eating solid foods, it's easiest to feed both babies at one time. You may find it much simpler to use one bowl and spoon for both. Although this runs contrary to my anti-infection instincts, if it's easier, do it.

BATHING

Although I love the look and smell of just-washed babies, when you have twins you may want to bathe them every other day and supplement their cleaning with sponge baths. Just be sure to keep the diaper area very clean with a soapy washcloth, followed by a very thorough rinse with another wet cloth. Also be sure to clean the neck as well, where folds of skin can hide dirt.

Until your babies can bathe together in a tub, it can be a real race to try to give both babies their baths without lots of crying and fussing from one or the other. The most important things to remember are to bathe your infants at the same time and to schedule baths when you have help in the house. Do baths one after another, but have your helper feed or hold one baby while the other is being bathed. Then switch. Make sure all diapers and towels are standing by, ready when bath time ends. If you don't have help, keep one safely in his crib or playpen while you wash the other and just try to close your ears to the screaming. Once the twins are old enough to sit up well, they can both go in the bath together. You may want to use plastic bath seats to help ensure against slippage. After all, you have only two hands!

SLEEP

Working out a sleeping schedule for one baby just home from the hospital can be a nightmare. Trying to get two to go to sleep and wake up at the same time will seem an impossibility! In the NICU, bright lights and noise were the infants' companions twenty-four hours a day. Often, just as they fell asleep, someone would come by and wake them up for a test or a treatment. In addition, the two babies probably responded differently to the NICU and developed different sleep patterns. One probably went to the intermediate-care nursery—and home—earlier. Once in a home environment, this premie's sleep patterns almost certainly evolved very differently from his twin's. Suffice it to say, long periods of sleep are not going to be second nature to these babies. Still, it's very important to try to extend sleep periods as soon as feeding schedules will allow. Two premies will simply exhaust you; you need all the uninterrupted sleep you can get. You will not survive this first year of premie-dom if one of the premies is always awake! In the beginning, you may have to wake one of them for feedings, thereby interfering a bit with his preferred sleep patterns. Within a few months, though, both babies should be in sync.

Parents of twins seem to be divided on the likelihood of one twin's waking the other one up at night. Some have told me that their infants can be in the same room and learn to sleep through disturbances made by the other twin. Some parents even put two twins into the same crib for the first few months. If you have only one crib and are waiting for a second, you might have to do this for a while as well, but also consider options like a travel bassinet. If you do have both twins in the same crib, you may want to fashion a midway divider, using a crib bumper tied across the middle.

Other parents of twins have told me that the toughest part of their first two years of twin parenthood was the constant waking of one twin by the other. (Interestingly, waking of one twin when the other twin's monitor went off was not a common problem.) If one twin *is* waking the other up every night, creative arrangements may have to be made, such as putting one of the twins in a bassinet in your bedroom. If you have sufficient room, the ideal would be to put them in their own rooms, or to put each in with an older sibling. Older siblings usually can handle the noise. For both night and day during the first few months, you may prefer to have the babies sleep in bassinets (separate ones, of course). Bassinets fit their size better than cribs, and if one baby is napping in the daytime while the other is awake, you can easily wheel or carry one bassinet to another room. Also, at night, this will give you more flexibility in trying out various sleeping options until you find one that works. Most of all, remember that you must get some sleep. If the above suggestions don't work and you've run out of your own ideas, ask your pediatrician and friends for advice.

LANGUAGE DEVELOPMENT AND SCHOOL

Twins are generally exceptionally close to each other as children, which has its good and bad points. Language may be delayed because twins can often communicate with each other through their own private language or without using any language at all. As mentioned above, this can leave both you and the other siblings out. More important, it means that your twin children will not have the breadth of relationships and experiences that might aid their development. So try various ways to get them to interact with others. Have each share a room with a nontwin sibling. Arrange individual play dates with other children, so that they have a reason to learn how to communicate and socialize with others. Remember that their closeness per se should not be discouraged. You just don't want them to limit their relationships to each other!

One twin will usually dominate the other. If this is the case with your twins, it may be to their benefit to have them in different classes once they enter school. This separation will also help their social development. Discuss this in advance with their teachers and principal. If there are not two classes at the same level in the school and it would be too expensive or time-consuming to put them in different schools, work closely with your children's teachers to maximize the individuality, special abilities, and development of each of your twins.

One mother of twins says she kept them in the same class for nursery school but is not sure yet what would be best for them in kindergarten:

"They didn't really separate from each other. Once when I was there, I saw all the other kids sitting down listening to the teacher read a story while Matthew and Grace were off doing their own thing. . . . They love being together. I think Grace wants to *be* a boy! . . . We try to take them on separate jaunts just to get them off by themselves. In kindergarten, I may put them in separate classes."

DIAPERS AND CLOTHES

Buying disposable diapers for twins is convenient but it can get very expensive. You might think about getting a large number of cloth diapers and using them. Ask your friends for all the old diapers they can spare. You'll need to have on hand enough to last two to three days; otherwise you'll be doing washloads continuously! Don't bother ironing or folding the diapers.

Do avoid the urge, and often the pressure from grandparents, to dress your twins the same way. They can share clothes, though, even into older life if they are of the same sex and approximately the same size. That way, you can have one set of drawers for both and don't have to worry about separating washed items into "his" and "his."

EQUIPMENT

You really don't need me to tell you that you're going to need two of everything: two carseats, two infant seats, two cribs, two walkers. If your home has two levels, you may also want some equipment upstairs and duplicates downstairs, so that you don't have to run up and down the steps all the time. It is especially useful to have two or three changing areas, with diaper pails, located strategically around the house. Unfortunately, this all means added expense. *Do* ask people if they might have some items you could borrow. Acquaintances may not think of it if you don't ask, but are sure to be more than willing to help out when you do ask. Also, buy used items when you can.

Double strollers are available—either side by side or front and back. Side-by-side ones can be too wide for some store doorways. Front/back ones can be cumbersome to open, close, and store. Since both tend to be expensive, try them out carefully before you buy. An alternative, at least for some occasions, is a Snugli or backpack for one and a stroller for the other. Also available is a Snugli front carrier for twins, so you can have one on back and one on front. (But as your twins get heavier, this is a good way to get shoulder aches; two backs—or fronts—are better than one!) Remember to alternate which child is in which location for all of these. Choose whatever combination works best for you. One mom of triplets suggested to me that a front/back stroller is definitely worth the investment. She pointed out that walks—and lots of them—are a great way to entertain twins or triplets without exhausting yourself. As for storage problems, her stroller was rarely closed anyway! She found both front and back Snuglis too difficult to use without help getting the babies in and out. When her triplets were older, she would put one into a backpack (you can lift it on by yourself from a table) and the other two infants into the front/back stroller and take them everywhere.

While I am not a playpen advocate, a playpen is a necessity for twins. A larger, fencelike "corral" is even better, if you can find one. (A corral can also be put around danger spots such as a Christmas tree, to keep the kids out of harm's way.) Once twins start crawling, it's just too hard to always keep an eye on both at once. Also, twins seem to enjoy playpens more than singles do—they have company when both are placed in it together. A playpen will give you a few minutes to do something for yourself or maybe even sit down! Take advantage of every moment of peace. If you continually fuss over your infants, you will never last the year! If you do use a playpen, begin putting your infants into it for short periods when they are three or four months old (corrected age), so that they get used to it.

Don't forget the importance of safety items. Childproof your house carefully: lock away medicines and poisons, cover outlets, and get gates for the tops and bottoms of all stairs. Two infants are impossible to watch every second—and accidents happen to people who are tired and stressed.

GETTING HELP

Far and away, the major comments I have heard from parents of twins have focused on their exhausting, all-consuming, never-ending childcare responsibilities. There is no time for yourself; there is no time for your spouse; there is no time for the other children; there is no time for sleep or pleasure. If you have twins or triplets, you *must* have help. You just can't take care of these babies alone. Maybe you can get a neighbor or a church member to help out if you can't afford to hire anyone. If you can't swing full-time help, get part-time help.

If your family can help with the babies, hire someone to help with the housework. Don't be proud. Call on all your resources—your mother, your relatives, your friends. But get help. You need it! One very wise mother with triplets *and* older children, who has survived her triplets' infancies, recommends that you take out a loan if need be to pay for help—and even for evenings out. She said that she and her husband initially felt embarrassed to tell anyone they did this, but in retrospect feel it was the smartest thing they ever did. Their loan is now paid off—and their sanity was maintained.

Enlisting help is good—taking everyone's advice is not so good. You may receive a lot of well-intentioned remarks from relatives and friends about how you should handle your situation. One mother bluntly tells how she feels about all this unasked-for advice:

"The best tip I could give other mothers is that no matter what you're doing, as long as you're doing something, you're not doing wrong. If your baby is responding, to hell with everyone else. Mine was a special situation. My feeling was, 'If you had triplets, I'd be glad to listen to you, but nobody knows what my babies are like.' "

Husbands and wives should support each other in this demanding job of being parents to two premature infants. Even if the mother is home with the infants and the father works full-time, he should participate fully in childcare during his home hours. Caring for twin premies is at the top of the list of stressful, exhausting jobs! Here's how one couple split up some of the workload in the early months:

"Mark is self-employed so he was able to work his schedule around our triplets. When two came home from the hospital and one was still there, we would take turns—one would go in and the other stay home."

If Dad cannot be there in the daytime, a lot can be done on evenings and weekends. Mom and Dad should encourage one another, not criticize. Now is not the time to be a perfectionist—remember that everyone is cranky. You should also remember to spend some time alone together as a couple; a cheap date is better than no date at all. So what if you end up talking about the kids all evening out? At least you're out!

Since a husband and wife often differ in their reactions to things, talk to each other about how you are feeling and why. It is especially important that the parents resolve their own feelings toward each premie early, since the twins themselves may need your help to resolve similar feelings of anger and guilt toward each other as they grow. This is especially true if one of them is healthy and the other either does not live or survives with long-term disabilities.

Your life will also run more smoothly if, as the children grow up, they learn to help out, too: by behaving. Says one mother of her children:

"There are certain things they realize as multiples. I can't afford as much leeway in discipline. They are aware that they have to cooperate. If they don't we can't go. There are no discipline problems. They realize this is the way it has to be."

HANDLING OUTSIDERS' QUESTIONS

Once you're the parent of a twin or other multiples, you come into the public eye. People are drawn to the sight of two or more babies, all the same age, out together for a walk. You may become known as "the triplet mom" or "the twins' mother." People may come up to you and talk to you— sometimes they will ask personal questions, make tactless remarks. Other times they may marvel at how well you handle parenting.

"Compliments are nice, but you get humbled when you hear other stories, about mothers of triplets with spina bifida," says one mother, whose children, now age three and a half, are physically and developmentally normal. Most of the time, though, she says, you do not hear compliments, only startlingly personal questions: "The fact is that people ask the stupidest questions. They'll say, 'Oh my God, did you find out early on that you'd be having triplets?' 'Do they run in your family?' 'Were you on fertility pills?' Most of the time I say, 'No,' but I *was* on fertility pills. My infertility is not anybody's business. I'm five feet tall and weigh 118 pounds. People say, 'You're so tiny—how'd you have them?' I was enormous when I was pregnant—170 pounds! How did I have them? What choice did I have not to have them?"

Your children may hear a lot of these same comments as they grow up. You will have to know how to help them handle their uniqueness. This mother was prepared for the worst—and took steps to protect her triplets. She says:

"I was very aware that what people said would influence them. I knew that people would say things like 'triple trouble' [in front of them] so I always answer, 'No . . . triple treasure!' When people moan, 'How do you handle them?' I say, 'They're excellent children!' Because I realize that what they hear about themselves is so important even at a young age."

SUPPORT

For information, support, and news, you might want to contact:

The Triplet Connection
P.O. Box 99571
Stockton, California 95209
209-474-0885

They have a quarterly newsletter and packets of information for expectant moms and mothers of newborn multiples. Or contact:

National Organization of Mothers of Twins Clubs, Inc.
12404 Princess Jeanne Avenue
Albuquerque, New Mexico 87112
505-275-0955

They have a quarterly sixteen- to twenty-page newspaper, and are a clearinghouse for information on multiples. They can send you information and/or refer you to a local chapter for support.

12. Ongoing Problems

As technology has improved, so has premie survival. Smaller and smaller babies are living, thanks to advances in the field of neonatology. There has been some concern that this increasing survival rate is being won at the cost of long-term disabilities for many children. But the statistics strongly suggest that this is not the case. Only 6 to 8 percent of babies born weighing less than 1,500 grams will have some ongoing disability, and rates of severe disabilities have declined in recent years.

Ongoing and long-term problems are often related to complications of, and therapy for, prematurity. Some premature babies are at greater risk than others. In this chapter, we discuss some of the ongoing disabilities premature children may face. The first half of this chapter includes problems that usually disappear in the first few years of a premie's life. The second half provides information on long-term, perhaps lifelong, complications of prematurity.

RESPIRATORY-TRACT PROBLEMS

Upper-respiratory-tract and ear infections are common problems for all young children, but occur more often in children born prematurely. These problems are relatively minor and your child will eventually grow out of them. Still, respiratory problems certainly make parents anxious and they can affect your premie's growth, plaguing him long after he is healthy in all other respects.

Several studies have shown that premies visit their doctors more often than full-term infants and toddlers do. It is unclear how much of this may be due to the high level of anxiety and concern felt by many premie parents. Studies also show that premies are treated for otitis media (ear infection) more often than full-term children. In one study, 19 percent of the premies studied had persistent ear infections (infections that did not clear up immediately with antibiotic treatment). Other studies have reported that as many as 50 percent of premies have recurrent otitis media (infections that recurred soon after medicine was stopped). Again, it is unclear whether premies are more susceptible to ear infections or whether parents of premies are simply quicker to go to the doctor when their child is sick. Many parents do say they are more cautious with children who were born prematurely than they might be with a term baby. One father confesses:

"I still have this feeling that anytime anything comes up I want to get her to the doctor right away. Objectively, I see she's passed all the major danger points. It's not a rational fear but it's there."

For all children, premie and full-term, problems with ear infections usually disappear by the time the child reaches school age. This is because the development of a child's facial/head structures make him less and less susceptible to ear infections with increasing age. In the meantime, though, parents learn to cope with more frequent colds and infections. One mother complains:

"David was born with immature lungs and had hyaline membrane disease. At age three and a half, he will still keep a cold longer than his brother and sister."

Another mother noticed that her daughter had a tendency

to get sick—and stay sick—more often than her brothers or sisters born at term. This mother says:

"She was very tiny for a very long time. She was always sick—pneumonia, bronchitis, ear infections."

One mother, though, found her premie surprisingly *less* susceptible to the common cold:

"He's a very healthy little boy. He has always been healthy. He gets maybe one cold a year. He didn't get his first cold until he was three years old. Once I told his doctor that I think it's because of all the medicine they gave him his first three months of life!" We hope that you and your premie will be as lucky.

Premies who had respiratory problems during the first weeks of their lives may be predisposed to pulmonary infections and/or to lung hyperreactivity (wheezing, "asthma," etc.) during the first few years of life. Problems that do occur appear to be related to oxygen and ventilator therapy. This therapy is changing rapidly, so it is not clear whether a premie born today would still be at risk for these problems. Also, as with ear infections, any problems that do exist usually disappear by school age.

A more serious problem related to oxygen and ventilator therapy is *bronchopulmonary dysplasia* (BPD). BPD occurs in 6 to 24 percent of babies treated with oxygen for respiratory distress syndrome. (See Chapters 3 and 5.) It is most common in the smallest, most premature infants, who receive prolonged ventilatory therapy, but it can occur in infants who were never ventilated. BPD is a complicated lung disorder that involves a maldistribution of oxygen in the lung tissue and, in severe cases, fibrosis (or scarring) of microscopic lung areas. The severity of BPD can be determined by X ray and by a child's degree of dependence on oxygen supplementation. It is, in general, a bad sign if an infant still requires oxygen supplementation after five months of age. A number of children do come home from the hospital on oxygen and this is something parents must learn to deal with. Says one mother:

"Justin came home on oxygen. Home nurses would come in and check on the oxygen. The worst part was, every day I had to rip the tape off his face and put new tape back on. But you do what you have to do."

In addition to oxygen therapy, children with BPD may also require theophylline and/or diuretics at home. Fortunately, lung tissue has remarkably good regenerating powers in the first year of life. Also, BPD frequently looks worse on an X ray than it actually is. Usually by school age, both the child and the X ray are completely normal. Until then, however, a premie with BPD may have problems with lung infections and/or hyperreactivity. A lung infection is extremely difficult to diagnose by X ray in these children, so if your premie has acute symptoms, your physician may sometimes treat for pneumonia, to be on the safe side. As many as 70 percent of infants with BPD require rehospitalization in the first two years of life, usually for respiratory symptoms. Children with BPD often require a diet high in calories, since they use up a great deal of energy just by breathing. At two years of age, children with BPD are generally in only the tenth percentile for weight and tenth to twenty-fifth percentile for height; but by three years of age the average weight of children with BPD does not differ from that of other children. Respiratory function is usually normal by three to ten years of age.

Some extremely premature infants need prolonged ventilator therapy over the first several months of life and, occasionally, this long-term intubation may cause the upper airway (trachea, or windpipe) to become scarred or narrowed. In this situation, it may be necessary to place a small hole (a *tracheostomy*) into the trachea below the area of narrowing, through which the premie can breathe until the narrowing resolves or can be repaired. A tube is placed in the tracheostomy site in the neck; the baby breathes through this tube. A parent will usually be frightened and intimidated by this tube at first, but should feel comfortable with it by the time the baby comes home. For one to several days before discharge, both parents should assume sole responsibility for the cleaning and care of the baby's tracheostomy. It is essential that the area be kept open and clean. This is done by suctioning the tube and airway and washing the area surrounding the opening.

HEART PROBLEMS

If your premie was born with a *congenital heart defect,* his surgeons may well have decided to delay surgical correction until he has grown somewhat. While he is growing, your premie may need to be on medication to help his heart function. As he grows, the doses of these medications may need to be increased; your baby's physicians will guide you. Doctors will also tell you about the signs of "heart failure," requiring a rapid evaluation by them. These signs include too-rapid weight gain (a sign of fluid overload, not real growth), breathing problems, wheezing, and/or arm, leg, and abdominal swelling. Once your premie has grown, his heart defect can probably be repaired and these worries will be in the past.

INTESTINAL DISORDERS

As discussed in Chapter 3, *necrotizing enterocolitis* (NEC) is an acute intestinal disorder occurring in the first weeks of life. NEC is more common in premature infants. If NEC was suspected in your premie, his oral or tube feedings would have been temporarily stopped; usually this solves the problem and there are no long-term complications. Occasionally, however, NEC may not improve with this therapy and instead the intestines rupture or necrose (die). In this uncommon situation, surgeons would remove the dead bowel (intestines) and can usually then reconnect the healthy bowel remaining. It doesn't take a great deal of bowel for food to be absorbed, but occasionally too little bowel remains for good food absorption. This is called *short-bowel syndrome,* a condition that can obviously interfere with weight gain and also causes chronic diarrhea with the undigested food. In extreme cases, the infant may need to be fed at home with intravenous hyperalimentation feedings, through a central intravenous line (see Chapter 5), or with a special liquid diet by mouth, which is easily absorbed and contains all essential nutrients and vitamins. In some cases, it is impossible to reconnect the bowel at the initial surgery when the dead section is being removed. In this situation, the lower end of the bowel is closed off and the upper end is attached to the surface of the abdomen. This is called a *colostomy,* through which the baby's stool can be collected in a sac. Children with colostomies will have a higher rate of symptomatic gastroenteritis (stomach flu) with certain viruses.

Happily, an infant's intestines have amazing recuperative powers. Thus, short-bowel syndrome usually resolves itself in the first few years of life, and babies with colostomies can usually have the ostomy removed and the bowel reconnected in the first few years of their lives. Eventually, you and your child will not even notice the small colostomy scar left behind. The emotional scars and growth effects can last much longer, however, so it is important not to think of your premie as abnormal or a "freak" during this time. It is also important to give him support if and when other adults and children make comments. (For more on scars, see the next chapter.) Reassure him that this will not last forever and that he is wonderful with or without an ostomy, with or without short-bowel syndrome.

If your premie has a central line in place for feeding, you will have to keep it and its site of entry into the skin scrupulously clean, as aseptic as possible, and covered. Your physician will tell you about signs of infection, requiring a trip to his or her office for an evaluation. These would include tenderness or redness at the site of entry, fever, etc.

If your premie has an ostomy, you must learn the art of caring for it. Keep the opening clean by washing with regular soap and water on a washcloth. Commercial wipes may be irritating; if you want to use them, opt for the hypoallergenic, unscented ones. Change the bags frequently. Both the intestinal fluid and the adhesive used to hold the bag in place can irritate the baby's skin; skin irritation occurs more than 40 percent of the time. Try lotions or ointments, such as petroleum jelly, on the irritated areas. Make sure you have a tight-fitting tube to help prevent leakage. Get more advice from the medical staff on how to avoid irritation; talk with nurses who specialize in handling gastrointestinal problems. Each one may have a trick to share or a recommendation for a good ointment.

For more information, contact:

> *American Digestive Disease Society*
> *7720 Wisconsin Avenue*
> *Bethesda, Maryland 20814*
> *301–652–9293*

LIVER AND KIDNEY PROBLEMS

Hepatitis is an inflammation of the liver, usually related to an infection or reaction to a medication. It may last for only several weeks or for months. Symptoms include jaundice, fever, vomiting, diarrhea, and general malaise. A premie is at heightened risk for hepatitis because of infection, medications, and the use of "intralipid" (an intravenously given fatty nutritional solution). The infections causing hepatitis occur either before or after birth, and include infections caused by viruses that may contaminate blood products used in transfusions (not the AIDS virus). There is no medical treatment for hepatitis, except removal of the cause and, possibly, giving the premie a restricted diet. Like premies' lungs and intestines, premies' livers have great recuperative powers. Rarely is damage to a premie's liver long-lasting.

Kidney damage may also occur, albeit rarely, in children born prematurely. Being born prematurely in and of itself does not increase an infant's risk of kidney dysfunction. However, a number of the problems associated with prematurity, such as infection and the side effects of some medications, can occasionally lead to kidney damage. Also, if your premie was very ill and had either extremely low blood pressure or a cardiac arrest, his kidneys might have been temporarily damaged. Again, kidney damage is usually not extensive or long-lasting.

For more information, contact:

> *National Kidney Foundation*
> *30 East 33rd Street*
> *New York, New York 10016*
> *212–889–2210*

LONG-TERM DISABILITIES

Some of the most heartbreaking complications of prematurity are most often related to central nervous system (CNS) bleeding or infection. (See Chapter 3.) The most common long-term complications related to the CNS are retardation, hydrocephalus, seizure disorders, and cerebral palsy. Hyaline membrane disease and intrauterine-growth retardation also put a premie at higher risk of these serious disabilities. In general, the earlier a premie is born and the less a premie weighs at birth, the greater the risk of his having these complications.

Intraventricular CNS bleeding (see Chapter 3) occurs in up to 50 percent of premies born at less than 1,500 grams or at less than thirty-three weeks gestation. Luckily, only the most severe bleeding is associated with long-term neurologic disabilities. Most severe disabilities will be very obvious in the first year of life. Rates of severe disability have been dropping in recent years and in most studies now run between 6 and 8 percent for premies born at less than 1,500 grams.

Hydrocephalus Hydrocephalus, as explained in Chapter 3, can occasionally occur as a result of CNS bleeding or infection.

Hydrocephalus is caused by a blockage in the flow of the fluid surrounding the brain. If the blockage does not resolve itself, a shunt is placed surgically to keep the excess fluid from pressing on the brain tissue by moving the fluid to a place where it can be readily absorbed, usually the abdomen. Fortunately, it's uncommon for a shunt to be needed. For example, in one study of 438 infants, only five of those with intraventricular hemorrhages developed hydrocephalus and none required a shunt. If your premie does have a shunt, your physician will tell you what to look for as an indication of possible shunt infection or blockage. Symptoms would include appetite loss, irritability, pain when moving the head or at the shunt site, vomiting, disorientation, or fever. You may also be asked to bring your child in for periodic sonograms (ultrasound) or X rays to be certain the shunt is working.

This system of checking on the shunt can be a real help, as one mother found out firsthand:

"We knew when they put the shunt in Eric that there was no guarantee that it would always work. As it happened, he developed a trapped ventricle. We had been going into the hospital every three months for ultrasound and we just happened to hit it when it happened. Otherwise, I would eventually have seen symptoms of a trapped ventricle—Eric would have become lethargic and begun vomiting. We were lucky that it occurred during an ultrasound. That was on Thursday. He went into the hospital for brain surgery the following Monday. Still, it felt like yet another setback. You have to wonder: When does it end?"

A shunt may be removed in a matter of months or it may have to stay in place for years. If it does need to be kept, it will be replaced every couple of years, to allow for your child's growth. The placement of a shunt is a serious, but not excessively dangerous, surgical procedure and requires the use of general anesthesia. A shunt per se should cause no long-term problems. While there is always a risk of infection, this risk should be weighed against the fact that hydrocephalus, left untreated, usually leads to mental retardation. Fortunately, many

premature kids with shunts have no problems with infection—
and no retardation.

Seizure disorders   Seizure disorders are usually controllable
with various antiseizure medications. If your premie has a seizure disorder, his seizure therapy should be followed closely by
a neurologist, who will alter medications and doses as needed.
Each of these medications usually has noticeable side effects,
which range from sleepiness to hyperactivity to skin rashes to
gum overgrowth. One goal of therapy is to minimize side effects, so do share your concerns and observations with your
child's neurologist. Changes in medication or dosages can be
made. The long-term outlook for a child with a seizure disorder
varies with the cause and nature of the central nervous system
injury that led to the disorder. Only your child's neurologist
can give you a prognosis for your premie, and this prognosis
will probably require repeated testing and observation over
time. Remember that a seizure disorder does not make your
child retarded; his intelligence can be completely normal. Try
not to be overprotective and try not to make him feel "different." Explain his problem and its cause to him, his friends,
his teachers, and his classmates. Try to help them all understand and accept his situation. As with all the problems we are
discussing, patience, understanding, and acceptance are key to
a healthy and happy child.

Cerebral palsy   Cerebral palsy is a disorder of muscular control. Premies are at an increased risk of cerebral palsy. Of
babies born with a birth weight of under 1,500 grams, about 2
percent will develop cerebral palsy, compared with about 0.4
percent for all babies. About 15 percent of those weighing less
than 1,000 grams at birth will have some degree of cerebral
palsy. As with retardation, hydrocephalus, and seizures, it is
the complications of premiehood, not premiehood itself, that
cause cerebral palsy. The lateral ventricle of the brain is the
area most vulnerable to CNS bleeding. This area is right next
to the nerves controlling the motor function of the legs. It is

thought that this is the reason premies have an increased incidence of leg spasticity, but usually normal arm tone. Cerebral palsy may be diagnosed early, sometimes before your baby leaves the hospital, but usually the first clues appear at around three or four months corrected age, when newborn reflexes would usually disappear and the baby would normally begin to use his extremities more actively and purposefully. Milder degrees of cerebral palsy may not be apparent until even later, when motor milestones aren't reached, especially when the child would normally begin to walk. The severity of cerebral palsy can range from uncoordinated clumsiness, to a slight tremor in one arm or leg, to "toe walking," to crippling handicaps. Up to a third of children with cerebral palsy may have a seizure disorder, but most children with cerebral palsy have normal intelligence. This intellectual normality can be at once heartbreaking and a comfort.

"When we left the hospital with our daughter, we were not expecting anything else to be wrong with her. But when Emily still couldn't sit up at the age of one year, we knew something was wrong. We took her to a university hospital to have her evaluated. The doctor there said, 'Has anyone ever told you that your daughter has cerebral palsy?' No one had, but we knew that, whatever you want to call it, something was wrong. She began to go to therapy. First, we were told that she'd be walking by her second birthday. But she wasn't. It made me feel like—what else should we be doing? She's three now and is able to walk about twenty-five steps independently, kind of on her tiptoes. She also crawls and walks on her knees. She has an imaginary friend who walks standing up. Now doctors want her to have surgery to cut the muscles in her thighs and heels, then put her in a cast. They say this will lengthen her short heel cords and correct her legs, which turn in. The therapists, on the other hand, suggest only some special metal boots and more therapy. We don't know what to do."

On other levels, though, her daughter is developing beyond her years:

"By twenty-four months Emily was talking at a three-year-old level. She was talking in paragraphs when most kids her age could only say a few words. We knew she was smart and that made us feel better.''

There is debate whether early physical therapy is effective in reducing the degree of handicap, but therapy beginning in infancy is usually recommended. An infant-stimulation program—including motor, sensory, language, and cognitive activities—may be equally effective. You should repeat with your child at home what the therapist does, either by setting aside a special time for the exercises or, even better, by incorporating them into daily activities and playtime. Until more is known about the effectiveness of physical therapy and of infant-stimulation programs, it might be best to participate in both these types of programs, especially if your child has spastic diplegia, which is the kind of motor defect most common in premies. (There are four main forms of cerebral palsy: spastic, athetoid, ataxic, and flaccid.) Sufferers of spastic cerebral palsy experience stiffness in their muscles and have trouble moving affected limbs. If facial muscles are affected, speech will also be affected. While cerebral palsy is not "curable," its prognosis is not necessarily bad. The outlook is highly dependent on the cause and degree of neurological deficit. For example, if a child has "mild" cerebral palsy at two years of age (e.g., is able to walk), the prospect of him "outgrowing" his cerebral palsy by school age is quite good.

For further information, contact:

The United Cerebral Palsy Association
66 East 34th Street
New York, New York 10016
212-481-6300

They can provide information and pamphlets explaining what cerebral palsy is, and other educational materials, as well as referrals to centers providing diagnosis and therapy in your area.

VISION PROBLEMS

Visual impairment, caused by retrolental fibroplasia (RLF, also known as ROP—retinopathy of prematurity), may be a sorry side effect of treatment in the NICU. (See Chapter 5.) The relationship between high levels of oxygen and the occurrence of RLF has been recognized only in the last five years, and the exact reason for this is not clear. It seems that high oxygen and perhaps other, as yet unsubstantiated factors—such as high ventilator pressures, time on the respirator, transfusion therapy—cause the blood vessels in the eye to proliferate (multiply), potentially leading to retinal scarring and detachment. Luckily, the incidence of RLF has decreased since its association with high levels of oxygen was discovered. Now, a premie's blood oxygen levels are monitored closely and only strictly necessary amounts of oxygen are given. As with the other long-term problems we are discussing, the risk of RLF increases as prematurity increases and birth weight decreases.

Each year about 2,600 infants have some visual loss and more than 650 are blinded by RLF. But more and more premies are surviving, so these figures, although sobering, mean that RLF occurs in only 2 to 3 percent of babies born weighing less than 1,500 grams (three pounds five ounces). The degree of damage from RLF is scored on the basis of serial eye examinations and is as follows: grade 1, often causing myopia (short-sightedness) correctable with glasses; grade 2, sometimes causing mild to moderate uncorrectable myopia; grade 3, localized retinal detachment with vision of 20/200 to 5/200 (significant myopia); grade 4, retinal detachment (often causing blindness). Ninety percent of cases of RLF will disappear spontaneously. Scarring from RLF will occur in 2 percent of babies born at 1,000 to 1,500 grams, but less than 1 percent of these babies with scarring will be blind. Of infants born weighing more than 1,000 grams, fewer than 1 percent will end up blind. As much as 90 percent of the time, infants with RLF simply improve by themselves, without treatment.

Early surgery can make a big difference in the outcome of

severe RLF, so the American Academy of Pediatrics recommends that all babies who were treated with oxygen and who were born at less than thirty-six weeks gestational age or 2,000 grams should have eye exams done at seven to nine weeks of age. Those born with a gestational age of less than thirty weeks should have an eye exam every three to four weeks until two to three months postterm, when the retina is mature. Although your baby was probably tested for visual loss while in the hospital, impairment may not have been apparent at that time. Vision problems can be difficult to notice until the child is older, so he should be checked again at six months. Vitrectomy, a type of eye surgery in which bloody fluid is removed from the eyeball, is often used in treatment of the advanced stages of RLF. Recently, cryosurgery has been proposed as a highly promising therapy for RLF, reportedly reducing the risk by half for infants with grade 3 disease of having retinal detachment, folding, or scarring. Cryosurgery involves freezing blood vessels that are growing excessively within the eye. So, between prevention and treatment measures, RLF promises to become an increasingly rare problem for premies.

Rarely, loss of vision is due not to RLF but rather to other problems such as CNS bleeding, an intrauterine infection, optic nerve atrophy (scarring down of the nerve to the eye) associated with cerebral palsy, or a vascular-embolic accident (a blood clot traveling to the brain). The severity of the visual problems may range from eye changes that improve with time to retinal detachment and blindness.

A blind baby will need to learn to use all the other senses available to him—touch, smell, sound, and taste—to relate to the world around him. With proper help and support, he can develop normally, although he may crawl or walk a little later than other children.

Premies have an increased incidence of minor visual problems, including refractive errors (nearsightedness, farsightedness, etc.) and ocular muscle (muscles around the eyeball) dysfunction. In many cases, this is related to RLF. Premies with even mild RLF have an increased incidence of myopia, strabismus (eyes not focusing together), amblyopia, and other oculomotor problems, usually correctable with surgery or lenses. Studies vary as to whether premies without RLF have an increased incidence of these problems. In unusual cases, the visual problems may be a result of cerebral palsy affecting the muscles of the eye.

At home, you might notice certain signs of eye trouble, which you should point out to your pediatrician. (Ocular motor defects may come and go, depending upon your child's level of fatigue, so these problems may not always be picked up in a routine examination.) If your child doesn't focus on his toys, doesn't respond to light, crosses his eyes all the time, frequently rubs his eyes, has red or watery eyes, or strains his neck and cocks his head in an attempt to see an object in front of him, you should mention this to your pediatrician. Some ocular problems cannot be corrected unless they are treated early. For example, if your child is unable to focus both his eyes together, he may have a visual defect known as strabismus. To be effective, treatment for strabismus *must* be given early and may include patching of the stronger eye to improve sight in the weaker one, surgery, or eyeglasses. Even one- to three-month-old babies can be fitted for glasses! Here's how one mother describes her toddler's adjustment to glasses:

"He started wearing them when he was eighteen months old. They told us [from the start that] he might need them because he'd had oxygen. They tested him and told us he was developing a lazy eye so we got glasses for him. He was real good about it. I told him he couldn't go outside unless he wore his glasses. So in the beginning, he didn't wear them in the house but he did outside until he got used to them. Now he wears them all the time. He can see better with them. One eye's real bad."

For more information contact:

American Foundation for the Blind
15 West 16th Street
New York, New York 10011
212–620–2000

National Association for the Visually Handicapped
22 West 21st Street
New York, New York 10010
212-889-3141

American Academy of Ophthalmology
Box 7424
San Francisco, California 94120
415-561-8500
Information on eye care and eye disease.

HEARING LOSS

Some hearing loss may occur in 1 to 4 percent of premies. It can be caused by a congenital defect unrelated to prematurity, an intrauterine infection, or a postbirth infection of the central nervous system or ear, or be the result of trauma (usually at delivery) or a complication of antibiotic therapy given for an infection or a suspected infection. Recently there have been reports of occasional hearing loss associated with therapy for PFC, or persistent fetal circulation, a type of pulmonary hypertension more common in full-term infants than premies, but not uncommon in the first weeks of life. The cause of the hearing loss is unclear, but it occurs after discharge from the hospital and progresses over a period of several months. There has even been speculation that some hearing loss may be the result of the noise levels in the NICU. Your baby's hearing will be tested while he is in the hospital, but you should have it tested again after you have brought your premie home, at around six months of age. Usually, the test used assesses the baby's response to, or movement toward, sound. A "brain stem evoke response" test can also be done. This measures a baby's brain-wave changes in response to sounds. These tests are quite reliable. Your pediatrician should have information on where these tests can be administered.

Very often, especially with progressive hearing loss, parents are the first to notice a problem, so you should also be attuned to signs that your premie may be having hearing problems (especially given the relatively high rate of ear infections in premies, which can be associated with treatable hearing loss). Does your premie turn toward a noise? Does he respond to noise in any other way? Does he respond to the sound of your voice? Did he coo and babble to himself at three months corrected age and up? Did he begin to talk at the appropriate age? Does he have frequent earaches? When he talks, does he always talk too loudly or too softly? (Be careful on this one: many normal children do not modulate their voices well. It's a learned art.) If you suspect hearing loss in your premie, even if previous tests were normal, ask your pediatrician to repeat them.

The only curable hearing loss mentioned above is one resulting from chronic ear infections or serous otitis media (fluid collected behind the eardrum) associated with ear infections. Certainly it would be a shame not to have this diagnosed quickly, since it is so easily corrected. Unfortunately, all other hearing losses are usually irreversible. But therapy is available in the form of hearing aids and speech therapy. Providing therapy as quickly as possible to a child with hearing loss is extremely important for maximizing his intellectual, social, and emotional development. A child with a severe hearing loss or deafness may need to learn sign language and lip reading, so that he has languages with which to communicate.

For more information contact:

The National Association for Hearing and Speech Action
10801 Rockville Pike
Rockville, Maryland 20852
800-638-8255
Information on hearing and speech problems and referrals to speech-language pathologists or otolaryngologists (ear, nose, and throat specialists).

National Association of the Deaf
814 Thayer Avenue
Silver Spring, Maryland 20910
301–587–1788

HOW TO FIND A SPECIALIST

If your child has an ongoing problem, such as one of the ones mentioned above, a pediatrician may not be able to provide you with all the care you need. You may need to find a specialist as well, one who should work closely with your pediatrician. Some of the reasons you might want to find a specialist include:

1. A problem for which your pediatrician is unable to diagnose the cause.
2. A problem for which surgery is suggested or necessary.
3. A chronic disease.
4. Any illness that your pediatrician believes would be better handled by a specialist.

As we have discussed in previous chapters, a specialist is a doctor who has not only received the usual four years of medical school and three to four years of residency ("specialty") training, but also spent an additional two to six more years concentrating on a particular "subspecialty." Some specialists see only children and are called pediatric specialists; others will see both children and adults. Illnesses that may require a specialist range from nearsightedness to recurring middle-ear infections to asthma to unusually slow weight gain. If your child needs a specialist, talk with your pediatrician about it. Your pediatrician will likely recommend someone with whom he or she feels comfortable. In the unlikely case that he cannot recommend someone, or if you are not comfortable with the person he recommends, here are some other methods of finding a specialist. (Remember to ask the specialist the same sorts of questions you would when interviewing a pediatrician; see Chapter 9.)

1.   Call a university hospital for a referral or to find out if it has a university clinic handling a certain problem.

2.   Get in touch with nonprofit organizations founded to assist in funding research and providing education on the medical problem your child has. These groups may be able to refer you to specialists in your area. They can also provide you with pamphlets and other educational materials and advice.

3.   Look in the *Directory of Medical Specialists*. This book, published by the American Board of Medical Specialties, is usually available in the reference section of your local library. Board-certified doctors are listed by specialties, along with a brief biography of the individual, including the name of his or her medical school, and the awards, honors, and positions that they themselves choose to list. (It is very personality-related; I put none down.)

4.   Ask another mother for a recommendation.

The following is a list of some of the specialists your child may come in contact with or need in the first few years of his life:

ALLERGIST/IMMUNOLOGIST: for problems in fighting infections, for recurrent or chronic infections, allergies, asthma, etc. (Not all allergists are also trained in immunology.)

CARDIOLOGIST: for congenital heart defects and other heart problems. A cardiologist does not do surgery, but does do catheterization studies. (A thoracic surgeon would do the heart surgery, if this was needed.)

DERMATOLOGIST: for skin problems.

ENDOCRINOLOGIST: for problems of poor growth, short stature, or metabolic defects. An endocrinologist deals with endocrine glands, most of which affect growth directly or indirectly.

GASTROENTEROLOGIST: for diseases of the esophagus, stomach, liver, and intestines.

HEMATOLOGIST: for anemias, low platelet counts, or malignant diseases (cancer).

INFECTIOUS DISEASE SPECIALIST: for the treatment of serious, rare, complicated, or recurrent infections.

NEPHROLOGIST: for kidney disease.

NEUROLOGIST: for the treatment of nervous system diseases, seizure disorders, etc.

OPHTHALMOLOGIST: for eye disease and surgery.

ORTHOPEDIC SURGEON: for noninflammatory bone, joint, and skeletal system problems.

OTOLARYNGOLOGIST: for chronic, severe, or recurrent ear, nose, and throat problems, especially if these will require surgical therapy.

PEDIATRIC SURGEON: for routine surgery, such as hernia repair, or subspecialized surgery, such as heart surgery. A pediatric surgeon has additional specialty training in surgery specifically on and for children.

PLASTIC SURGEON: for cosmetic or reconstructive surgery, including the repair of external congenital defects.

PSYCHIATRIST: for mental, behavioral, and psychosocial disorders.

RHEUMATOLOGIST: for inflammatory joint, bone, and skeletal disorders, such as arthritis.

UROLOGIST: for diagnosis and treatment of problems of the genitals and urinary tract.

Some organizations that may provide you with information or referrals to physicians in your area are:

American Heart Association
7320 Greenville Avenue
Dallas, Texas 75231
800–527–6941
Information, educational materials.

American Society of Plastic and Reconstructive Surgeons
233 North Michigan Avenue
Chicago, Illinois 60601
800-635-0635
Information, brochures, referrals.

American Psychiatric Association
1400 K Street, N.W.
Washington, D.C. 20005
202-682-6000
Information and educational materials.

American Academy of Orthopaedic Surgeons
222 South Prospect Avenue
Park Ridge, Illinois 60068
312-823-7186
Information, publications, no referrals.

American Academy of Dermatology
P.O. Box 3116
Evanston, Illinois 60204-3116
312-869-3954
Information, referrals.

American Urological Association
1120 North Charles Street
Baltimore, Maryland 21201
301-727-1100
Requests for information answered by personal letter.

American Lung Association
1740 Broadway
New York, New York 10019
212-315-8700

13. How Healthy Is Healthy?

It is possible that even some healthy premies may face some long-lasting problems, such as learning problems and behavior disorders. We all want the best for our children; it is difficult to accept the fact that our premie may have done better in school or life if he had not been born early. It is hard not to ask "What if?" Obviously, you desire "only the best" for your children and, as such, you may find parts of this chapter distressing to read. But in reading it, keep in mind that all the information currently available about school-age premies is, by definition, somewhat outdated. All the long-term studies we have at present reflect NICU care from ten to fifteen years ago. They are not necessarily relevant to children who have been in an NICU of the late 1980s or early 1990s. So the data I will be sharing with you pertain to your premie in only the most general way. Advances in and refinement of premie care may lead to shorter, less traumatic, less dangerous stays in an intensive-care unit and fewer complications from a premie's early birth. There is every reason to think that this will add up to fewer long-term differences between premature children and term children.

A quick look back at the history of premie care will show

you how far we have already come and how different the outcome is for today's premies. Prior to about 1965 there was really
no such thing as "newborn intensive care." Ventilators were
not used routinely until after the early 1970s. Respiratory therapy is still advancing, with surfactant therapy and, on the next
horizon, something called extracorporeal oxygenation therapy
(in which blood is oxygenated outside the body, through a machine). Other medical advances in premie care have occurred
in the recent past and continue to occur. Intravenous lines also
began to be used in the 1970s, and central-line technology and
hyperalimentation continue to advance. Sophisticated newborn
surgery has been possible only in the last five years. So, in a
very real sense, any conclusions made about "long-term" outcome for healthy premies is based on premies whose care was
very different from that of your own. The problems that a
premie born ten to fifteen years ago faces may be very different
in nature and degree from the problems your premie may be
facing in ten to fifteen years.

WHAT WILL THE FUTURE HOLD FOR YOUR CHILD?

Many parents wonder, long after the medical crises of
prematurity have been resolved, if their child will continue to
develop normally. Will the effects of prematurity or its related
problems be more far-reaching than originally thought? It's
very hard to tell, from the available statistics, what the future
will hold for your child.

We do know that premature children now in school seem
more likely to have learning disabilities and may perform slightly
below the level of term children in school. We also know that
premies' motor skills, even using corrected ages, tend to lag
behind those of full-term children. In addition, visual and spa-
tial perceptions and skills are not as good as those of full-
term children of comparable corrected age, even as late as seven
to nine years of age. Studies also show that premies' IQs, as a

group, are several points lower than those of full-term siblings, even at ten years of age. Most of the studies on development, however, do not take into the analysis the very important fact that many premature babies are born to poor, young, uneducated, single mothers (a population group that is at greater risk for having premies). Disadvantaged backgrounds are associated with delayed development even in term babies. Also, developmental differences at ten years of age do not necessarily persist into adulthood. And, as stated above, we have no idea how changes in modern medical care may affect development, in either a negative or a positive direction.

There are, however, no good ways to predict which premature child will develop slowly, have a low IQ, or have a functionally important problem (other than those with obvious retardation or nervous system damage in the hospital). There is really no way for you to know where your premie will eventually lie on the developmental spectrum.

It's best to consider your child's development as unique, rather than as being "behind" other children or "slower." A premature baby is *different* from a term baby in early development because he has a *different* start on life. But the term baby is not better and the premie is not backward. Whenever you start to look at your child as being behind, there's the risk that you can turn it into a self-fulfilling prophecy. This is not to say that your expectations should exceed your child's abilities; rather, they should not fall short of your child's abilities. This can sometimes be a difficult balance to strike.

Without a doubt, NICUs are not ideal places for newborns to be. With a heavy concentration on the baby's physical needs, the NICU staff must often overlook the emotional and developmental needs of the baby, and this may result in developmental problems later in life. This is of course part of the reason we stressed your role as a parent in counteracting the effects of this environment. For example, remember that one of the most outstanding problems facing a premie's early emotional and intellectual development is thought to be the constant level of stimulation in the NICU. This little baby who is

extremely sensitive to any kind of stimulation is by medical
necessity subjected to fairly constant and often painful stimuli—bright lights, mechanical noises, blood drawing and other
procedures. He is handled by multiple caretakers. He has poor
visual stimulation, between the glare of bright lights and the
barrier of his isolette's Plexiglas. He has no day/night cycle of
light and activities. Depending upon his state of alertness, development, and health, he may retreat from stimuli and be
unresponsive or, alternatively, overrespond to stimulation.
Some parents find that their children continue to have trouble
dealing with too much stimulation on into early childhood.
This mother of an eight-year-old explains:

"Daren prefers to focus on one thing at a time. Something
really catches his interest and that's it. Whenever Daren got
excited as an infant, he'd get stiff and shake—almost like a
spasm. He still does this. We're working on that. The only
thing I can do is remind him not to do that. He's getting older
and I think he's growing out of it."

Another mother found that her son had a similar reaction
to excitement and stimulation. She says:

"We have seen in Matthew some problems with irritability, overstimulation. Sometimes he'll be dancing around to
music and just lose control of himself. He starts sobbing at the
same time. I have to hold him real tight and take him to a
quiet place. Now that he's four it doesn't happen too much
anymore but the other day he was dancing to 'La Bamba' and
he just lost it. It was very frightening for him because he knew
what was happening, he knew [he was out of control]."

You, like these mothers, may notice some aspect of your
child's behavior or development that seems to be the result of
his prematurity. You may see some differences between your
baby's development and a term baby's development. These
differences don't have to stop your premie from being successful or happy. This may sound very pat, but it is the only
way to live comfortably as a premie parent. Try to make peace
with the fact that sometimes differences do exist; you will never
know if they are related to your child's "premiehood," but

putting pressure on your child or trying to make the differences "go away" can only be harmful to you, to your child, and to your relationship.

This does not mean that you should not get him all the help you can. If he is having problems in motor, speech, or perceptual development, therapy may help in a very tangible way. Ask your pediatrician or school personnel for referrals and advice about special developmental or educational programs, therapists, or tutorials. Most important, look for your child's singular abilities; praise him and encourage him in these. Children want nothing more than to please their parents; your premie will sense your anxieties about him and interpret them as disappointment in him. As he gets older, he will be aware of "how he measures up" to the other kids. Like all children, your premie needs to feel good about himself or his development *will* falter, but not because he's a premie—rather, because he sees himself as a loser.

SCHOOLING

Your premie should start preschool whenever you feel he's ready, but let the school know he's a premie and remind the teachers of his corrected age. Trying to place a two-year-old premie in a class with other two-year-olds may begin a cycle of frustration and isolation that should be avoided. Allowing your premie to be the oldest child in the class, especially during preschool through kindergarten, may be a wise idea. As with all judgments, it depends upon your premie.

Schools should be told that your child was born prematurely, so that they can use his corrected age when gauging your child's developmental level. One mother from New York City, where admission to private schools is competitive, says she hesitated telling the school about it during the admissions process:

"I wasn't going to volunteer the information until after she was accepted because I didn't want it to prejudice them.

But when I was filling out a school questionnaire, I came to a question that asked, 'Was there anything unusual about the pregnancy or birth?' I thought a moment about what to do. What should I say? I answered honestly. She got in anyway in spite of it, maybe because of it. The director of admissions was very impressed by my answer. She called me and said, 'We don't foresee any problems with Caroline but we felt that if there were a problem, you were the type of parent we could work with.' "

Once in the school, you might want to make sure the teachers are keeping an eye out for any learning or developmental problems. Says one mother:

"I told the teachers, 'If you see something, tell me. Don't assume that it will go away. Tell me about it.' For example, I saw that she wasn't as adept at beads and basket weaving as other kids, but when I spoke to the teachers, all I got were platitudes. 'She's fine,' they'd tell me. It turns out some of her muscle strength needed building. She was in therapy—squeezing tennis balls. Now we give her piano lessons—that's more fun than the tennis balls."

Teachers may also need to be reminded occasionally of your child's prematurity when problems or difficulties crop up. For example, one mother who says her son is academically on a par with the kids in his class but socially very immature, says the prematurity often needs to be brought up again with new teachers:

"Teachers know what being premature means. Some are real good at coping with kids who are a little different, but others aren't. His kindergarten teacher was. But in first grade, his teacher called me to say Daren was rolling in the aisles and that she couldn't control him. I called his old kindergarten teacher and she said that he just needed a little extra time to cope with a new environment, that he would settle down in a few days. Sure enough, he did."

Sometimes, teachers may be too hard on your child and this has to be dealt with, too. As a parent, you may have to step in. As one mother explains:

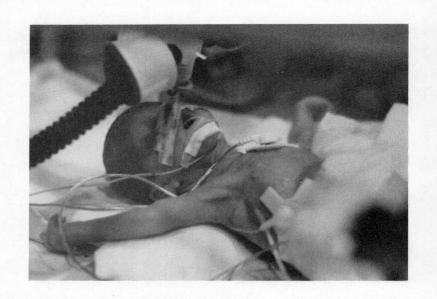

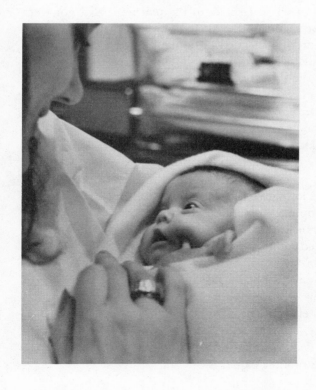

"In kindergarten, they noticed that Caroline holds her pencil in a slightly unorthodox way. I felt it was possible that, because of her prematurity, she just didn't have the muscle or nerve control to hold it any better. The teacher's mindset was that my daughter was just being obstinate. I stepped in and talked to the school about it. I said, 'Her handwriting is fine . . . can't we just move on?' In third grade it came up again because of how she holds her pencil. They always want to improve her grip. I'm not opposed to their trying, as long as we're not just playing the same old record."

Another school issue that may come up: deciding which age group to keep your child with. It's not always easy to know what grade to place a child in or when to keep him back. As I said before, it's usually better to make some allowances during

Caroline: at two weeks, at thirteen weeks, and again at eight years, with her six-year-old brother.

the early years, when possible. As the child gets older, though, the decision becomes more difficult. As one mother says:

"Daren acts very immature and is a real loner. The school suggested we keep him back a year. But he can do the work. I don't know what to do. I think Daren would know we had kept him back and that wouldn't be good. He's very bad at math, though, and staying behind might help that. I need help deciding."

At school, physical education and sports may be another area where your premie has some difficulties. Often, the gross motor skills are slow to develop. Many parents complain of problems climbing, skipping, swinging, and the like. One mother I know of sums it up by saying; "She can no more do a sit-up than fly; she's not a jock." Another finds that not being good at sports has caused some social problems for her eight-and-a-half-year-old son. She says:

"The other kids want to run and play tag. He doesn't. He pretty much keeps to himself. His gross motor skills are awful. He still has trouble swinging. He can't get the top part of his body and the bottom part of his body going at the same time. Sports are not for him. He can't seem to coordinate his arms with his legs. Something just doesn't seem to connect. He used to run on his toes—little itty-bitty steps—because of stiff muscles in the back of his legs. Now he's good at running."

As your child grows up and the effects of his prematurity or related problems are diminished and become inconsequential, you will not need to mention prematurity to a school. In other words, he's not going to be writing it in on his college application!

LEARNING DISABILITIES

"She's a horrible speller!" says one mother of her daughter, now eleven. "I try to blame it on the prematurity," she laughs.

It *is* hard to know whether learning problems are related to prematurity or whether problems would have existed even if your baby had been born on time. There is some evidence to suggest, however, that premies may be at greater risk for certain learning disabilities.

Learning disabilities are neurological disorders affecting a child's motor, visual-spatial, perceptual, language, cognitive, and/or abstract reasoning skills. This definition of learning disabilities is long and complex, in part because learning skills are not independent of one another. From birth, a child learns by interacting with his environment—the people and the things around him. It is very unusual for a child to have an isolated learning disability. Skills used in exploring toys are related to skills later used in reading; language skills are related to all the complex interactions you have with your baby, even from before his first coo and smile. Abstract reasoning is related to all these, as well as to all the whys and hows your premie asks as a toddler and growing child.

Physicians usually cannot point to a single brain lesion or defect that causes learning disorders, so these disabilities are instead described in terms of the child's responses to standardized tests. When we go over studies on learning disabilities and behavior disorders, remember that the results are based on standardized testing. While these tests are related to how your premie functions—for example, how he is doing in school— they are not great predictors of how he will be doing in school ten years from now or in later life. When done as a battery, rather than singly, these standardized tests are useful in three ways: (1) in describing a child's learning function *at this time* (longer-term prediction does improve as the child's age increases, but, then, so does prediction based on school grades and observation!); (2) in pointing out areas in which a specific child might need special help; and (3) in comparing *groups* of children (e.g., premies versus full-term).

The risk of learning disorders increases with decreasing gestational age and birth weight. Also, like other disabilities, learning disorders are associated with the complications of prematurity—respiratory problems, fetal hypoxia (poor oxygen levels prior to delivery), infection, and CNS problems. Five to 20 percent of nonretarded premies weighing less than 1,500 grams at birth subsequently have some learning disability. In one study, 49 percent of premies in this weight group had some problem in language comprehension and/or visual-motor integration. It is not possible to predict which individual infants and toddlers will have enduring disabilities.

Let me explain this point in a bit more detail, since I am sure that you, like me, eagerly wish someone could predict your premie's future. First, a premie with mild problems in infancy—even if these are associated with clinically apparent neurological dysfunction—may do perfectly well at school age. Unfortunately, the converse is also true: normal development in infancy does not guarantee a normal IQ or normal intellectual functioning. Now let's go on to studies that tested school-age premies, as opposed to younger children.

The children tested in these studies were usually born in the late 1970s, long before many medical advances that are now routine. Now that we have been reminded of this, let's look at the results. In one study, 92 percent of premies performed normally, in normal classes. But 47 percent of these normally performing children were also receiving special educational assistance after school hours. In another study, teachers assessed 32 percent of nine-year-old premies with birth weights of less than 2,000 grams as needing special education, compared to 12 percent of full-term children. A third study evaluated premies born at less than 1,200 grams when they were four, eight, and eleven years of age. It found that 28 percent were delayed more than six months on their receptive vocabulary scores, 43 percent were delayed this amount on their visual-motor integration skill scores, and over 20 percent were delayed this much on achievement testing. These percentages didn't go down as the children got older. Studies comparing the IQ test results of school-age premies to those of children born full-term consistently show the premies scoring five to twenty points lower, but these studies rarely take into account the economically disadvantaged backgrounds of many premies. Studies comparing premies to their own sibs, however, do show that premies *as a group* score ten to fifteen points lower on IQ testing than do their siblings.

So what does this all mean in terms of your premie? Well, if you're like me, it means that you have taken some deep sighs in reading the above paragraphs. First, let me point out again that individual children can change radically over time. For example, in one study of premies more than eight years old who had IQs in the normal range, about a third improved on subsequent testing, about a third stayed the same, and about a third declined. Also, even if your premie seems to be lagging developmentally or in school performance, early intervention—by you and by therapists—can make a difference. This is part of the reason I have gone into so much detail on your role as a premie parent, and why I have described how you can interact with your premie, to help his development from the day of birth, through toddlerdom, and now through school age.

Share your concerns with your premie's teachers; seek their opinions and advice. Be sure they know your premie's background in preschool. By school age, however, your premie's teachers will not be making allowances because of his premiehood. What they can and should do is help you in having your premie evaluated; assist in getting him special education and/or therapy, if this is indicated; and work with you and his therapists in maximizing your premie's potential. Help him accept the fact that society will not make allowances for his early birth, much as you might wish it would. Life is not fair, and he has had to deal with that reality from the day of his premature birth. Second, he must feel that he has your love, respect, and support, for all the wonderful things about him as an individual. He must feel secure that you will help him maximize his own potential—and that you will be proud of him in the process.

For more information, contact:

> *The Association for Children and Adults with*
> *Learning Disabilities (ACLD)*
> *4156 Library Road*
> *Pittsburgh, Pennsylvania 15234*
> *412-341-8077*

Dyslexia.   Dyslexia is a learning disability that makes it difficult to perceive written language correctly. Reading problems occur. A dyslexic may see a *b* but perceive it as a *d,* for example. This inverting is very common and normal for all children below the age of five or six. Contrary to what some people think, premies are no more at risk for dyslexia than are term babies. One cautious mother tells how she discovered this firsthand:

"I noticed my daughter reversed her *b*'s and *d*'s. The teachers told me it was normal for that age and it is . . . but I wanted to watch it. She outgrew it."

BEHAVIOR DISORDERS

Problems such as hyperactivity, attention-deficit disorders, and sleep disturbances are more common in children born prematurely. These difficulties are more apt to surface in boys than in girls. Males, both premie and full-term, are at higher risk for behavioral disorders. As with learning disabilities, early intervention is the key, but it should be based on a competent and thorough medical evaluation, diagnosis, and follow-up. Medications may be indicated, but should not be prescribed unless a thorough medical evaluation is done first and an appropriate medical specialist recommends it. One mother is now trying to decide whether or not medication may be of help in her son's case. She says:

"Daren is very bright verbally—he's been reading since he was four—but he's a little hyperactive. He's always running circles around me. They suggested Ritalin for hyperactivity. They said it would help him control his excitement. Maybe we'll try it. Maybe if he has it for a little while, he'll be able to look around and see what the other kids are doing.''

HEIGHT, WEIGHT, AND APPEARANCE

As we mentioned in Chapter 10, your premie child's height and weight may lag behind those of his peers and may not be comparable to those of his siblings, even in adulthood. You can never know how much of this might be due to his premie birth. Certainly these differences can be upsetting for a growing child, but reading about the severe problems in Chapter 12 may help you see your premie's growth from a slightly different perspective. Being short is not a handicap unless you and your premie turn it into one. Review Chapter 10 for advice on how to deal with this problem and which specialists can advise you as to your premie child's growth potential or predicted final height. Remember that being tall is simply not all that important, even in our macho society—and then work with your premie to convince him!

Some premies will have to live with physical scarring as a result of their time in the NICU and operations as a child. This may or may not pose a problem for you or him. Other children may notice the scars when he grows older and ask about them. If you have always treated the scars in a matter-of-fact way, your child probably will as well.

''My son still has a little X-mark in his chest from where they cut in to get to a main artery. He also has pockmarklike scars on the bottom of his feet from all the times they took blood gas tests. He had a central line out through a vein in his skull as well and there are spots where his hair doesn't grow. (The rest of his hair covers this now.) He never has questions about the scars. [Children] accept a lot. Rather than being teased, I would think he'd get sympathy. My premies also had little flat heads. That lasted a long time but they grew out of it."

Another parent, a father, has developed a wait-and-see attitude:

"She's covered with scar tissue. It doesn't bother her yet. But I hope someday to give her plastic surgery—maybe when she's thirteen or fourteen."

A mother whose daughter has no scars noticed, though, that her daughter's eyes seem unusually big:

"Premie eyes—I think all premies have it. The eyes kind of bulge out. I think it stays with them, though it becomes less pronounced."

I'm not sure there really is such a thing as "premie eyes," in a long-term sense. "Premie eyes" are probably due, at least in part, to a lack of fat on the face. In the beginning, the prominence is more noticeable. Later, a lot of people find prominent eyes a very attractive feature.

14. Should We Have Another Baby?

When we had Ashley I was shocked that two premie dads whose children were in the nursery with Ashley—"older" but first-time fathers—were electing to have vasectomies rather than risk the emotional trauma of another premie child. Two fathers at one time may have been unusual, but it was heartbreaking to see these two couples make a permanent decision during a time of crisis. I strongly encourage you to think through your decision about having more children *after* this immediate crisis has been resolved.

If you are now at a stage when you are ready to consider having another child, there are some issues you must face in making your decision. The most important of these is to realize that now that you have given birth to one premature baby, you are, at least theoretically, at increased risk of having another, if you become pregnant again. To be more precise, you have a 25 to 50 percent chance of going into preterm labor with your next pregnancy. This statistic alone can be enough to frighten you away from the idea of another pregnancy. Keep in mind, though, that this risk is for *all* women who have a premature delivery, no matter what the underlying cause. Many causes of premature delivery can be treated or managed medically or by behavior changes. If you go back to Chapter 1, you will quickly get a feel for this. Also remember that the statistic above means that *most* women classified as high-risk have normal pregnancies and deliver term babies. In one study, 40 percent of mothers of infants weighing less than 1,000 grams decided not to get pregnant again. Of those who did become pregnant again, though, more than half had healthy term babies. A little over 20 percent had another premie. Twenty-eight percent miscarried.

You will have an advantage in this pregnancy: because you know that you are at risk for premature labor, you and your doctor will be able to take extra precautions to prevent another premature birth.

One mother gave birth to her first child, Emily, at only twenty-nine weeks gestation. By the time she was twenty-two months old, Emily had a new baby sister:

"We always wanted to have more children. I didn't really plan to have them this close together, but that's the way it happened. When I got pregnant, I was sure I'd have another premie. I chose a doctor for high-risk pregnancies, and was even more cautious than the doctor. I didn't exercise, I didn't travel, I didn't drink Cokes, I didn't eat junk food. Ansley was born on time and healthy on February 20. She's a year old now, walks, and says a few words." This mother says she will go on to have more children.

Before you (and by this "you," I mean both Mom and Dad) consider another pregnancy, you'll probably want to give the possibility of another premature birth some very serious thought and discussion. Would you, your marriage, your family, and your finances be able to cope with another premature and possibly sick or disabled baby? How would another premie affect the children you already have? If your premature baby has any long-term difficulties as a result of his prematurity, will you have the time and energy to mother a second child, even if that child is born at term and healthy? Are you concerned about your own health? Have doctors cautioned you about becoming pregnant again?

"I would never ever have another baby," says a mother of three. Her first two children were born on time but her last child, Jonathan, was born eight weeks early, weighing five pounds two ounces. He spent three weeks in the hospital before he was sent home with a clean bill of health. She says:

"If I got pregnant again I'd be afraid the same thing would happen. I had a horrible pregnancy, contractions on and off since the fourth month of pregnancy, constant fatigue, high blood pressure, an unidentified rash all over my whole body, and a month on complete bed rest in the hospital. Everything went wrong."

Despite all these sorts of concerns, some of you may long to experience the joys of another child. I understand this well. For the first two years after Ashley was born, I felt that fate had been kind to us once and I would never again take a chance of having another premie. But children are such delightful creatures that even impressive risks seem worth taking, after the memories of those early premie months have finally dulled. One couple who thought they couldn't have children saw the birth of their first, a premie, as an especially happy event. As the father explains:

"We didn't think we could get pregnant the first time but we did. After Jessica was born prematurely, bam! A surprise! A second pregnancy. We were concerned . . . and very much afraid, but we wanted another. My wife really took it easy. A lot of bed rest. Julia was born on time. There was no stark terror. I'm so glad it happened that way. My wife really enjoys motherhood so it was nice for her [to have a term birth]."

So, for whatever reasons, you may decide to get pregnant again. If you do, you probably want to choose a perinatologist, or a specialist in high-risk pregnancy, to provide your care in this pregnancy. You will want the most advanced care possible, to avoid another premature birth and make the event of a premature delivery as safe for you and your baby as possible. You should probably scout out an obstetrician or perinatologist before you actually become pregnant again. Talk with this doctor about your last pregnancy and get some advice about how a second pregnancy would be managed.

HOW TO CHOOSE AN OBSTETRICIAN OR PERINATOLOGIST

You might want to stay with the same doctor who delivered your premie. On the other hand, you may prefer to look for a doctor who routinely handles high-risk deliveries. Get recommendations from friends, from your obstetrician, from the state medical association, and from the neonatologist who cared for your premie. Then call and try to arrange a few interviews. (Realize that obstetricians may charge you for this visit, so ask ahead of time about the fee. It is unlikely that it will be covered by your medical insurance.) As mentioned above, choosing your doctor should be done *before* you get pregnant, so that you aren't under any pressure to make a snap decision about your doctor and so that if anything can be done to decrease or eliminate your chances of a preterm delivery (e.g., surgical procedures), there will be time to do it. Ask him or her many of the same sorts of questions you asked your pediatricians: Where did you go to medical school? Where did you do your residency in obstetrics? Do you have additional training in high-risk pregnancies? If so, from where? Are you board-certified in obstetrics? Are you board-certified in perinatology? What is your fee? Where do you deliver? Does that hospital have an NICU? Who are your partners, what is their training, and where did they train? Who sees your patients on routine visits? What is the delivery rotation when patients go into labor at night or on a weekend?

Most important, you should get a sense of whether you want to be with this person through pregnancy, labor, and delivery. Can you talk to him or her? Does he or she discuss things and explain clearly? Are both you and your husband comfortable with him or her? After all, this could be a stressful pregnancy and delivery.

Make sure you talk with the doctor's nurses as well. It may be the nurse who will speak with you when you call in with questions or symptoms. How do the doctor and nurses seem to respond to patients' questions? Do they appear to take patients' complaints seriously? Much of the success of your second pregnancy depends on your ability to recognize premature labor and your doctor's ability to trust your instincts and to see you immediately, no matter how many times it turns out to be a "false alarm."

Once you have selected an obstetrician, he or she will need your old records, will examine you, will do some tests, and will ask you to come back to discuss his findings. At that visit, voice every question or concern you might have. It might be good to have these written down in advance and to take notes on the answers. If your husband cannot be there, you may wish to record the conversation. For example, ask the obstetrician how your pregnancy will be monitored. What, if anything, can you do to decrease your chances of another premature birth? Would your high-risk status mean that you can't use a birthing room even if all is going well? If you had a cesarean section last time, does this doctor feel you could have a vaginal birth this time, if all is going well? At what gestational age does the doctor aggressively intervene to save the baby? For example, if you went into labor extremely early, at twenty to twenty-five weeks, what steps would the doctor take? Would your wishes or desires be included in the decision? The doctor probably will not be able to give you a pat answer to all this, but you will get a feel for his or her philosophy.

This pregnancy will be much more carefully monitored than your last. If you have a chronic disease that may have contributed to your first preterm delivery (e.g., diabetes mellitus, hypertension, kidney disease), your doctor will want to follow and treat that disorder carefully, beginning even prior to conception. Depending on the details of your previous pregnancy and family history, your doctor may suggest genetic counseling before you try to get pregnant. A genetic counselor will take a detailed family health history and possibly run some laboratory tests to determine whether or not you are at risk of having a child with certain abnormalities. Or your obstetrician may feel that surgery may decrease or eliminate your chances of another preterm delivery. For example, if a malformation of the uterus is found to be the cause of your first premature birth, this can often be surgically corrected, bettering your chances for a term delivery next time. Or if you're diagnosed as having an "incompetent" cervix (one that dilates without labor contractions), your doctor may suggest suturing, or sewing, the cervix to prevent it from dilating too soon. This operation, performed under anesthesia in the hospital, is called a cerclage. The stitches would usually be removed about two weeks before your due date. Occasionally, stitches from a cerclage are not removed and the baby is delivered by a cesarean section.

If nothing can be done surgically or medically to reduce your chance of premature labor, your pregnancy would simply be monitored more closely and you would be instructed to keep on the lookout for signs of premature contractions. The sooner discovered, the more likely these can be stopped and the less invasive the methods used to stop them. Often, bed rest alone can put an end to early labor. You will be instructed on the signs of premature labor, but recognizing the beginnings of preterm labor is not as easy as it sounds. Preterm contractions are often painless and may last only twenty seconds. Premature contractions are really only "tightenings" of the uterus. If you put your hand on your uterus, you'll be able to feel it getting hard. If it gets hard on a regular basis, about two to three times in one hour, you can suspect premature labor. At first, it may be difficult to differentiate between the baby's movement in the womb and a contraction. The difference is really the length of time the uterus stays hard and the regularity of the hardening. A fetal movement may pass in ten seconds. A contraction will probably keep your uterus hard for twenty to forty seconds—a subtle difference but one you can learn to recognize. Also, a labor contraction must be differentiated from Braxton-Hicks contractions, common in all pregnancies; these are painless "practice" tightenings of the uterus that last *longer* than true contractions, usually one to two minutes. Some doctors have their patients wear an electronic fetal monitor at home. A woman straps it on once a day to find out whether or not she's experiencing any contractions. She gets a digital readout and calls that number in. Other doctors strongly feel that the use of this monitor at home is unnecessary and overly expensive.

Whenever you even *suspect* premature labor, you should call your obstetrician immediately. The key to success here may be not being afraid to "bother" your doctor. A few extra and possibly even unnecessary visits to your doctor are a small price to pay for a healthy term baby. If you hold back, thinking you'll wait or that it's "just your imagination," you could end up in the same position as before—too far into premature labor to effectively stop it from happening.

Other, albeit subtle, signs of premature labor include increased vaginal discharge; lower back pain; feelings of pelvic pressure; pressure in the lower abdomen, back, or thighs; and diarrhea or indigestion. Vaginal spotting or loss of the mucus plug should also be reported immediately.

For more information, write for a copy of "Premature Labor: A Teaching Guide for Pregnant Women" from The March of Dimes, 303 South Broadway, Tarrytown, New York 10591.

If you are diagnosed as being in labor, don't panic. If you act early, there are many ways to prevent birth from occurring too soon. The preventative steps your doctor takes will depend on how far the labor has progressed. (See Chapter 1 for details.) In as many as half of premature labors, contractions will stop with bed rest alone. (See Chapter 1.) Unfortunately, standing up again can often bring the contractions back, so complete or partial bed rest may be prescribed. Obviously, bed rest is not as restful as it sounds. It takes hard work and stamina to stay in bed, especially when you have another child toddling or running around the house. But you know the work involved in the care of a premature baby. Bed rest, however difficult, has got to be easier than having another premie! It's important that everyone in your family know about and understand the importance of this bed rest. You won't be able to accomplish it without support from your husband and understanding from your children. If your husband works full-time, you're going to need some outside help—family, friends, or hired—to ensure that you'll be able to stay in bed. If you are working, you are going to have to arrange sick leave for complete bed rest or arrange more flexible or part-time hours for partial bed rest. Ironically, it is often much easier to obtain this leave than it was for you to get leave to care for your premie!

To give your baby the best chance of being born full-term and healthy, there are some things you can do by yourself, even before you become pregnant—and certainly before any sign of trouble starts. First, do not get pregnant too soon after your last pregnancy. Ideally, give yourself a year or two to get back into shape. At the very least, discuss with your obstetrician whether he or she feels your body is ready for another pregnancy. Second, eat a balanced diet, drink only in moderation (one glass of wine a week), if at all, and if you smoke or use drugs, *stop!*

If you are a smoker, try to stop before you even get pregnant. Smokers have a 50 percent greater chance of having a low-birth-weight baby, more often because of poor growth in the womb than because of premature birth. Remember that the outlook for these children is even worse than for premies, and is especially bad if they are both small for gestational age and premature. (See Chapter 3 for a review of these problems.) Premature labor and premature rupture of the membranes are also more likely to occur in smokers. If you can't stop completely, at least cut down. The effects of smoking on your unborn child are related to the amount you smoke, so the fewer cigarettes you smoke, the greater your chance of a term baby with a good weight. Everything you read above about smoking is even more true about drug abuse, but in addition you have the very major risk of your baby's being born addicted.

Although malnutrition was almost certainly *not* the cause of your previous preterm delivery, nutrition is extremely important for all pregnant mothers. You might want to examine your normal eating habits by making a list, just once, of everything you eat over the course of a few days. Divide your list into categories: proteins, dairy foods, grains, fruits and vegetables, fats. This list will help to pinpoint weaknesses in your diet. Show the list to your doctor. He or she should be able to help you improve your nutrition. Follow your doctor's prescription for vitamins, iron, and calcium, but don't overdose. Too many vitamins can be more harmful than too few. Drink plenty of fluids to aid in digestion, circulation, and waste removal. Four to six glasses of water a day are recommended. A slow, steady weight gain is best. The number of pounds you gain will vary depending on your body makeup. Rapid weight gains or low weight gains will be watched by your doctor.

Strenuous exercise should be avoided throughout a high-risk pregnancy. Ask your doctor about more moderate forms of exercise—stretching, swimming, walking. Sex may be prohibited at some point as well; do not be shy about asking your doctor about this. This might be done because some obstetricians feel that orgasm can occasionally lead to contractions. Although orgasm would not cause premature labor in a normal pregnancy, it is not clear if it may have an effect in a high-risk pregnancy. Nipple stimulation can also bring on contractions. Some doctors will advise against sex during the entire pregnancy; others may ask you not to have intercourse in the last trimester.

You will not want to travel during the early months, when risk of miscarriage is high, or during the late months, when premature birth might occur. Travel itself will not cause premature labor, but you have spent a lot of time carefully choosing the doctor and the hospital for this birth—and you don't want to end up having the baby away from these carefully chosen supports.

Conclusion

By the time you have finished this book, you have already survived a great deal. You have lived through a preterm delivery, life in the NICU, and your premie's early development. You can look forward to more peaceful years with your premie and set your sights on the future, leaving much of the legacy of your baby's prematurity behind you. Your child may soon go to school, play with friends, and cause you all the normal anxieties any child his age causes a parent.

Your premature baby will always hold a special place in your heart, and you probably won't ever forget the difficult way he came into the world or the unusual beginning he had. But you and your family have survived it. Congratulations! We hope this book helped along the way.

Acknowledgments

I would like to thank Drs. Janice Johnston and Barbara Croft for helping me through my premature labor and delivery, and Dr. Len Sacks, Ashley's neonatologist, for helping her come home early and for introducing us to many of the parents who contributed to this book (see below). Also, thanks to Dr. Ben Sachs, for reviewing the early chapters of the book, and to Dr. Deborah Pearson, for helping us contact parents of premature children with ongoing problems. I appreciate the hard work of my co-author; the support and understanding of our editor, Channa Taub; and the insightful contributions of the premie parents who allowed my co-author to interview them. Most of all, I wish to dedicate this book to my beloved Bill, Danielle, Ashley, and Brandy. —*Janine Jason*

To my family—Peter, Nicolaas, and Natalie—for their encouragement; and also to Ardene B., who helped me to have the time to write this. —*Antonia van der Meer*

Thanks to all the parents who spoke with us at length about their children, their experiences, fears, and hopes: David Casey, Jennifer Derby, Jackie Henry, Doris Ivey, Donna Leeb, Mimi Markel, Carolyn Moise, Mary Moore, Mary Ellen Parise, Cynthia Smith, Naomi Steinberg, Karen Rice Thomas, and Kathy W.

Index

interacting with premature infant, 143–44
parents', 155–56
reactions of, 138–42
separation from parents, 137–39
sleeping arrangements, 144–45
twins and, 209
Sight. *See* Vision
Single parents, 152
Size, 25–26, 28. *See also* Weight
child's self-image and, 200–201
head circumference, 36
Skin, appearance of, 29–30
Sleep, 168, 169
newborn, 50–51
twins and, 214–15
Sleep/wake cycles, 191–92
Smell, 51–52, 80, 116–17
Smiling, 190–91
Smoking during pregnancy, 266–67
Social workers, 73–74
Sodium, in antibiotics, 37–38
Sonograms (ultrasound), 5, 71
Specialists, how to find, 240–42
Spoiling, 204–5
Steroids, for baby's lungs, 10–11
Stimulation, 53, 80, 88, 92, 98, 99, 116, 132–33, 179, 186–88, 190, 192
Stomach irritation, 39–40
Stranger anxiety, 194–95
Stress, 4, 51, 179
Sucking, 33–34, 66
Sudden infant death syndrome (SIDS), 168
Supplemental feedings, 134
Support (supportiveness), 145–46, 156, 204
Support groups, 157–58, 221–22
Surfactant, for respiratory-distress syndrome, 69
Surfactant therapy, 245
Surgery, 245. *See also* Cesarean section
CSF shunt and, 45–46
pain and, 54
for patent ductus arteriosus, 43
Swallowing, 33–34

Tachycardia, 39
Talking, 88
Tantrums, 199
Tasting, in newborn, 51
Technicians, 73
Tests, 69–71, 90–92. *See also specific tests*
Apgar scale, 20–21
blood, 69–70
discussing results of, 102
pain and, 68–69
painful, 55
sonograms (ultrasound), 4, 71
ventilators and, 68–69
weighing, 69
X rays, 70–71
Theophylline, 39, 40
Tocolytic agents, 8–10
Touching, 52–54, 79, 88, 188
fear of, 111–12
Toys, 198
Tracheostomy, 226–27
Transfusions
for jaundice, 62
white blood cell, 42
Travel during pregnancy, 267
Triplets. *See* Multiple births; Twins
Tube feeding at home, 172–74
Twins, 3, 206–22
bathing, 213–14
bottle feeding, 212
clothing for, 207, 216–17
diapers for, 216
differences between, 207–8
equipment for, 217–18
feeding methods, 210–13
getting help with, 218–19
guilt and, 208–9
language development, 215–16
outsiders' interest in, 220–21
school and, 215–16
siblings and, 209
support groups for parents of, 222

Ultrasound (sonograms), 5, 71
Urinary catheter, 64–66